THE
RABBI
IN THE
GREEN JACKET

THE
RABBI
IN THE
GREEN JACKET

MEMORIES OF JEWISH BUCKINGHAMSHIRE
1939 – 1945

VIVIEN AND DEBORAH SAMSON

Matador
9 Priory Business Park,
Wistow Road, Kibworth Beauchamp,
Leicestershire. LE8 0RX
Tel: 0116 279 2299
Email: books@troubador.co.uk
Web: www.troubador.co.uk/matador
Twitter: @matadorbooks

ISBN 978 1785890 093

British Library Cataloguing in Publication Data.
A catalogue record for this book is available from the British Library.

Printed and bound in the UK by TJ International, Padstow, Cornwall
Typeset in 11pt Aldine401 BT by Troubador Publishing Ltd, Leicester, UK

Matador is an imprint of Troubador Publishing Ltd

This book holds memories from Jewish evacuees and refugees who crossed borders to reach Buckinghamshire during World War Two.

With thanks to those who enabled survival and freedom and to our fantastic contributors – to life – L'Chaim!

Thank you to the Jewish Historical Society of England (JHSE) for choosing us to be your Award recipients, and so enabling our research material to be made public.

An extra special thank you to Ivan Jakar, for your generosity, made in memory of Frank and Eve Ross, wonderful people, who took him in when he was evacuated to Amersham.

And Gabrielle – we thank her too.

Thanks to the Amersham Museum for our Wartime Jewish Amersham webpage: http://amershamhistory.info/research/wars/wartime-jewish-amersham/

★

If only you could have seen this, Ruth (Isaac) and William Lowenthal. How we would have loved your hugs, kisses and Mazel Tovs!

In memory of our cousin, Sir Martin Gilbert, who listened intently to details of our emerging book. We didn't know it was going to be the final time, but for that last spell of laughter together, we are thankful.

COPYRIGHT INFORMATION

Jewish Museum London, Oral History Collection Transcript, interview with H Lipschitz; *Picture Post*, January 12, 1946, Maurice Edelman, '*SMALL TOWN THEATRE*', R. Abrams; Bloch, S. (1980) *No Time for Tears: Childhood in a Rabbi's Family,* London: William Kimber; Capristo, L, ed. (2004) http://web1.smcm.edu/mulberrytree/_assets/PDF/summer04/growingupingermany.pdf, '*From Hitler's Hamburg to Hollywood: Growing Up in Germany*' *The Mulberry Tree*; V. Samson, *Landsleit of Amersham and surrounding areas: A History of the Amersham Hebrew Congregation 1939-1945.*

TABLE OF CONTENTS

Table of Contents

TABLE OF FIGURES

(Thanks to Dennis Rapaport (Fig. 3), Bournemouth Hebrew Congregation's Centenary Gallery (Fig. 4), Della Worms (Fig. 5), Fritz Lustig (Figs. 6 & 7), Carolyn Williams (Figs. 8 and 9), Norman Franklin (Figs. 10 – 13), Silvia and Paola Rosselli (Fig. 14), Jeremy Godden (Fig. 15), Geoff Freed (Fig. 16) and Judith Joseph (Fig. 17).

Introduction –
An Anglo–Jewish
Country Garden

Refugees from Nazi occupied Europe, and evacuees from London, looked upon new vistas. The cityscapes turned into open fields, ancient woodlands and the rolling Chiltern Hills of the County of Buckinghamshire, (Bucks) in South East England.

People who came as refugees had their homes, jobs, belongings and financial assets confiscated by the Nazis. Jewish refugees to the UK paid for their own health care as did all British citizens. There was no welfare state. Support was generated mainly through Jewish charities. To ensure refugees entering this island would blend in, and not be a burden, each new arrival was given rules from the Anglo-Jewish community with strict instructions on how to behave in a British manner, such as observing a dress code and only speaking English in public.[1]

Several assimilated, even anglicising their names to sound more British. Others, as those in the Chesham community, focused on the survival of a rich, deep, and ancient religion. Some of the religious changed their names to sound more Hebrew. Others became Zionists, realising most countries shut their doors to the persecuted. There needed to be a Jewish homeland, a safe haven, with a Government prepared to defend the right to life for Jewish people.

Country life – what a contrast to the urban lifestyle! Cows needed milking, chickens feeding, and animals helped with birthing. One evacuee recalled a particular cultural shock involved the Boxing Day Meet. Since the sixteenth century tradition upheld that on the 26th December, a public holiday, fox hunts would take place across Britain.

Holocaust survivors with Post Traumatic Stress Disorder may find uniforms to be triggers to anxiety and panic. The colours of the hunt are red, black and white. The Swastika was black, on a white disc, with a red background. The Nazis fashioned theatre to gather crowds. During the 1936 Olympic Games in Berlin, Hitler Youth and military bands also used bugles. People were disturbed by the hunt; barking dogs, the crowd of spectators, the thrill of pleasure on the faces of willing participants of a blood sport and cries of 'Tally ho' as they exhausted a fleeing fox. It was, for them, less splendorous ceremonial rite and more abuse of power. Hunting animals for sport is against Jewish law.

One Jewish evacuee to Buckinghamshire loved animals, and hated cruelty. Fox hunting was one of his nightmares. From an early age he wasn't attracted to the colourful clothes or the rituals. When he was five or six a fox came, terror-stricken, into their garden, immediately followed by horse riders and hounds. They were led by a large ugly woman who had a red face. She was (he believes) the Master. The little boy rushed into the house and brought out a hot poker from the fire. He used a cloth to cover his hands, but afterwards saw they had been burned. The Master of Hounds was half standing on her mount, and her large posterior was in the air. He stuck the poker into her rear and, screaming, she fell off. The hounds ripped the poor fox to pieces. The sight for this child was never forgotten. Later, the police constable came around with his notebook at the ready. The boy's mother argued that he was only a small child and didn't understand country ways. The policeman was angry and warned he would keep his eye on the child. After lecturing the mother, whilst the boy hid behind the door, he went away.

DIGGING FOR VICTORY

Some refugees and evacuees were housed on farms. Flint Hall Farm was used as a training centre by the YMCA under a scheme, British Boys for British Farms, during the 1930s.[2] Jewish families wrote pleading places for their children. Successful applicants could only partake in agricultural training, on the farm near Hambledon, working alongside the Christian trainees if they paid twenty pounds a head. On completion they were to be sent to work abroad within the British Commonwealth. Barbara Vessey described '…the spartan conditions in the cottage, the primitive living and working conditions…' and noted Austrian and German refugees struggled with English. Kosher requirements were not met.[3]

One of the Flint Hall Farm boys was Lewis Erlanger, there until early 1940 before moving to another farm. Erlanger reported the two farms didn't really train the boys but used them as cheap labour.[4] Others who dug for victory included the German-Jewish Strauss family, Victor, Marianne and sons Helmut and Kurt, who were evacuated, with other refugees, to Andridge Farm, Radnage, near High Wycombe.[5]

And who would have thought that Kibbutzim existed in Buckinghamshire? Historian Yanky Fachler provided a fascinating account from the memories of his parents whose formative teen years were spent in Bachad Kibbutz Buckingham.[6] They recalled Amersham residents, Holzer and Horovitz, and in Chesham, Eisemann and Kohn.

The following is sourced from Diana Gulland's excellent research. Tythrop, near Princes Risborough in Buckinghamshire housed 'Basque children escaping the Spanish Civil War, followed by Jewish refugees fleeing from Nazi persecution in Europe.'[7]

The Central Council for German Jewry had set up a special Agricultural Committee to deal with the growing number of young Jewish women and men brought to England for agricultural and industrial training. The *Reichvertretung der Juden in Deutschland* [National Representative Agency for German Jews] in Germany and the *Kultus-Gemeinde* of Vienna were

1

responsible for selecting pupils and for preparing them for departure to England. By early 1939 16 training centres had been set up and one independent one was established at Tythrop House, Kingsey.

Tythrop House was leased from the owners Magdalen College, Oxford, by the Langham Committee with four trustees: Angel Botibol, proprietor of the firm A.Botibol & Co., which owned 91 tobacco shops in London; Bernard Nathaniel Waley-Cohen [1st Baronet]; Howard Samuel, Estate Agent and Henry Solomon, Solicitor. The refugees lived in the house and farmed at Foxhill Farm, a short distance away, working under the guidance of Professors Alexander Moch and C.S.Orwin from the School of Rural Economy, Oxford.

Press reports December 1938 and January 1939 stated:

"First German Jewish refugee agricultural institution in England to be run on a self-supporting and co-operative basis. 100 young people, aged from 16 to 21, who have been studying under Director Professor L. Moch on a farm outside Berlin will take over Tythrop House and the surrounding farmland of 200 acres. Fifteen hundred acres of farmland have been allocated to Professor Moch and Dr Leonore Goldschmidt in North Carolina [for the refugees to emigrate to after training]."

"Tythrop House Scheme. The main outlines of a practical scheme for training refugees in agriculture were announced at a party given last week by Miss Pamela Frankau, the novelist."

A visiting, Jewish, journalist wrote, "The food …is dispensed by a Kitchen Committee… run by the students themselves with the aid of a few German women who shoulder the burden of cooking for the whole community."

Dunstan Skilbeck, from Oxford School of Rural Economy, May 1939 reported, "The house looked clean and well painted, the kitchen garden had been tackled and the farm improved. There is no doubt that the refugees are an asset to the estate and materially improving it."

Henry Solomon, in a fund raising letter to a Rotary Club, wrote, "We have already purchased some £1500 worth of stock and we are producing very nearly 50 gallons of milk per week… we have 60 students, in addition to the 40 trained agricultural workers… we are expecting a further 100 boys within the next few weeks."

The Wheatsheaf, Journal of the Oxford Co-operative Society (OCS) recorded, "Twenty-five of the homeless and unfortunate young men arrived some six months ago. Some of them straight from Hitler's concentration camps... At the time of writing [September] there are now 117 residing there and being trained as agriculturalists and when more fully competent most of these will be transferred to British Dominions and overseas. They will then be replaced by others now living in destitution and misery in Germany... Within five months they have performed miracles. The gardens are well stocked with all kinds of English vegetables, fields of corn, well-stocked pigsties, chicken-sheds, cattle-sheds, and stables...There are at present 150 fattening pigs and 10 breeding sows, three horses, 80 sheep, 40 heifers, and a multitude of chickens and still more to come..."

Three of the Tythrop boys were survivors from a German emigration training centre which had been set up at Gross Breesen on the German/ Polish border, in 1936, to train young Jews in agricultural practices and to prepare them for emigration. After *Kristallnacht* all the trainees over 18 were sent to Buchenwald concentration camp but were later released and many made their way to other countries. Two of the Tythrop boys contributed to a journal called *Rundbriefe* which had been established to keep survivors of Gross Breesen in touch.

One of the Tythrop boys, Otto Weil stated:

"...pleased with circular-homesick for Breesen. Lately I have been working at a neighbour's farm. [This may have been in Towersey, the next parish to Kingsey...] In the morning and evening, each time I have to milk 14 cows there, look after the calves and before noon from 9.30 until 1 o'clock I work with a team of horses. At present we cart manure onto the hay pastures; if the weather is all right tomorrow we will bring in our oats, which, is already cut for three weeks and meanwhile sprouts. But one can learn much all the same..."

Heinz Jacobsohn from Tythrop wrote:

"Now I am already 2 months in England and find it so lovely and splendid here and am completely happy in my surroundings. I have no loneliness or yearning for Gross-Breesen, as we are three here at one farm [a third boy

3

known as 'Schwips' [Wolfgang Huelsman] was expected at Tythrop on 23 August]. I am working for the Tythrop-House with a farmer and actually earn money. My workplace belongs to the most beautiful sceneries of England...I sit on a hillock, the sun shines, I have a lunch break (1 hour)... around me sheep and young cattle...My farmer, too has essentially a dairy farm, a grass-farm. Make only hay, right through the whole year."

THE RABBI IN THE GREEN JACKET

It's quite possible, that after the hot poker incident, as described in *Introduction: An Anglo-Jewish Country Garden*, the Master of Hounds found herself under the care of Katie (Katharina) Krone. Katie lived alone but wasn't isolated because of her circle of friends. She was in constant demand, sought out by those wishing to unburden themselves. When resolved, she would throw her hands in the air in great relief, and utter, 'Gott sei dank!'

St Mary's Hospital of London evacuated to Amersham Hospital to avoid the Luftwaffe bombs. Katie was a nursing sister who helped transform the old workhouse into an emergency hospital.

Decades later our Samson family would often pop in to see Katie, a close family friend. With a beaming smile she would welcome us, measure us against her, and joke about how she was shrinking and we were growing. Indeed, to examine her patients, as a Sister in Amersham Hospital, she used to stand on a stool to be able to reach them!

Her cosy flat of memories displayed a beautiful hand-crafted menorah made by Katie's brother. There were photographs; one of her family in pre-war Germany, Katie in her nurse's uniform and others of her *adopted* Samson girls. Always, on the anniversary of Kristallnacht we would see a memorial candle burning. Coincidentally, as the mother/grandmother of the authors of this book Katie too had fled Stettin in Germany, now Poland.

Katie was heavily accented. Her English conversation was often punctuated with German 'Naja's', 'Ach nein's' and 'Y' sounds that replaced the English sounding 'J'. In 1993, Katie Krone was in her early nineties, when she talked of wartime Amersham, and referred to the 'rabbi in the green jacket', which she pronounced as 'yacket'! However, who this rabbi was she just could not recall.

Further research, with daughter Deborah, and illustrations by daughter, Gabrielle, resulted in Vivien Samson's booklet, *Landsleit of Amersham and*

Surrounding Areas: A History of the Amersham Hebrew Congregation 1939-1945.
The Yiddish word 'Landsleit' is not just a definition of Jewish people
living in the same village or town, but the sense of a deep emotional bond,
of sharing experiences, and looking after each other. Vivien organised a
reunion, on 10th July 1994. Amongst those present was ninety-two year old
Ben Grossman, past Secretary of the wartime congregation. He was the last
person to lock up the old synagogue.

At a time when Jewish people, religious or not, were being chased out
of their homes and countries, and being subjected to genocide, building
a new synagogue was in part a statement of survival. The humble pre-fab
that became the Amersham synagogue was also a symbol of hope. It may
have been unique, the only synagogue built in Great Britain during WW2,
though Haversham in Buckinghamshire may also have a claim to sharing
the title. The synagogue was a place of inclusion. All were welcomed in to
share in prayers, socials and public talks.

Katie Krone, a member of the wartime Amersham Hebrew Congregation,
did not live to see the reunion, but her donation made the printing of the
booklet possible.

Memories became the foundation for this book which has expanded
to cover the whole of wartime Jewish Buckinghamshire. As to whom the
rabbi in the green jacket was, well, that continued to be a mystery for a very
long time!

PEOPLE IN PERIL

'My brother was arrested on suspicion of burning down the Reichstag. None of my family survived, not even my brother.'
Katie Krone

The burning of the German parliament building, the Reichstag, 27th February 1933, followed arrests of those who did not fit the German ideal. Held in forced labour concentration camps, when no longer needed they were murdered. Sanctions, from a totalitarian state, came swiftly. Jewish people were systematically disenfranchised. Some escaped.

At the Evian conference, on the 6th July 1938, world representatives met over a refugee problem but more specifically, another Jewish problem. No country wanted them. Yad Vashem recorded, 'The British delegate claimed that Britain was already fully populated and suffering from unemployment, so it could take in no refugees.' He made an apology to Germany for interfering. The solution, inaction, let Hitler deal with them.[8,9]

Eli Fachler, refugee to Buckinghamshire, reflected, 'I well remember the 9th of November 1938 (Kristallnacht) in Berlin, when teachers from our school were sent to Sachsenhausen and came back half their size, made to hand over their bank accounts and shareholdings to the State (Gestapo). Those who could emigrated.'

The violence against Jews pushed Britain into accepting ten thousand Jewish children aged five to seventeen. The entrance fee was fifty pounds per unaccompanied child. Most left behind were murdered. The authors own mother/grandmother, Ruth Isaac and twin sister, Eva, came on the Kindertransport, from Stettin, when their father was in Sachenhausen concentration camp, hence their prioritisation for a place on the train. Many children had already become orphaned by murderers who were once their neighbours. They didn't know if they would ever see their families again, most did not. For anyone who questions allowing child refugees into

Britain, they had to commit to pay for education and care. Private sponsors, Jewish charities and the Quakers paid.

Christian convert, Sir Nicholas Winton, a former student of Stowe School, Buckinghamshire, came from Jewish parentage. Sir Nicholas' daughter, Barbara explained, 'he was baptised by his parents during the First World War and then chose to be confirmed in his teens.' He helped save six hundred and sixty-nine mostly Jewish children from Czechoslovakia in 1939, after the Germans invaded, by organising the Czech Kindertransport. They resided with British foster families and some found safety in Bucks.

Meanwhile, the crème de la crème of international society were fine wined and dined in Lord Waldorf and Lady Nancy Astor's Cliveden mansion in Taplow, Buckinghamshire. The soirées combined an unlikely mix of characters from film actors to high ranking visiting officials from around the world, which included Ribbentrop, Foreign Minister of Germany and German Ambassador to Britain. Lord Astor even met with Hitler in Germany. The Astors and their closest inner circle felt sympathy toward Germany for the 1919 Versailles Peace Treaty and the harsh reparations. [10]

Resentment festered toward influential aristocrats out of touch with modern Britain. Many foresaw the inevitability of war and that delaying would put the world at a disadvantage against Germany. Influential people wanted peace. Hitler was not appeased and invaded Czechoslovakia on the 15th March 1939.

Several guests became labelled, by Claud Cockburn in 1937 as the 'Cliveden Set'. The media bandwagon continued to report on the right-wing ideas, accusing the exclusive set of influencing Government with a pro-German agenda. Allegations of anti-Semitism were hotly denied by Lady Astor and she helped fund an appeal for aiding Jewish refugees.

High society dressed in their finery, sipping champagne and putting the world to rights, may not have been as shocked as others, when Hitler invaded Czechoslovakia. Even though Nazi abuse was fully documented in the world press, some aristocrats may have viewed this as just a hiccup in international affairs. However, champagne bubbles burst on Hitler's broken word, when on the first of September 1939, Germany invaded

Poland. Britain declared war with Germany on 3rd September. Thousands of Jews were murdered. The remainder were forced into ghettos and starved.

After Britain became an enemy of Germany, Lady Astor, a Conservative MP, voted against Chamberlain, so that Churchill could become prime minister in May 1940. She denounced dictatorship and housed evacuees at Cliveden.

DETENTION WITHOUT TRIAL

'Collar the lot!'
Churchill 1940

Those who were fortunate enough to enter Britain in time were faced with a new label, 'Enemy Alien'. People were rounded up without trial, aged from sixteen to seventy.

Jewish people, many of whom had been stripped of their German citizenship, were interred in camps, behind barbed wire. Being labelled as an 'alien' had disturbing parallels with Nazi Europe where they were outcast as sub-human – 'untermenschen'. In Britain, people, mainly Jewish, evidently not spies of the Third Reich were arrested. They were forced apart from their families, threatening dependents with impoverishment for losing the breadwinner. The survivors of Nazi persecution were the least likely to be anti-Britain. Hitler may have been delighted to hear of Jews being rounded up and transported.

There were many camps, the largest on the Isle of Man. Its flag, with three kicking-out legs, taken from the Celtic sun sign, shares a symbolic resemblance to the swastika. What was awaiting them on an unknown island prison? Was suicide an option? Not all managed in conditions that made some physically and mentally ill.

Slowly the inmates were released. Many Jewish internees went on to fight for Britain against Fascism. Those who were allowed to make Britain their home continued to do everything they could to support their adopted country. Their descendants continue to love Britain, raised to take responsibility for looking after their country and the world, through knowledge, learning and charity. In Hebrew repairing the world is called, *'Tikkun Olam'*, a core value to Judaism.

Thirtieth June 1940 the Channel Islands were occupied by German forces. The executioner was on British shores.

Fighting Back

'Enemy Aliens' were unwilling sitting targets. Indeed, in France they were conveniently detained so all the Nazis had to do was kill them.

Refugees, imprisoned, stateless, and desperate to fight for Britain joined the Auxiliary Military Pioneer Corps (AMPC). Initially it was 'the only part of the British Army that a friendly enemy alien was allowed to join.'[11] Frustrated with their limited role, they proved themselves, and were entrusted into armed combat and Intelligence roles.

Nazism would be defeated and Jewish people vowed to do all in their power to help Britain into victory. Many were engaged in war work, too many to name individually, even when limited to the County of Buckinghamshire. Britain stood firm against the onslaught of bombs; the Navy held off the Nazis from crossing the Channel; others worked, sometimes secretly, on the Home Front and abroad, and the Royal Air Force (RAF), though heavily outnumbered, fought the Luftwaffe from the 10th July to the 31st October 1940 and won the Battle of Britain. Defeat would have seen the implementation of anti-Jewish laws and almost certain death, just as in the Channel Islands and Europe.

One determined German Jewish refugee, Fritz Lustig, was put in a positon of absolute trust, having signed the Official Secrets Act. Working for the Intelligence Services, he became a Secret Listener into bugged conversations of captured German Prisoners of War. These high ranking Nazi officers were held in Trent Park and two Buckinghamshire locations, Latimer and Wilton Park in Beaconsfield. Their hosts (warders) gave them every luxury to lull them into a false sense of security and learn their secrets. Historian Dr Helen Fry invited the authors of this book to her book launch, *Spymaster: The Secret Life of Kendrick,*[12] at Latimer House in the Chess Valley, Buckinghamshire. Sir David Jason and Helen Fry explained the history of wartime Intelligence led by the spy Thomas Joseph Kendrick. Fritz Lustig was one of many Jewish people who served under him. Rumour has it that Rudolf Hess, Deputy Leader of the Nazi Party, was held at Latimer House.

Egon Brandt (later Ernest Brent), a member of the wartime Amersham Hebrew Congregation, also worked in Intelligence at Latimer House. Due to the Official Secrets Act he was not allowed to talk when interviewed by Vivien Samson in 1993, though we accidently bumped into Brent's daughter at this event! American Intelligence was also Latimer based, later evolving into the Central Intelligence Agency (CIA). At the end of the war Churchill visited to thank Personnel for their vital war work.

Post-war, German Jewish refugee Heinz Koeppler ran Wilton Park, Beaconsfield, as a centre of rehabilitation for German POWs and European civilians. A dialogue of education and understanding was opened so people could voluntarily choose to undertake the customs and lifestyles of democracy. Sir Heinz's work helped to create the birth of a democratic Germany.[13]

Another essential war operation in Buckinghamshire was at Bletchley Park. The house belonged to a Jewish couple, Sir Herbert and Lady Fanny Leon.[14] The Government purchased the fifty-five acres of land where people worked tirelessly to crack the German codes. Debbie Gardner, a relative of the authors of this book, was a code-breaker amongst many other Jewish personnel. London born Debbie was educated in Germany but trapped when WW1 broke out. According to her cousin, Bernie Lowenthal, 'Debbie was brilliant but peculiar! She was a bohemian, wearing very unfashionable, loose and flowing clothes. She spoke at people not with them and liked a drink. She was fluent in English and German. She was asked by the British Government to work on the Enigma Code at Bletchley Park.' The Enigma machine allowed the Allies to decode what the Nazis believed was impossible-to-crack secret messages. Decryption helped Britain to win the War.

Head of a Bletchley Park translation unit was Walter George Ettinghausen (later Walter Eytan, Director of the Israeli Foreign Ministry and Israel's Ambassador to France).[15]

Dame Miriam Louisa Rothschild worked at Bletchley on the Enigma project near where her famous Buckinghamshire relatives, from the banking family, lived.[16] Halton House, near Wendover, was owned by the Rothschilds, and designed by William Rogers (was Rodriguez), a Jewish architect.[17] The Rothschilds allowed it to be used by the armed services during both world wars. The RAF continues to be stationed there.

Leo Marks (MBE)[18] was based at Grendon Underwood in Buckinghamshire. He wrote poetry as code for spies in order to improve safeguards against detection.

Hanns Alexander, whose Jewish family lived in Chalfont St Peter, took it upon himself, initially against orders, to hunt down Nazis, including the Kommandant of Auschwitz, Rudolph Höß. The British, on liberating Europe, did not make proper provisions for capturing, taking evidence, and seeking justice. Hanns, bold and confident, was determined to take up the mission of Nazi hunter to gain some form of justice. Thanks to his heroic strength of mind, and detective work, he tracked down Rudolph Höß who went to trial at Nuremberg. Höß was found guilty of war crimes and executed in 1947. Further details are in the book, *Hanns and Rudolph,* by Thomas Harding published by Cornerstone.[19]

Roald Dahl, the famous writer, lived in Great Missenden. The *Jewish Chronicle* reported he was an unapologetic anti-Semite.[20] The brave contributions of the Jewish people fighting to protect Britain clash with Dahl's claim he 'never saw a Jew in the front line'. [21]

Many Jewish people risked their lives for the Allies. In connection to Chesham, Buckinghamshire, The Commonwealth War Grave Commission[22] recorded the death of Pilot Officer (Observer) Frank Samuel Day. Martin Sugarman listed him on his website as Jewish. We paid our respects at Chesham War Memorial.

The Mystery of the Missing Airman

The Chesham Memorial commemorates seventy-seven men. Frank Samuel Day is not inscribed.

Why the absence of a young Jewish man?

On a website in memory of airmen killed in a crash[23] there is information that Frank Samuel Day was born 'Deitchman'. He changed his surname, possibly to be thoroughly assimilated into Britain.

Pilot Officer (Observer) Frank Samuel Day joined the RAF voluntarily just short of the outbreak of war in 1939. He was promoted to Sergeant. He navigated, aimed bombs and photographed targets. Three days after his twenty-eighth birthday, on the 21st July 1942, his plane crashed, probably due to a failing of an engine. He and three others, of a heroic team, died, avoiding a Cornish town to protect the civilians. Frank Samuel Day is buried in St Illogan churchyard. There is no Star of David on his stone and no record of him being a member of The Association of Jewish Ex-Servicemen and Women (AJEX).[24]

Day is missing from Chesham War Memorial because of a misunderstanding. Frank's final address was in Golder's Green. He did not live in Chesham. However his father, Nat Day, aka Nathaniel Deitchman, (MBE) resided in Chesham with Nora Bancroft, a variety performer known to be in 'The Three Merry Widows'. In 1940 Nat married divorcee Nora Bancroft, in Paddington. Nat and Nora had a home in Chesham from around 1942, first at 'Hill Crest' on Nashleigh Hill, moving to 'Bancroft', on the same road, around 1949. Nora died there on 18th August 1975.[25]

Franks's grandparents were Israel and Sarah Deitchman, born in Russia and came to London. Their son Nat married his first wife, a Dutch Jewish girl, Rika, in Amsterdam in 1912 and came to London.

Nat died on 27th January 1982 in his 97th year. His funeral at Golders

Green, two days later, was attended by representatives of the Grand Order of Water Rats, the theatrical associations he was involved with, and Equity.

Frank's Will was made in Golder's Green. The executors were Margery and Joseph Toeman. The surname rang a bell for us. The Toemans were active members of the Amersham Hebrew Congregation. Could they be the executors? We traced Maurice Blaug, whose mother was Sarah Blauaug née Toeman. Maurice's two brothers lived in Amersham with their uncle Joe and his wife Rosa. Maurice believes it possible the executor was his uncle, Joe Toeman, as the surname is so unusual, though Maurice never heard mention of the airman's death. Day was not related to the Toemans.

Could the Toemans and Days have known each other in London and escaped the Blitz to Amersham and Chesham? Members of the wartime Amersham Hebrew Congregation have spoken of the Toeman family with great respect. Mr J Toeman was a name referenced, in a Jewish context, in the local newspaper, the *Bucks Examiner*.

Frank's father, Nat was involved in theatre; another connection with the Toeman family? Sure enough, Maurice Blaug revealed, 'The great family secret was that Uncle Bob, Joe's brother, had been in Vaudeville as a youth. He played 'with' Charlie Chaplin before Chaplin went West. I've taken the 'with' with copious amounts of salt.'

Maurice Blaug's first cousin, Zerka Toeman Moreno helped develop, with her husband Dr Jacob Levy Moreno, the theory and practice of psychodrama. She is the author of books including a memoir, *To Dream Again*.[26] Zerka explained:

My parents were Joseph and Rosa Gutwirth Toeman. I came here as a 22 year old by myself in October 1939, and was the only Toeman in the U.S.A.

Father grew up in the East End but he left for the Netherlands as soon as he married my mother and settled in Rotterdam with his parents, as my mother, who lived in Antwerp, refused to come and live 'in dirty London'. Later we moved to Amsterdam. In 1931 we moved to London and lived in Willesden Green. During the early part of the war, they moved to Amersham. They had Charles, my younger brother, Sabine and my older brother Rudy. My parents were highly respected.

Uncle Bob was a successful music hall actor in London until his name appeared on a program listing outside on the street by the theater. Grandfather Morris pulled him out because he thought theater was indecent. He was furious to see the family name in public. But in this generation we have an actress who made a movie.

The reference to Amsterdam gave rise to another Toeman connection. Further communication with Zerka and the connection was sealed:

Rika Day was one of Mother's friends in London. Her son was Frank. He was a very clever young man, a reporter, but unhappily a victim of the war. His parents were divorced when he was a young teenager. Rika had a sad life. Frank Day was a single child. I never met his father, whom Frank kept in touch. Rika never married again. My parents met Rika in the Netherlands and Rika was there when we came to London from The Hague in 1931.

The Toemans lived in the East End. My mother Rosa was born in Antwerp where her father was in the diamond business. My father was a baby when his parents came to London and became a British subject. My aunt Sarah, father's youngest sister, married Blauaug, later contracted to Blaug. Their children, George, Marc – a name he chose instead of an English name he rejected – and Maurice with whom you are in touch. Their parents came to the U.S. with Maurice, aged about four or five years; George and Marc stayed under the supervision of my parents. They too came and grew up here.

My father had an older sister, Leah. She married in The Hague but her husband Gerard, divorced her. She had two daughters, Erna and Ruth. She refused to emigrate, probably in the delusion of many of Dutch Jews, who believed that the Dutch would protect them against the Nazis. Her brothers begged her to come to London. She and her family suffered the dreadful consequences.

In summary, Frank Samuel Day, a young man from a Jewish family, fought and died for Britain. His mother was a family friend of the same Toemans who came to Amersham, and were executors of Frank's Will. The two families were connected through culture, history, place, friendship and possibly theatre. In addition, Frank's father Nat was resident in wartime

Chesham, his son was not. Hence Frank's exclusion from the war memorial. Nat was only a short distance from the Toeman/Blaug family of WW2 Amersham. So the mystery of the missing airman has been solved.

★★★

Uphill from Chesham, in Chesham Bois, commemorated on the war memorial, is the name of a Jewish man who fought on the Front Line. Sergeant Harry Kleiner was an air gunner in the Royal Air Force Volunteer Reserve (RAFVR). He flew in a Lancaster with 57 Squadron and was shot down over Holland on the 23rd May 1943. [27] He was a member of AJEX along with his brother Mark. Mark explained their parents, Esther and Joseph Kleiner, moved to Dorset House, Long Park, Amersham. Mark was married to Phyllis, daughter of Tina and Alex Hirschfeld. They also moved in 1941 from Hampstead, London, to avoid a nearby noisy anti-aircraft gun battery, to White Gables, Copperkins Lane, Chesham Bois. The Hirschfeld family donated the ground for the Amersham synagogue, and Mrs Hirschfeld supervised a kosher canteen in Chesham Bois.

Mark's father and father-in-law 'went from door to door' to revive 'the mainly dormant Amersham Jewish Community' to establish a centre for the Jewish community. Indeed, resident Rose Liebmann confirmed pre-war attendance, for High Holy Days, at a very orthodox congregation around Woodside Road. They disbanded as there were not enough people to form a minyan (ten men required for communal prayers).

Another member of AJEX was RAF Flight Lieutenant George Frederick Loewi. His death is recorded, 4th March 1944, by the Commonwealth War Grave Commission, but he died from a disease unrelated to the war and was not killed in action. His nephew, Geoffrey Schott, whose parents lived in wartime Gerrards Cross, explained, 'there was not enough penicillin around to save him, the antibiotic only recently having been discovered'. The reason for the war record is he probably worked in Military Intelligence. He was only thirty-two. His parents were Paul R. Loewi and Dora M. Loewi, of Gerrards Cross. His sisters were Margaret and Erica, who lived in the town, with her husband Dr Schott. The Lieutenant's father was first cousin to Nobel Prize winner Dr Otto Loewi (see *Famous Bucks* chapter).

Sam Rubinowitz, Jewish airman and co-pilot, was flying with his five-man crew, the 321st Transport Squadron of the 27th Air Transport Group, United States Army Air Forces (USAAF), when his life was cut short.[28] On the 21st October 1944 the Americans experienced aircraft failure. By diverting from the town of Princes Risborough, they prevented civilian casualties. This was not the first time pilots had done the same and lost their own lives. The crew could not clear the top of Kop Hill. All five died. They are memorialised in the high street, where poppies are laid in memory and thanks.

CASUALTIES OF WAR

Seventh August 1943, 3am, a Lancaster Bomber crashed in Winslow. A row of cottages and the Chandos Arms were hit and caught fire. Four airmen, and their cat, Wimpey, died. The navigator survived. Thirteen residents and evacuees lost their lives.[29] Four of them were Jewish. Israel (aged 67) and Annie (aged 66) Goldberg were evacuees from Stoke Newington. Their married daughter Lottie Hoberman was aged 41. Victor, Lottie's son, was only seven years old. They were buried in the Jewish Cemetery in Edmonton.[30] Lottie's husband, Jack, served in North Africa. The *Buckingham Advertiser* reported 'Mrs Hoberman and Victor Hoberman were rescued alive; but later died from their injuries.' Mrs Hoberman died after arriving at Northfield House and Victor in Aylesbury Hospital. Six Rose Cottage was demolished. Many died from severe burns. Local residents and services fought hard to save them. Some of the rescuers had to recover the bodies of their own relatives. The Jewish family had come to seek safety 'after bereavement and suffering in the Battle of Britain.' The *Buckingham Advertiser* described the whole family helping with the Evacuee's hostel at Market House.[31] The Winslow community were a shining example of people giving aid in times of need regardless of religion or politics.

Historian Dr David Noy additionally stated, '…my late friend Mrs Peggy Carter (née Pipkin) lived at Burnaby House, North Marston during WW2, and they had a Jewish couple from London staying with them. I think the man was a tailor and continued to work in London, coming to North Marston at weekends. Two other men, staying in this same large house, presumably, after the Jewish people had left, were Hans and Michael, German Prisoners of War who did agricultural work.'

When London hospitals were full to capacity patients were taken to hospitals further afield. North West London is about thirty miles away from Amersham. Thirty-seven years old (Jewish) William Supran of Kilburn, died in Amersham Emergency Hospital on 17th May 1941. His spouse was Maisie. He was an 'Auxiliary Driver, London Ambulance Service.'[32]

Sarah, (Jewish) mother of Goodman King, of Laburnum Cottage, Bow Brickhill, Bucks, must have been devastated to learn of the death of her Air Raid Warden son, at the Lord Stanley, Hackney on 16th October 1940 aged forty-two, leaving behind his wife, Dinah.[33]

Also, Frederick, Grete and Rena Sulzbacher of Stoke Newington, a Jewish family, who were due to leave for Chesham, were killed, more on this later.

Famous Bucks

Buckinghamshire became home to film stars, writers, musicians, dancers and artists. A community of exiles socialised and worked together no matter their class. The concentration of intellect and creativity, combined with countryside freedom and the darkness of war, nurtured talent and deep-thinking. Many children became inspirational figures in adulthood.

New arrivals included Austrian Jewish Expressionist painter, Marie-Louise von Motesiczky, who persuaded friends to move from London to Amersham in 1941.[34] They were Sephardic Jews from Vienna. Bulgarian born, Elias Canetti was already a well-known author before he came to England. In 1981 Canetti became a Nobel Prize winner in Literature. His wife Veza was also a published writer. She was related to the Secretary of State of War, Leslie Hore-Belisha, who was attacked as a 'Jewish warmonger' by Denham resident, Oswald Mosley. The latter became leader of the British Union of Fascists.[35] Stepney Jewish Primary School evacuated to Denham and Heimi Lipschitz recalled banter about not knocking on Mosley's door, as they all knew he was leader of the Blackshirts![36]

The Canettis visited Marie-Louise and her mother, Henriette von Motesiczky (born von Lieben) in Chesham Bois. The Canettis rented various rooms, the longest tenancy being at 'Durris' Stubbs Woods, in the same village, within walking distance of Amersham station. A few Jewish families lived in Buckinghamshire for centuries but never an influx so big, of around three hundred Jewish children, at the height of evacuation.

Some of the Canettis friends read as a list of intellectuals.[37] One of these was WW1 poet Herbert Reed of Seer Green, Buckinghamshire, a librarian and later curator of the Victoria and Albert Museum. The internationally acclaimed poet Denise Levertov met Reed in Seer Green, whilst she was a pupil in the ballet school next door to his house. Reed was to become a strong influence on her poetry.[38]

It was to Marie-Louise Motesiczky's Amersham studio that Canetti's books were entrusted for safe-keeping from the London bombings.

Despite his affairs with other women and his continuing married relationship to Veza, Marie-Louise remained closely involved with Canetti for many years to come. Their friend, Austrian Expressionist painter, Oskar Kokoschka, who was not Jewish, fled the Nazis after being decreed as a 'degenerate' artist. He visited Amersham. Kokoschka revealed to Canetti that he harboured a sense of blame for Hitler's political rise to Fuhrer. They both applied for the same scholarship at Vienna Art Academy. Kokoschka was accepted. Hitler was rejected. The future of the world took a new direction.

In 1941, artist Marie-Louise Motesiczky and her mother purchased a house, 'Cornerways', 86 Chestnut Lane, with vegetables and chickens in the garden. The artist's mother, Henriette, wrote about the house being 'in a road with an old dairy, with very old Chestnut trees, cows grazing and horses opposite'.[39]

Another lover of Elias Canetti, long after the war, was writer Iris Murdoch, who had been briefly engaged to his friend, refugee Franz Steiner, until his early death in 1952. Canetti featured in Murdoch's novels and Motesiczky painted them all.

Amersham resident, artist of some renown, and German Jewish refugee, Harry Weinberger, also came to know Iris Murdoch and painted her portrait. Weinberger had a narrow escape from the Nazis, first from Berlin, and then from Czechoslovakia, on Nicholas Winton's kindertransport train to Britain. He fought in 'the Queen's Own Royal West Kent Regiment in 1944 and then transferred to the Jewish Brigade, serving in Italy.'[40]

Harry Weinberger's daughter, Joanna, provided extra information about her father who as a boy had witnessed the Reichstag on fire:

> My father attended Amersham College when he arrived in England at the age of 16, and stayed to take his matriculation exams. He was a boarder, and there full-time, including weekends and possibly holidays. He spoke warmly of his head teacher, who encouraged his art making, and also his love of classical music.
>
> He had a brother and sister, but his brother was older so had finished his schooling, and his sister, who was younger, went to school elsewhere. His parents survived the war in Switzerland. After my father finished

school he then left the area. He never spoke of other Jewish people in the school, or the area. I think he spent most of his time on the school premises.

Returning to the artist, Motesiczky, The Marie-Louise von Motesiczky Charitable Trust *Biography* recorded, 'The family also made an impact on the origin of psychoanalysis, Motesiczky's grandmother Anna von Lieben being one of Sigmund Freud's early patients.' [41]

Freud was not known to have visited Buckinghamshire. However, Otto Loewi wrote to Anna Freud from New Chilterns, Amersham Common, Bucks, September 23rd 1939, to offer condolences on the death of her father, Sigmund. Otto Loewi, and his friend, Sir Henry Dale, won the 1936 Nobel Prize for research into nerve endings. Otto was dismissed from the University of Graz for being Jewish, went through Nazi imprisonment [with two of his four children, Victor and Guido], and was forced to relinquish all his work, prize money, and possessions to the Nazis.[42] The Jewish refugee was a pharmacologist and pioneer of neuroscience.[43] The Royal Society confirmed Loewi was with friends in England, on holiday from his place of work in Brussels, when he was caught by the outbreak of the war. Interestingly, he had relatives residing in Gerrards Cross. (See *The Mystery of the Missing Airman*)

Professor Josef Donnerer explained in correspondence: [44]

In the summer of 1939 Otto Loewi spent some months at the country seat of friends in England. One of his sons, Guido Loewi (Geoffrey William Low), was sponsored as a refugee by a distant relative in England. He (the distant relative) arranged a place at a language school for Guido Loewi. The priest in a small village in Buckinghamshire arranged a job for him in a car maintenance station outside London.

Completely unexpectedly, he [Loewi] received a cable from Canada informing him that not only the entrance permit but also a paid ship ticket and a job in the laboratory of C.H.Best are waiting for him. Who was C.H. Best? His father explained he was the close co-worker of Sir Frederick Banting in the discovery of insulin. No doubt that Sir Henry Dale had been instrumental in the arrangements for Guido. With the support of Sir Frederick, Guido was soon accepted in the Royal Air Force for training

as Navigator. Upon completion he was transferred to the UK. For safety
reasons, as a member of the aircrew, he changed his name to Geoffrey
Low. Subsequently he flew for four years as Flight Lieutenant with the
R.A.F. in the Far East.

Returning to the aforementioned Sigmund Freud, Otto Loewi did
meet him in Vienna. Loewi recalled Freud 'filled the whole room with
his personality.'[45] Furthermore, the Amersham house, from which Dr
Loewi wrote the condolence letter to the Freud family, was the address,
according to a 1943 obituary notice, of John and Margery Simmons.[46]
Is it merely coincidence that a Margery Simmons from Amersham is
referenced in correspondence between Felix Frankfurter, Associate
Justice of the United States Supreme Court and his sister Estelle who was
in Washington? The Widener Library at Harvard University confirmed
Frankfurter was in Amersham. 'Felix was in the US a month before and a
month after the letter, so it was a short stay.' The 1939 letter 'is on printed
stationary headed Chilterns, Amersham, Bucks.' Furthermore, a second
letter from the same address (1948) 'was written by Margery Simmons
[spelling uncertain] and enclosed in a letter to Felix for forwarding to
Estelle, then in Washington.' [47] We know nothing about the Simmons
of Amersham, yet they had a connection with these Jewish people who
made significant achievements.

Jewish families visited Amersham Repertory Theatre where a string of
stars began their careers. In *Picture Post*[48] Local resident Maurice Edelman
penned 'SMALL TOWN THEATRE', a four page spread complete with
photographs of the Amersham Rep Theatre and staff. Edelman wrote,
'There is no balcony at the Playhouse, and the remotest member of the
audience could easily whisper a message to his favourite actress.' Edelman
continued, 'A Club, attached to the theatre, enables audience and players
to meet and discuss drama. A tea-lounge adds comfort to their informal
mingling in the intervals and at any other time that you care to drop in.'
There was debate about a move to a bigger theatre but not all Amersham
dwellers agreed, 'We like it the hard way. We like the clatter and the rush
and the fug and the crowds and the turmoil. That's what makes our theatre
unique. That's what gives us vitality."

Sadly, the theatre closed down in the 1956. George Marks, another member of the Jewish community, founded today's Amersham Playgoers. He directed and acted in over one hundred plays.

Buckinghamshire was a hub of creativity. Brian Tesler would go on to become influential in British television. Richard Toeman was in the music business. German Jewish émigré, Allan Gray changed his name from Joseph Zmigrod. The first proof of him residing in the area is 1947 when he naturalised and is recorded as, 'Music Composer; "Glen view," Bois Lane, Chesham, Buckinghamshire.'[49] He composed scores for several films, many made during the war years. Later he wrote the music for *The African Queen*. Walter Goehr lived in Amersham, and also composed music. His son Alexander followed in his footsteps.

Walter Goehr taught at Morely College, where Henrietta (Netta) Franklin née Montagu was Principal. Netta married into the Jewish Franklin family of Buckinghamshire. A cousin of the Franklin's, Eva Hubback, also became head of Morley College, in which many excellent musicians were refugees. Non-Jewish Michael Tippett was a wartime music director at Morley College (Kensington). He composed *Child of Our Time* after being moved by the plight of Herschel Grynszpan who killed the German diplomat, following the expulsion of Polish Jews from Germany. The assignation was the excuse needed to trigger violence against Jews – Kristallnacht. Tippett also taught at Little Missenden Abbey, Buckinghamshire; a boarding school for children with challenging behaviours, run by psychologist Mrs Lister-Kaye. Another teacher was Jewish New Zealand poet, Charles Brasch, who came with his ailing sister, and recorded his experience in his memoirs.[50] The school had distinguished teachers, including visiting artists and musicians. Jewish artist and Buckinghamshire resident, Mark Gertler, who commited suicide partly out of fear of the Nazis, was according to Brasch, said to have admired the work of a pupil.

Sir Alexander Korda lived in Denham, where he owned film studios which later merged with Pinewood. Imagine the list of stars working at the studios and visiting his home! It has been suggested Alexander Korda 'downplayed', in public, his Jewish identity for British assimilation.[51]

Denham was also the home of German Jewish actress Lilli Palmer and her husband Rex Harrison, whose brother, according to past Jewish pupils, was the headmaster of Dr Challoner's School. Siblings Bernard and Rose Kops were evacuated to Denham. Fame was contagious in this locality because Bernard Kops grew up to be a playwright, novelist and poet.[52]

Gerrards Cross residents, refugee Walter Zander, expert in law, and son Benjamin, who became a famous music conductor, may have crossed paths with Jewish actress Renée Asherson. She was raised in Gerrards Cross, acted in many films including WW2 released, *The Way Ahead* and starred with Laurence Oliver in *Henry V*. She recalled 'taking the early train from Marylebone to Denham and tramping through muddy fields from the station to report for work with Laurence Olivier in 1943'.[53]

Modernist Jewish architect Elisabeth Benjamin designed, with Godfrey Samuel, The St George and Dragon House, Hedgerley Lane, Gerrards Cross, built in 1937. [54]

Architect Erich Mendelsohn was a refugee from Nazism. His Russian colleague, Serge Chermayeff, was also Jewish. They designed the modernist 1934 concrete dwelling, *Nimmo House* in Shrubs Wood, Gorelands Lane, Chalfont St. Giles. Refugee, Marcel Breuer, co-designed buildings for Eton College, which used to be in Buckinghamshire.

Pinewood Studios was requisitioned for the Army Film and Photographic Unit in 1941. In the same year, Hughenden Manor (once owned by the Victorian Prime Minister, Jewish-born, Benjamin Disraeli) was requisitioned. Britain was on the brink of losing the war. Day, and even night raids, on Nazi occupied land, were not successful. Hughenden, otherwise known as Hillside, became one of the key locations in altering the outcome of the war. It was all very hush-hush. The Official Secrets Act prevented talk until the National Trust, who now own Hughenden, were able to convince the MOD to reveal the story of the secret map-makers. Danesfield House, near Medmenham, is where the RAF studied the photographic intelligence that came in, some of which was sourced by resistance fighters. They passed on the relevant material to the small team at Hughenden Manor.[55]

Edmund Frederick Warburg, of the famous banking family, was an influential botanist. He found new species in Britain and served at RAF Medmenham, interpreting the aerial photographs, taken from RAF planes. Edmund's father Oscar was the first member of his family to marry outside the Jewish faith.[56] Edmund was not Jewish on his mother's side. There is newspaper evidence for another Warburg in the area:

"Eva Warburg fined 10/ – for a car lighting offence, and PC Lake stated that the car was left outside a butcher's shop in High Street, Great Missenden after lighting up time without having proper lights."[57]

Eva's distant cousin by marriage, Will Warburg, confirmed, Eva 'was the wife of Siegmund Warburg, of S G Warburg the merchant bank in London. Her maiden name was Philipson and she came from Stockholm.' Eva was from a Jewish banking family too. Further investigation revealed that the Warburg family, with their two children Georg and Anna, lived in The Hyde, Great Missenden, in April 1939.[58] Another cousin, John Warburg stated, the Jewish family roots went back centuries, to Simon Von Cassell in Italy. Edmund was cousin to Siegmund.

Whilst Edmund Warburg interpreted the aerial photographs, the cartographers, at Hughenden Manor, used stereoscope lenses to enhance the features, making them 3D and then hand-painting target maps, which were sent to Bomber Command at nearby Walter's Ash, Naphill, High Wycombe.[59]

Alice Anson (née Gross), worked underground at High Wycombe Bomber Command. Upon the request of the Intelligence Unit she would take a photograph of the photo and with the resulting negative would enlarge the print to reveal more detail. Alice Anson stated, 'I was a Jewish refugee from Austria. Aged fourteen, I came over to England on my own and spent four years in the WAAF during the war, stationed in High Wycombe for about one year.'

Without the departments working together D Day may not have happened.

RAF photographic interpreter, Edmund Frederick Warburg, German Jewish refugee was a botanist. Otto Leeser was a botanist and a homeopathic practitioner. His nephews Hans and Gerhard came on the Kindertransport in January 1939, after their father was murdered by the Nazis. They stayed with their uncle Dr Otto Leeser.[60] The Leeser family are registered as 'Leeser, Hans Alfred Bernhard (known as John Alfred Bernhard Leeser); Student; "Riversleigh," Loudwater, High Wycombe, Buckinghamshire. 29 September, 1947.[61] This is also the location of Leeser's 'London Homeopathy Labs'. Otto Leeser became extremely successful in his field, throughout the war and beyond.

Education was a key to success for many. During the war, girls and boys were admitted to Dr Challoner's school in Amersham. Many pupils of the Amersham Synagogue used to attend and who was there with them? 007, James Bond! Although he wasn't Jewish, Sir Roger Moore, who acted as James Bond, in the films, was also evacuated to Amersham. A bomb landed in the school field. Thankfully no one was hurt, and the pupils had a chance to go on to be stars in their specialised areas.

James Bond was created by Ian Fleming. Historian Dr Helen Fry reported that Fleming, Naval Intelligence Officer, liaised between Bletchley Park and Kendrick, a British spy who came to Latimer, after saving thousands of Jewish lives in Vienna.[62]

Imagine being the only boy in a girl's school. The Lelyvelds, a Little Chalfont Jewish family, had a son, Anthony, who could not be found a place at overcrowded Chenies School. He was sent to join the girls at Belle Vue School in Little Chalfont, the very same school attended by non-Jewish Jennifer Worth, famed author of *Call the Midwife*, which was serialised for television. She also became secretary to the headmaster of Dr Challoner's School, Amersham.

Even the famous had to shop. With no competition everyone paid the same. Amersham Wartime Food Office issued ration books, renewable every six months. Intellectuals and celebrities could have been spotted there! There were window displays of dried milk, concentrated orange juice and cod-liver oil. Close to the Wartime Food Office was the Regent cinema, an air raid siren and a shelter.

One affair of Elias Canetti's was with Jewish novelist, refugee from Vienna, Friedl Benedikt (pseudonym Anna Sebastian). They went to 'beautiful' Fingest near High Wycombe.[63] Jewish, impoverished painter from the East End of London, Barnett Freedman (CBE), created *The Barn at Fingest, Buckinghamshire* (1933), and as an Official War Artist, designed posters which are familiar to this day'.[64]

In local pubs these creative types may have bumped into non-Jewish horror writer, Arthur Machen, who had retired to Old Amersham. Having looked at various title pages, it soon became evident that if they didn't know each other, they certainly had dealings with the same Jewish publisher Alfred A. Knopf. He represented Machen, Canetti, Roald Dahl, and others vaguely connected to Bucks, such as Sigmund Freud, and Iris Murdoch. Knopf also published John Lehmann (of Jewish heritage) and his sister, novelist Rosamond, long-term residents of Bourne End. Furthermore, The Franklin family of Chartidge (since 1899) consisted of famed bankers, suffragists, scientists and academic publishers – Routledge, which operated from a garage in Chartridge during WW2.

The Sobell family evacuated to Buckinghamshire. Michael Sobell, businessman and philanthropist, was married to Anne Rakusen. Their daughter, Netta, married Lord Weinstock. Michael Sobell's granddaughter, stated he 'lived in Fulmer and his business, *Radio and Allied*, which made televisions and radios, was in Denham. They weren't religious. My uncle, Arnold Weinstock, lived in Gerrards Cross.'

Over in Chesham lived the well-known Baghdadi Sassoon family. One was seen, by an evacuee, wearing a sari at a Jewish wedding in Chesham. Rabbi Dessler, who lived in Chesham, tutored the Sassoon children. Trading across Iraq, India, China, Britain, and beyond the Sassoons were a significant force in the business world.

If all this name dropping is headache inducing, reach for an Aspirin and think of the Australian Jewish family tablet manufacturers. George Garcia came to Slough, then in Buckinghamshire, and opened the Aspro factory in the late 1920s, making much revenue for the UK, as painkillers were always needed.[65]

Rosalind Preston (née Morris), her mother, Marie and her brother, Lionel, lived in Beaconsfield. Rosalind became the first female vice-president on the Jewish Board of Deputies and president of the Jewish Volunteering Network. For a more detailed biography see the Jewish Women's Archive.[66]

Rosalind neighbours were 'very anti-Semitic'. She attended a private school 'up a small lane not far from our house (rented) in Clover Hill'. The family did not attend synagogue but Rosalind has 'memories of my mother going to the station to pick up kosher meat and chickens each week.' She recalled 'knowing one other Jewish family – refugees by the name of Segall.'

Rosalind Preston always had a love for the countryside. Aged about six, she 'spent most time in the garden or cycling around local lanes.' The 'house seemed large' but points out she was only small. Rosalind's aunt and two children lived with immediate family. Sometimes her maternal grandparents would join them. Rosalind felt 'war did not impinge on our young lives and the sun always seemed to be shining.'

Also in Beaconsfield lived Madeline Albright, of Jewish heritage, who would grow up to be the first female American Secretary of State. Albright's father, Josef Korbel,[67] worked for Edvard Beneš, exiled president of Czechoslovakia, who was residing in Aston Abbotts near Aylesbury in Buckinghamshire.[68]

Alice Hildegard Margolis was evacuated to Waddesdon village. She became Professor Alice Shalvi, a feminist and social activist, winning prestigious awards for her work. In nearby Quainton, Jewish feminist and famous writer, Amelia Pincherle Rosselli lived.

According to another evacuee, Jewish Londoner Michael Fox evacuated to High Wycombe. Fox helped found the largest Israeli law firm, Herzog, Fox & Neeman. His partner Chaim Herzog became President of Israel.

Rolf Decker played for Aylesbury United Football Club and his brother, Otto, for Wycombe Wanderers. Both Kindertransport children were signed to the U.S national team as professional soccer players.

German-Jewish child refugee Vernon Katz, who became a writer, lived in a hostel in Loudwater, High Wycombe. He enjoyed idyllic holiday time with a family in Great Missenden, as recorded in his memoirs.[69]

A King in Exile

King Zog of Albania lived in exile in Parmoor House, Frieth, Buckinghamshire, renting from 1941 until 1946. The King fled Albania in 1939 when Mussolini invaded. King Zog was a Muslim who saved Jews. Dr. T. Scarlett Epstein OBE wrote an autobiography, *Swimming Upstream – The Story of a Jewish Refugee.*[70] She kindly explained how important King Zog and the Albanians were for Jewish people:

> Albania was in 1938 the only country that followed besa, their Code of behaviour, and disregarding their religion offered asylum to persecuted Jewish Refugees. They saved about 3000 European Jewish Refugees before and during the last war of whom my parents and myself were part. I thus now feel that I owe my life to Albania and use my professional developmental experience to improve the efficiency of Albania's development activities.

King Zog was not a very good housekeeper! His pet goat made a feast of the furnishings, his dogs were bathed in the bath tub and rats climbed up the foliage, on the external walls, to make a living space for themselves of the upstairs.[71] We can forgive the King his lack of domestic discipline when we think of all the Jewish lives that he and his fellow Muslim Albanians saved.

BRITAIN'S MOST WANTED

The Nazi invasion of Britain plan was for September 1940. SS General Walter Schellenberg produced a list of names of their most wanted.[72] Authorisation had been given for Einsatzgruppen, killing squads.

Some of the most wanted included those connected to Buckinghamshire; Chamberlain and Churchill who's Prime-ministerial retreat, was 'Chequers' in Wendover (Churchill also stayed weekends with the Winants, an American Ambassador and his wife, in a Latimer farmhouse). Others were Lady Astor, Benes (exiled President of Czechoslovakia), Kendrick – who saved thousands of Austrian Jews and oversaw a spy operation in Latimer and Beaconsfield, Alexander Korda (film magnate), Dr Max Sulzbacher (German Jewish refugee), Leslie Hore-Belisha (MP related to Veza Canetti) and members of the Rothschild family. Philip Woolf, who managed Rothschild's Waddesdon estate, could have discovered his Jewish brother Leonard and sister-in-law, writer Virginia Woolf, on the list. Distinguished historian George Peabody Gooch, who lived in Chalfont St Peter, helped many refugees and so was not favoured by the Nazis. John Jagger was recorded as Jewish ('Jude'). The labour MP, and trade unionist, as soon as Hitler came to power, advocated for world assistance for Jewish people. Tragically, Jagger died 9th July 1942 in Beaconsfield, when his motorbike was in collision with a car, near his cottage. [73]

LET MY CHILDREN GO

Life was to change for the children who became evacuees. One day they were going along with their normal routine, the next an uprooting began of such proportions that leaving home would be an exciting adventure or a terrible mistake. Parting from home had the power to shape the direction of their lives into something completely unexpected and new.

The Government advocated non-compulsory evacuation for children, and vulnerable adults, which began on the first of September 1939, a Friday. Dusk turned into Shabbat, the holy Sabbath and lasted until sunset on Saturday.

Parents of evacuees worried about the goodness of host families. They would wait for the postman every day for their pre-stamped, addressed postcard to arrive. It was hoped siblings had not been homed separately, as happened to Jewish Chesham child evacuee, Hilda Baxt.

In addition to homesickness young children would have difficulty in understanding their feelings and making sense of the strange and unstable world around them.

And the food – what would the children have to eat? Children from kosher homes might have no choice but to eat forbidden food. Some children obtained places in Jewish hostels, as did Bernd Koschland, so they did not have to worry about dietary laws.

Jewish Life

There were wartime orthodox synagogues in Gerrards Cross, Beaconsfield, High Wycombe, Haversham, Bletchley, Chesham and Amersham.

Sue Blake extensively researched the history of Haversham:

> I found out where the synagogue was, and would you believe, it stood in the garden of the house where my cousin lives at number 2 Wolverton Road, Haversham. It was a wooden building. His old neighbor, who died some years ago, said they also stored food in there. My cousin pulled the building down when he bought the house and put up a brick garage. Giles Randall built the houses in Wolverton Road and on the Crescent, they weren't selling, but as soon as war seemed on the horizon Jewish families came down and bought them up and some rented. The men spent the week in London and came home weekends. My cousin has found the details, "Timber built garage with electric light and 3 power points measuring 16' 3" x 9' 6" workshop at the rear." He remembers it was built of cedar wood planks. Although it was sold as being a garage in the particulars of the early 1970s, during the war not many people had cars, so was perhaps purpose built as a synagogue at the time.

Before them came Moses Margoliouth who wrote *The History of the Jews of Great Britain* published in 1851. He was born a Polish Jew, converted to Christianity, and became the vicar of Little Linford parish, a part of Haversham![74]

The Amersham Hebrew Congregation (1942 – 1968) was loosely based on the United Synagogue. The consecration of the New Communal Hall, a pre-fabricated hut, was on Sunday, 23rd August 1942. It was established by the United Synagogue Membership Group of Amersham and District. During the war years, three ministers were appointed; Reverend Sebastian Morton Bloch (known as Sonnie), Rev. Izaak Rapaport PhD, (appointed 1941) who was also the secretary, and Rev. Jonah Indech (appointed 1st April 1944 – 31st December 1945).

Woodrow High House, Cherry Lane, Amersham used to be called Woodside House. The sanctuary housed the wife and children of Oliver Cromwell during the English Civil War, in the mid seventeenth century. In 1665 Cromwell re-admitted Jewish people for the first time since the 1290 expulsion, a major event in Anglo-Jewish history. Interestingly, the sanctuary for the Jewish people of WW2 Amersham was the synagogue, similarly named Woodside Hall.

Close by Woodside Hall was a canteen hut in Bois Lane, Chesham Bois. It was run by a committee of Jewish ladies. Children could get a good dinner for 4d, and adults for 1/-. There was a second kosher canteen in Chesham Cricket Pavilion, a Saturday kosher meal for service personnel in the Amersham synagogue and kosher meals available in Amersham Hospital. The woods surrounding Amersham were filled with Prisoner of War and military camps. The Home Guard trained locally, complete with broomsticks instead of guns! They also dug trenches, signs of which can still be spotted around the woods and fields today, such as in Rectory Wood.

In Chesham, an orthodox congregation affiliated to the Federation of Synagogues, was formed about 1941. They met in the Chesham Cricket Pavilion off Amy Lane. People from both Amersham and Chesham very often knew each other, socialised and held services together. Post-war, numbers dwindled, and they officially united as the Amersham, Chesham and District Hebrew Congregation. Other services were held in various locations across Buckinghamshire, such as at the Methodist church in High Wycombe, and even in a train carriage!

Back to the original question, raised from talking with Katie Krone, who is the rabbi in the green jacket? Well, you're not going to be told yet! However, it can now be revealed that it was one of these three reverends, and none of them were rabbis at the time! A reverend is not yet qualified to be a rabbi. A few members were mistaken in the belief that they were rabbis. This suggests how good these three men must have been in their roles as teachers.

Bombs over Buckinghamshire[75]

Buckinghamshire County Council archives noted the 'fires of the London blitz could be seen as far away as Waddesdon'. The area was at risk but much safer as figures prove. During the Blitz, 26th June to 31st December 1940, London's death toll was twenty – three thousand compared to thirty-three in Buckinghamshire. The archives recorded:

When a flying bomb hit and demolished a house in Chestnut Lane, Chesham Bois in July 1944, rescue parties came from Amersham, Great Missenden and Chesham to help clear the area. Sandbags were used to help soften the blast and minimise damage.

The Women's Voluntary Service (WVS) were on call day and night providing help to victims and rescue workers with mobile canteens, clothes and blankets. Buckinghamshire archives recorded that on 'Sunday 2nd July 1944 a V1 bomb landed on the house Red Leys in Chestnut Lane, Chesham Bois. Red Leys was the home of Sir Arthur Scott, a distinguished veteran of the Boer War and World War 1.'

Several people died when the doodlebug exploded in Chesham Bois. As a younger generation it can be difficult to comprehend what it would have been like to be caught in the midst of a world on fire. The courage and generosity of the community may have elevated confidence to a general belief that, even if they had to take a few hits first, Britain was going to win the war.

***

MEMORIES

Primary sources include recollections through interviews with the authors, some originally published in *Landsleit of Amersham and surrounding areas: A History of the Amersham Hebrew Congregation 1939-1945* by Vivien Samson. Secondary sources have been provided with equal generosity by families, knowledgeable individuals and organisations.

Where possible we have decided not to include news of those who are no longer alive. The memories portray youth and vitality, and that is the way we think of everyone involved.

The only truly dead are those who have been forgotten.

Jewish saying

KATIE KRONE

When Hitler became Germany's Fuhrer, I and my friend had to leave the country in order to survive. As a trained nurse I got a post at Amersham General Hospital. My friend only got as far as Holland. The war had started, and she missed the boat. We did not hear from each other anymore for a long time. Later, I received a letter through the Red Cross, from my friend, who had reached Palestine. She had been released from Belsen Concentration Camp in exchange for a German Prisoner of War. She had written:

"If the war lasts longer you will lose your whole family…"

And so it happened.

My friend settled in Israel after her terrifying experience in Belsen Camp.

During the war I and other German Jewish ladies met at the Quaker Meeting House every Sunday to have a drink and chat. I went in my nurse's uniform. They were surprised I worked in Amersham Hospital next door as a nursing sister. I helped to create Sunday meetings, for women only, which the refugees really enjoyed.

At Amersham Hospital we had wards in corrugated huts as well as the main workhouse. Our congregation still holds services at the Meeting House. When working in the hospital, I always wore my B'nai B'rith badge[76] and Magen David (Star of David) necklace. One wartime patient, non-Jewish, said to me 'I am proud of you for wearing these. I know many Jewish people.'

I occasionally attended services in the synagogue at Woodside Road.

Before leaving to be a chaplain to the Forces, Sidney Bloch's brother, Sonnie, was the rabbi [reverend] for a short time. Although there were three rabbis serving the congregation at different times during the war, I remember that one of them always wore a green jacket, and that he rode a motorbike.

One barmitzvah that I remember was that of Mrs Cohen's son in 1943.

His portion was taught to him by Mr S Tabor, who also conducted the service. I remember Mr Tabor as being a teacher of Barmitzvah boys.

After the war the services ceased because there were not enough men present to form a minyan.

Figure 1: Katie Krone, 1924.

Nathan Family –
Else, Kurt and their
children Renate and
Clemens[77]

By Liz Ison.

When Else and Kurt discovered that children in Wembley were likely to be evacuated, they decided to move to a rented cottage in Amersham, Buckinghamshire (this was on the Metropolitan Line) in the summer of 1939 (war broke out in September), following Sandy Goehr and his parents [friends] who had moved there. They lived in White Cottage on Grimsdell's Lane. It took Kurt about an hour to commute into his office in Central London.

Sandy's father, Walter Goehr, a well-known composer and conductor, having lost his job at Berlin Radio because of his Jewish origins, had come to England to work as a music director for The Gramophone Company (later EMI). Sandy – Alexander Goehr – is now a well-known composer. When playing at Sandy's house, Renate recalls the children spying on Sandy's father through the keyhole of his bathroom door as he practised his conducting in front of the bathroom mirror.

Renate and Clemens had lots of fun playing in the garden their first summer there. The cottage had a big hedge at the front which was great to use as a secret hiding place. They built dens out of sticks and used cloth samples that Kurt brought home from the business to cover them. Kurt organised for an air-raid shelter to be built in the back garden. The children watched the progress of the large hole that was dug for the shelter as they played their games out in the garden. It was a prefabricated 'Anderson shelter' made out of curved corrugated steel panels placed on a concrete base, with two points of access. They bought bedsteads and mattresses to sleep on. There were even shelves inside.

Kurt also made 'blackout' screens himself for the windows of the house, by soaking wood in water, and bending them into frames, which he covered with blackout material.

It was a pretty cottage but terribly cold in the winter months. To stop the taps freezing overnight, Kurt would put a lit candle in a milk bottle under the tap in the big sink in the pantry in the evening. There in White Cottage they settled down, buying a puppy, Topsy, and chickens so they could have fresh eggs every day.

They were very fortunate to have their grandparents so close. Their grandmother Regina Nathan came to live with them on her arrival from Germany. At first, [their other grandparents] Ludwig and Otti settled in Harrow-on-the-Hill in outer London. When it became a Protected Area (meaning anyone not British could not reside there), Otti and Ludwig moved to Amersham and rented a place [Grimsdell's Lane] in order to be close to Else and the family. Opa [German for grandfather] Kanin would continue his mesmerising stories about der Kleine Mann and der Grosse Mann, on condition that Renate and Clemens, and their friend Sandy who often came round, would let him finish reading his newspaper.

Renate and Clemens were initially enrolled in the local state school. On his first day, Clemens witnessed one of the boys being beaten in front of the class by the headmaster for setting fire to a bird's nest. The children were treated by the school nurse for lice. After a time, Else and Kurt decided to take their children out of the school and send them to a private school, The Turret School.

Like many others, the family helped with the war effort. Though they weren't allowed to join the Home Guard as they were German and they were required to handle weapons, Else and Kurt did join the Air Raid Precautions (ARP). They had night duty as air-raid wardens when they patrolled Grimsdell's Lane for two hours in the middle of the night, armed with large torches and a whistle. Kurt also had monthly night duty on the roof of the office buildings in Oxford Circus Avenue. Else helped make camouflage cloth with some other local women. Once, recalls Renate, Kurt invited a local friend to come and see his garden; the friend replied that he already had been in it, to put out an incendiary bomb.

Renate and Clemens usually walked the short distance home from The Turret School by themselves. Their route was across an unmade road bordered by a ditch, where they would often linger to splash in the puddles and then along a passage between two gardens to reach White Cottage. Once they heard a plane overhead and, terrified, Renate pulled Clemens into the ditch by the side of the road to wait for it to pass.

During this period they slept nightly in the air-raid shelter. The children went to sleep in there on their own, and their parents didn't come in till their own bedtime. The Anderson shelters were not at all soundproof and the two children would spend evenings terrified, listening out for every creak, Clemens suspecting that German spies must be at the door and Renate pretending not to be scared as she was the big sister. Indeed, the sound of distant bombing reverberated through the ground, and they could hear the echoes of bombs exploding in London. They also heard the terrible noise of the anti-aircraft guns (known as 'Ack-acks') that were stationed on lorries which would have been driving around trying to shoot down the planes. Finally, their father took their fear seriously and installed an electric bell that they were allowed to ring if they were feeling really scared. Often, their parents would sit with them too, and Clemens remembers Else playing her accordion to them to drown out other noises. They also played memory games like I packed my bags … to pass the time.

As well as being a gifted pianist, Else acquired a Swiss accordion which she endeavoured to master. The Swiss accordion has buttons at both ends (rather than a keyboard on one side) and Else struggled to learn it. One day, on the train home, Kurt got chatting to a man with a large black case. He found out that it contained an accordion, of the usual sort with buttons and a keyboard, and Kurt got off at Amersham station with the case and accordion and with rather fewer pounds and shillings in his pocket. Else, accompanied by Renate, took lessons from a local female accordion teacher. Later, not only did she help drown out the sound of bombing in the shelter by playing tunes on the accordion to her children, but she also played it at St. John Ambulance dances.

When the air-raid siren went off, they would have to go to the shelter immediately and could only return to the house when the siren had signalled the all-clear. Walking across the garden back to the house, they would often look towards London and see the sky glowing red: they could see the fires that had been caused by the bombing. Once, after the all-clear, the family emerged from the shelter and walked across the lawn back towards the house when two planes suddenly flew overhead. Else threw herself on top of the two children in an instinctive maternal gesture of protection. It was a gesture never forgotten by her children. Overhead, a Spitfire was engaged in a dogfight with a German Messerschmitt. The German plane machine-gunned in all directions until eventually it was shot down.

Like many others who used air-raid shelters, as the summer came to an end, conditions in the shelter became increasingly damp and unpleasant. The ground upon which their shelter rested was clay and, one day, they found it filled with water. So they abandoned the shelter and gathered in the hallway of the cottage which had no windows and the ceiling of which Kurt had had reinforced with metal. The children, parents and grandparents, who were living with them at this time, all sat there on the floor. Renate remembers the crocodile case that was always brought there too on these occasions. She didn't know why it was so important to have it with them but now realises that it must have contained their most important papers and documents. There was also a spade in the corner of the hall in case they needed to dig themselves out of trouble. During loud bombing, or even a thunderstorm, Else often played the piano to reassure the children.

Food was rationed during the war. They had a plentiful supply of eggs from their chickens, and other food was bought using coupons distributed to all the population. Clemens recalls that their second dog Rio (a sheepdog who replaced Topsy who was run over) once managed to eat up the family's entire cheese ration, upsetting Else but with Kurt taking it philosophically and telling the dog to enjoy it. Occasionally they had to eat whale meat, and Else, like many English mothers of that generation, was keen to give the children cod liver oil – considered an excellent source of Vitamin D; she even tried adding it to jam tarts but the children refused to eat them! Otherwise Else and her mother Otti continued to cook in the German continental style. Clemens remembers red cabbage, duck and goose being favourites; wiener schnitzels were another favourite. One of the few things that Kurt cooked and loved preparing was lemon cream, not a particularly German dish, but Clemens loved it.

Many German refugees were interned in camps during the war, suspected of being 'enemy aliens'. Else and Kurt had to attend a tribunal, as did other potential enemy aliens, after which they were recorded, together with the vast majority of other refugees, as 'Category C', the lowest risk of being a threat. However, when the political atmosphere changed in 1940 and the threat of a German invasion became greater, they knew the family was at risk of being arrested and interned. In anticipation, they sold all their chickens in case there would be no one to look after them if they were sent away. It was about this time, in April 1940, that Hitler invaded Denmark, and Renate found her mother crying at the news, one of the few times Renate recalls Else crying.

Very early one morning, Clemens and Renate remember vividly the police arriving at their house to take their father away. The policemen were extremely polite. Their grandfather Ludwig was also arrested on the same day and was interned for a short time. Luckily, Else and the children weren't (their great friends the Hochfelds and their young son, George, were all interned on the Isle of Man for a long time).

Kurt was taken to an internment camp in Paignton on the South Coast which was ordinarily a holiday camp. He stayed there for some months before his release. Kurt had rather poor health there, with damp conditions and an ongoing gall bladder problem. Kurt shared his room with a count, Count von Ostheim, who had been in the German cavalry – he was excellent at polishing shoes, so he polished the shoes, and Kurt made the beds. Afterwards, the Count visited the family in Amersham – to the excitement of the children who wondered whether he would arrive on horseback in full regalia. In the event, he turned out to be a very polite white-haired man with a heavy German accent. There wasn't much to do at Paignton, so some of the inmates – a rather cultured group of German Jewish refugees – organised concerts and lectures. Kurt opposed these events. He felt they shouldn't create a new community because that might prolong their internment.

Efforts were made to get Kurt released, citing his business responsibilities and his poor health. Kurt's secretary Phyllis McPherson wrote a letter asking him to be released, explaining about his business obligations and how his employees depended upon him. The Chief Rabbi intervened on his behalf.

Renate remembers that she and Clemens prayed each night for their father and grandfather's release. They always said a short nightly prayer before they went to sleep and, while they were away, they added a bit to the end: 'Please let my father and grandfather out as soon as possible' – they had a long debate as to whether they should be saying this in English or German. Otti [grandmother] stayed with them whilst Ludwig was away: she would sleep in Renate's room. Sometimes, Renate remembers, she would get up in the middle of the night and get fully dressed. When Renate asked what she was doing, she would reply "Nothing", but then go and look out of the window, probably to investigate some noises which she suspected was an air battle.

Kurt was released early, possibly due to his ill health, and he returned to Amersham. Clemens recalls an amusing story of how he got home – escorted by a nice young soldier, Kurt handcuffed to him. When they changed trains, the soldier offered to go and buy them teas at the railway station. He undid the handcuffs, telling Kurt, "Hold on to my rifle while I get the tea." So Kurt sat on the bench on the platform, holding a rifle, waiting for the soldier to come back with his mug of tea. After they'd finished, the soldier said, "I'd better put the handcuffs back on again."

Back in Amersham, they bought some more chickens and life returned to how it had been. The episode had been a difficult one, and Kurt's worsening health was often blamed on the conditions he had experienced in the camp.

Shortly after Kurt was released, the family bought a house, Torwood, Clifton Road, in the village of Chesham Bois, close to Amersham, that Ludwig had seen for sale for £2,500 [they lived there until 1956]. By this stage, Kurt's business was established, and the outbreak of war had created a shortage of cloth in England that had allowed Kurt's business to flourish.

Clemens remembers his nice bedroom, which had a bed that folded into the wall, a big couch, a round table for his books and a desk facing the front of the house. Renate's much larger room was at the other end of the corridor. There was a large garden that adjoined a wood, with bluebells in the spring.

Kurt was a founding member of the Jewish community in Amersham, the 'Amersham Hebrew Congregation' and served as Chairman of the small congregation for a time. The congregation was formed primarily of London evacuees, some of whom had come from Germany. Else served on committees, looked after poorer Jewish families, administering grants for food and clothing. At first, services were held in White Cottage then Kurt hired a church hall, St. Leonard's Hall in Chesham Bois, where services were held. During one of the first services, a member of the congregation let out an exclamation when he spotted a crucifix on one of the walls. The crucifix was duly covered up with a cloth.

Later on, a permanent synagogue was created in Woodside Hall in Amersham. The decision was made, after some discussion, not to become affiliated to the United Synagogue but to remain non-denominational. Synagogue furniture was, however, acquired from the United Synagogue. It was a small, friendly community, with a happy mix of the Orthodox and the less Orthodox.

The family would attend Shabbat Services every two or three weeks. Clemens remembers the pleasant walks with his father to and from synagogue, which gave them time to chat. Despite Kurt's commitment to the Jewish community, he had no qualms about eating non-Kosher, including pork or bacon. He maintained that many of the dietary laws had come about because of the difficulties of hygiene and food safety in hot countries, and that now in the days of modern refrigeration this made the need for keeping these laws redundant. Festivals were marked with the usual celebrations. Else and Kurt held a large seder at Torwood for Passover. Else organised Hanukkah parties for WIZO (Women's International Zionist Organization) in Amersham. On one occasion, to her horror, Else discovered a few minutes before the guests arrived, that the caterer, though briefed on kashrut laws, had put shrimps on top of the sandwiches. She quickly removed them and said no more.

Renate and Clemens learned Hebrew with a private teacher, Mr. Robant, an Orthodox man, who would come to their house every Sunday. Clemens remembers him teaching them to read prayers and then timing them to see how quickly they could get through them. He never taught them to translate them or to try to understand their meaning. Lessons were often a time to be naughty. Once, a neighbour and friend of theirs agreed to let the air out of the tyres of the teacher's bicycle during the lesson time. They could hear the noise from their bedroom where they were having their lesson and the teacher was satisfyingly cross. Another time, Clemens played a remarkable conjuring trick on poor Mr. Robant. Before the lesson, Clemens drilled a hole through the wall from one bedroom to the next, and tied the rug onto a piece of string. During the lesson, Renate demonstrated her magical prowess, while Clemens pulled the string from the other room and made the rug rise off the floor. Their father was very angry and deducted the cost for the repair work from Clemens' pocket money.

Clemens' barmitzvah in 1946 was memorable. He had been taught by the Reverend Indech. Rabbi Italiener came to officiate for the service itself at Woodside Hall in Amersham, the same Rabbi who had married his parents back in Hamburg. He treated Clemens with great kindness. After the service, Clemens' father called out, "Refreshments in the Committee Room!" and everyone bustled into the room. There was a lovely atmosphere, his parents so proud of him, with everyone complimenting the barmitzvah boy. Presents are often an important part of the barmitzvah rite, and Clemens recalls receiving rather too many fountain pens, which people considered a novelty in those days. He was thrilled when, back at Torwood, his father presented him with his first-ever watch. Else organised a lunch and tea back at their house. With rationing still in force, this was no easy feat. Clemens recalls that she had saved up their butter ration for months and months in order to make huge quantities of 'butter cakes' for all the guests. Clemens and his friend Sandy Goehr, not used to such a plentiful supply of cakes, and with their parents too busy chatting to notice, gorged themselves on the cakes till they had to rush out into the woods at the back of the garden to be sick!

Clemens's Jewish childhood experiences were happy ones. Involvement with the synagogue and a strong Jewish identity were balanced by his parents' strenuous efforts to assimilate into English society. They had many non-Jewish friends, and their involvement in St. John Ambulance, in particular, allowed them to make friends from all walks of life. Else and Kurt's involvement in Jewish life seemed to really develop on a continuum from their previous life in Hamburg: they wanted to be actively involved in the Jewish community but it was not their whole life.

Particularly because Else's sister, Lotte, lived in Palestine, the family always felt very positively towards Palestine and later the State of Israel. Else became active in WIZO when they lived in Amersham and she organised and supported many WIZO fund-raising events. She became WIZO Chairman of the local branch. Her association with the movement continued for the rest of her life, even travelling on her 80th birthday to Israel on a WIZO tour.

Kurt was rather less interested in Palestine-Israel until he visited for the first time and he discovered what a remarkable place it was.

Many lifelong friends were made through the Jewish community including Arthur Harverd, one of Clemens' oldest friends, John Farago and Shirley Samuel.

Renate and Clemens remember a constant stream of visitors coming to stay in Amersham, Their cousin Ushi, who had come over via the Kindertransport, visited from Liverpool and Leeds when she could. Ruth Heiman, Steven Adler and his brother Ralph had also come to visit at weekends. They were like older sisters and brothers to Renate and Clemens.

Ruth had come to England on the Kindertransport, and often visited or stayed with Otti and Ludwig or Else and Kurt in Amersham, when she had any spare time from working 50-60 hours a week in a war production factory at the age of 17.

Ralph Maier, a cousin of Kurt's, had moved to America and then came over to England with the army. He went over to Germany on secret missions, parachuting in or going by submarine. He passed as a German army officer and was able to extract important information and documents about the Nazis' war plans. The family also developed a lifelong friendship with his commander, Arthur Simon, Arthur was a keen singer and he used to stay for weekends at Torwood, and sing to Else's accompaniment on the piano. There were many musical afternoons when the sound of Schubert Lieder (songs) echoed through the house.

Kurt's first cousin Bella Snowman also moved to England from Hamburg with her husband Tel and three children, Werner, Inge and Ellen. The families were close.

The German Jewish community was close-knit. Else and Kurt made many friends amongst this community and they were an eclectic and intelligent group. Renate remembers, for example, Thea Hochfeld, who was an anthroposophist, a follower of the philosophy of Rudolph Steiner that influenced her work with handicapped children.

Kurt's main interest outside his working life was St. John Ambulance, the main function of which was – and still is – to provide first aid training and support. In Germany, he had been involved with the Red Cross and had organised summer camps for children there. In England, he worked tirelessly for St. John Ambulance in the Amersham area, and within a short time all the family had got involved.

Kurt's initial role in the organisation was as a Cadet Officer in charge of the cadets, the young boys who joined St. John Ambulance. In 1943, he helped set up a Cadet Division of St. John Ambulance in Amersham. He later became Superintendent of the cadets and continued to recruit many children to the movement: boys became cadets, and girls nurses. The nurses focused on simple nursing and the cadets learned a bit more about the outdoors. Clemens and Renate were duly enlisted. The cadets and nurses had to learn first aid and pass exams in them.

Kurt also helped to organise the summer camps for the Buckinghamshire County Cadets (some two to three hundred young people took part each year). For ten years between 1948 and 1958, he was Camp Commandant and Officer-in-Charge of the county camps. The cadets and nurses were often from working class or farming backgrounds and the camps were sometimes their only opportunity for a holiday. Clemens recalls that Kurt subsidised the camps from his own pocket so that the rates were very cheap for families. Kurt loved to give these children a great holiday. Renate recalls wet holidays in muddy fields and laying down straw under the tent so that she didn't completely sink into the mud. Occasionally, Lady Mountbatten would visit a camp and chat to Kurt. Renate remembers that Lady Mountbatten taught him a method for killing wasps!

Another important role for Kurt and St. John was organising volunteers to run the ambulance service (Central Ambulance Division) in Buckinghamshire, which at that time was run entirely by volunteers and serviced the population in all the surrounding villages; only with the advent of the National Health Service after the war did the ambulance service become professional when the great body of volunteers fell away. Clemens thinks it was a great mistake to lose these skills and with it the spirit of voluntary service. As a cadet, Clemens was required to help one evening a week with carrying stretchers and other tasks.

Else also became involved. She was also very proud of her uniform. She would muck in as required, making sandwiches for parties and washing up the dishes afterwards. At the camps, she would assist Kurt with checking that the tents were pitched correctly and that there were the right quantities of provisions for the stores; she would also help in the camp kitchens. Kurt and Else were a 'wonderful team'. In 1951, she became Honorary Vice-President of the Amersham Nursing Cadet Division.

Kurt later became County Staff Officer and subsequently Deputy Commissioner for Bucks. In 1954, in recognition of his contribution and on the recommendation of the Council of the Grand Priory in the British Realm, he became an 'Associate Serving Brother' of the Venerable Order of the Hospital of St. John of Jerusalem.

He found his work with St. John immensely fulfilling; he was proud to wear the St. John Ambulance uniform and to meet people from all walks of life. He was a popular and much-loved member of St. John. It was certainly an admirable way of contributing to something very English even though Renate recalls that some of their German Jewish friends were rather mystified that Kurt and Else would want to be part of an organisation of the Order of the Hospital of St. John of Jerusalem (founded at the time of the Crusades) where black uniforms, a cross insignia, parades, and youth camps were part of its characteristics.

After the end of the war, and ten years after arriving in England, in November 1946, Kurt received his Certificate of Naturalisation which, as the Certificate declared, gave him 'to all intents and purposes the status of a natural-born British subject'. He duly signed his oath of allegiance to 'His Majesty King George the Sixth, His Heirs and Successors'.

Kurt was 54 years old when he died. The funeral took place at the Jewish Cemetery in Hoop Lane in Golders Green. The street was lined by St. John Ambulance men in uniform. After Kurt's coffin had been placed in the ground, each of the men went up to it in turn and saluted it. The Rabbi commented that, despite officiating at many funerals, he had never seen anything so moving.

An Autobiographical Sketch

Clemens N. Nathan

[Extract from *The Changing Face of Religion and Human Rights*, Martinus Nijhoff Publishers, 2009]

My own personal concern for the relationship between human rights and religion stems from my upbringing and background. I was brought up in the Jewish tradition in Germany and became a refugee child in England at the age of three. My status as a refugee taught me that you can adapt to wherever you live, and in so doing experience a breadth of human society which enriches you. This was made possible for me through the concerns and caring attitude of others.

We kept the major Jewish holidays and went to synagogue, and although we were more liberal than orthodox, my father kept traditional values. He was a remarkable example of a person who adapted to his new environment as soon as he came to England to escape the Third Reich – not only to find a way to earn his living, but to do voluntary and human rights work in his own way. The same was true of my mother.

My father was active in the St John's Ambulance and became a member of the Order of St John. He offered to read the Old Testament lessons at camps for children, and even did so in the church where they held the service for the St John's Ambulance, which was his great love. He always said that the greatest gift from God was to hear children laughing at the camps that he and my mother voluntarily organised in Buckinghamshire where we lived. This brought 200-300 children together every year. My mother would help with the cooking while my father, together with groups of other volunteers of St John's men and women, organised the camp. My mother's family kept what could be called 'middle-of-the-road Judaism' in the Ashkenazi tradition. I was fortunate that my grandparents on my mother's side also came to England with us, and my grandfather went to synagogue every Saturday.

My mother was one of the first female students to receive a doctorate in political economics at Konigsberg and Heidelberg University. She was an active young woman in Germany before meeting my father in Hamburg. After emigrating to England, she enjoyed doing voluntary work and even played the organ in a Baptist church in Chesham when they were short of an organist. She would cycle there on Sunday mornings. She was also extremely busy in our local synagogue, a mere hut in Amersham, Buckinghamshire, and helped to organise everything with my father. We used to walk to synagogue – a Jewish tradition – on Saturdays.

The Jewish high holidays and Saturdays played an important role in my life, in a multi-faith way, especially during the war when we were in Amersham. There were Jews who were extremely religious and others who were liberal, yet we all managed to work and co-operate together. My mother also ran the Amersham Woman's International Zionist Organisation (WIZO) in the early 1950's, which collected money for a baby home in Jerusalem.

We lived in a charming cottage in Amersham and later my parents bought a very comfortable house. During our cultural afternoons, my mother used to play the piano at which she was extremely accomplished. She could read any score and we often heard Schubert Lieder sung by friends of ours. Walter Goehr, an eminent conductor of the BBC Symphony Orchestra who also came from Germany, often used to come and help out during these afternoons. His son, now a lifetime friend, has become Professor of Music at Cambridge and a prominent composer. We were probably too young to appreciate the romanticism of Lieder! This was wartime and people did not go to London for concerts, so our home became very much the Sunday afternoon place for people who created music.   During the Second World War, many different people living in London came and stayed in our house. My mother put down mattresses in all rooms so that people could be comfortable and safe away from the bombing. With our nanny, who was also a refugee and who was like a second mother to us, my mother worked very hard preparing food and baking cakes so that everyone had enough to eat. We had our own chickens, geese and ducks, with special feed rations to sustain them and provide eggs for our neighbours and family. From time to time one of these fowls would appear on the dining room table! This feeling of community spirit was nurtured at many lunches, dinners and concerts in our home. People of every profession and walk of life were there, especially refugees like ourselves from Germany and Austria. Many were from the Kinder Transport, including some of my cousins. I felt secure but was aware that there were many worlds outside of my own which I would want to explore when I grew older. The 50th Anniversary of the Kinder Transport who came to England in 1939 (10,000 children) was organised by a group of dynamic women and I was asked to help with this remarkable reunion which I opened in Harrow-on-the-Hill.

At the beginning of the war, we children had a great shock when the police took my father away early one morning. He was interned as an enemy alien, despite the fact that he was a Jewish refugee from Nazi Germany. Fortunately, he came back after six months, but he was extremely ill and never really recovered. He was also terribly shaken and depressed by the whole experience, which affected him much more than many other people. The lack of freedom, the degradation of being locked up and not being with his family, the injustice – all this was brought home to him when non-Jewish Germans from circuses who had elephants were allowed leave to feed their animals, whereas internees like himself were not even allowed home to look after their own children. My mother coped with this period by letting virtually every room in our rented cottage and expanding our chicken flock in the garden. In this way, we managed to survive quite well.

We as children were not aware that money was extremely tight, but we were aware that we could have been interned any day. My mother had packed rucksacks which were in the hall, just in case the police came again. We would otherwise have been unprepared, as my father had been when he was arrested and interned. He was also very bitter that having done so much voluntary work since he arrived in England in 1936, he was still classed as an enemy alien due to Home Office procedures. Fortunately, he recovered from his depression and rejoined the St John Ambulance throwing himself into its work. It was, in some ways, a haven – just knowing that once again he belonged, when in fact everything had been taken away from him – once in Germany and now nearly again through internment in Britain.

I joined the Officers Training Corps. I had already been a member of the Scouts and the St John's Ambulance Cadets in Amersham.

During the Second World War I hated the Germans so powerfully that I would have killed them in my dreams, although my feelings now are totally opposed to killing and capital punishment.

I became more aware of the development of emancipation for Jews in this country. It was possible to have a deep religious belief and to co-exist here. I met my wife at the Anglo-Jewish Association…and subsequently through them, under the guidance of the late Maurice Edelman MP I became the AJA's Treasurer. [The Anglo-Jewish Association provides funds to UK Jewish students in financial need.] Both my wife's family and mine have a sense of spirituality and concern for people of all faiths, which of course is part of Judaism… I am part of a religious body, a people marked out in their identity by their religion. As I live today, I consider myself to be a spiritual person. Perhaps I do not pray enough for my own well-being, but I prefer to be an activist in dealing with intolerance wherever it occurs. I believe my passion for this has come partly from having heard of the horrors of the Holocaust and those members of my family who were killed, and through the suffering of many of my relations who had to start completely anew in their middle age. It is remarkable how many of them learnt English and were able to find positions to develop their personalities and careers, but it was certainly not easy for any of them. Some, like my father, were able to bring their expertise in business management and textiles to this country and developed this talent enthusiastically.

LIZ ISON REMEMBERING HER GRANDMOTHER, ELSE:

Just as at Kurt's funeral some forty years earlier, St. John Ambulance men and women in full uniform attended the funeral of Else [aged 93]. They very movingly followed the coffin (in which her St. John Ambulance President's hat had been placed) to her final resting-place beside Kurt in the Jewish cemetery in Hoop Lane, Golders Green – a fitting tribute to Else and her husband, two Jewish immigrants who did so much for their local community.

… End of material from Liz Ison's book…

ELSA NATHAN
(CLEMEN'S MOTHER)

I was the local WIZO chair and my husband was active in the Jewish community as well as being the founder of St John Ambulance Brigade in Amersham. As a result WIZO and St John Ambulance Brigade used to get together for functions. [There is a room named after Kurt Nathan in the St John Ambulance Amersham building.]

The Jewish community had a coronation party. Parties were sometimes held at the Mill Stream restaurant (now a dress shop) in Amersham.

Interviewed 1993

BARBARA FRIEDLANDER AND THE ANGYALFI FAMILY

One day I saw a lady I thought I recognised from Germany. We had known each other from kindergarden. I'd been bullied and she always made it her business to protect me. The name of my friend, who lived in Chesham during the war, was Lotte Angyalfi. Her husband, a jeweller, taught barmitzvah boys and led services in the Amersham synagogue. Her son Rabbi Yeremiya Angyalfi, Director of Chabad Lubavitch Leeds said, 'My 1963 barmitzvah was in Amersham. I was taught by my father. By that time Mr Tabor [wartime barmitzvah teacher] had ceased running classes.'

ALAN COHN

I never knew my own grandparents. Almost our entire family were wiped out, thirty to forty people. My mum and dad wouldn't talk about it but life was awful for us. Mum, Hannah, escaped Nazi Germany. My Mother's brother fled from Nazi Germany to Palestine now Israel. All I know was that my mum was arrested on Kristallnacht and taken to prison, where she was left naked. My father, Fred, managed to get to England. One of my Father's brothers fled to U.S.A. and the other one also to Palestine. My parents could not speak English. They found each other amongst strangers and married not for love but for companionship in a foreign country.

My father had no skill so became a farm hand. My mother was a housekeeper, washing, ironing and cleaning. She worked for the Goehrs, Else and Kurt Nathan and the Angyalfis. I'm not sure if she was paid or just given a room in return for her work as we lived with the famous Goehr family, Walter the music composer, and his wife Laelia, the well-known photographer.

I was born in 1943 in Shardeloes. I was first made famous when Laelia Goehr took photos of me playing the piano with my hands and feet. She took the photographs to London. On the 24th March 1945 I became the centrefold of *Picture Post*!

My parents struggled to learn English, and my mother's accent never disappeared. We moved nine times, but always stayed in Amersham, until I moved, in more recent years, to Chesham. My mother knew lots of female Jewish people in the area and was a very kind person. She was friends with Betty Coleman who was married to Coleman Coleman. They lived in Old Amersham in the flat over the location of the original Challoner's Grammar School of 1624. My mum was also friends with Sister Katie Krone (lived near Amersham Hospital on Whielden Street), Friedl Hayman (a nurse at the same hospital), Margaret Brodie (of Stanley Hill), Barbara Freidlander, Rose Liebmann, the Halberstadts (lived for a time opposite Chesham Bois Post Office). There was Mr and Mrs Schatz with their son Ivan [changed his surname to Shaw] who lived in South Road Chesnut Lane, and Jennette Tabor, whom I remember for making sweet things, especially for Purim. She was married to Simon who taught me my barmitzvah. They were both highly intelligent.

Amersham synagogue was always packed for festivals such as Purim and Pesach. My mum didn't go. My father took me. There was a peculiar aroma in there, not unpleasant, but not pleasant either.

When the bombs were dropped they put me under the table and they had to shelter elsewhere. My mum and dad sacrificed food so that I could eat. It was a rotten life for them.

Harold Lazarus

I was Barmitzvah by Rabbi Rapaport at the WVS hut, with eighty families. I lived in a council house, Bell Lane, Little Chalfont. Amersham was very rural – fields all around – one cinema. People walked or cycled. I remember walks in the snow and everyone wearing balaclavas.

Ben Grossman

I was a trustee of the synagogue during the war years. The furniture came from a bombed out shul in London. The money made on the sale of the shul went to several charities. As a trustee I had meetings with Rabbi (later Lord) Jacobovitz.

George Marks

George lived in Amersham since 1938. His cousin was Frances Winston, who also lived in this district during the war. He was a founder member, producer, publicist and president of The Amersham Playgoers, formed in 1946. His wife Vera was responsible for refreshments.

The Amersham Playgoers is an offshoot of the former Amersham Repertory Players, who used to put on plays during the war, at the Amersham Playhouse Theatre. I acted with Lesley Shaiman (later Filer). I was President of the Amersham Chamber of Commerce for years until 1981. My mother was looked after by Sister Katie Krone. I remember her well.

Frances Winston

Bombed out in London, I came with my parents to Amersham, from 1941-1946, where family already lived. We had to make the best of everything as we were all in the same situation, and still continued with the Jewish traditions as much as possible. I partook in a Purim play. A few of us stood at the back of the stage holding a pole. I wore a white blouse and navy skirt. I have a book – a prize for Hebrew.

Donald Wolchover

Shul trustee Ben Grossman was a chemist. He had a pharmacy opposite Aldgate East Tube Station. My family were members of the Amersham Rep and whenever there was a show we went. There were some excellent productions.

IVOR DELMAN (WAS DEITCHMAN)

I had already been evacuated several times to Staines on the outbreak of war, Cornwall (Constantine) and Wales, and finally joined my family in Amersham from 1940-1954.

My mother, Rebecca, and father, Samuel, were born in this country having parents from Russia and Poland. We lived in one room at 5 Lexham Gardens, after the Blitz, in late 1940. My younger brother, Melvyn, aged three, slept in a cot. The house has 1909 on first floor frontage. There were trees at the end of the road which led to Chesham Bois, pronounced, "Chesham boys" and the common where I played was beyond.

One of my favourite things was playing on Amersham Common, which was not far away, hiding and being found. The other was, later in the war, playing table tennis for lengthy periods with my friend Manfred. We developed into quite reasonable players.

On arrival in Amersham, primary school was mornings, or afternoons, as I believe we had to share premises. One day we were called in to sit the 11+ scholarship. I started secondary school at AGS (Dr Challoner's) in January 1942 a term late. I have the impression that they were not too pleased with the additional pupils, which included girls from Chiswick School.

Dr Challoner's Grammar School took both boys and girls in those days. The people I went to school with were Della Rosenberg, Anne Weber, Ann Mays, Jack and Gerald Wolchnover. My best friend was Manfred Weidenfield but his English was not up to scratch and he went to Wycombe Tech instead of the grammar School. Ann Mays was my girlfriend. Della Rosenberg married Fred Worms. He became well known in the wider Jewish community, including the B'nai B'rith and many other associations. I remember Donald Walker – Wolchnover was a bit younger than me – a fresh-faced boy, whose dad was in the rag trade, and I think he went into it too. He attended Amersham College opposite Orchard Lane.

I enjoyed school, where there were older male teachers (others were in the forces) and younger, just out of college, lady teachers. As a punishment for say, talking in class, one would have a detention or a ruler slap (by females) over the knuckles. I don't recall any anti-Semitism except once when in a school queue having a stone thrown at me.

Some of the classrooms were huts from WW1 with a heating stove in the corner of the room. When he returned from the forces after the war, the headmaster Mr. Harrow (I believe he was the actor Rex Harrison's brother) admonished me for wearing a camel hair lumber jacket my father had made me, because he likened it to being "on a ranch", not appreciating the clothes rationing situation.

One of my class mates, probably first and second forms, was Michael Ehrentreu – older brother of Dayan Chanoch Ehrentreu [a senior rabbi and a religious judge]. Chanoch left school early and went to Yeshiva. They belonged to the Chesham Jewish community. Chanoch became Senior Dayanim. Mr Stamler, also of Chesham Jewish community, became the head of Carmel College, a Jewish boarding school, now closed. His older brother became a senior QC. I myself became a bursar at Carmel College. I knew the Sakals, who had a hotel in this area.

We Jewish pupils had separate prayers each day. At one time Maurice Bloch was Head Boy of Dr Challoner's. He became a London doctor. At the time, Mr Bloch belonged to the Chesham Jewish Community, which was even more orthodox than the Amersham Congregation.

I love cricket and played matches during those days. I was selected to play cricket earlier than usual age in the school, and later in the 1st X1 1946, was given my cricket colours having taken 71 wickets in the season. I played for Amersham Hill Cricket Club on Woodside Road. I have the school magazine ALAUDA for 1946. My cricket hat has a large A G S above the peak. AGS was colloquial for Dr Challoner's School. When I played for them against the Chorleywood team, I played on the beautiful green at Chorleywood on the main road. Similarly, I played at Eastcote for five seasons after leaving school, 1947-51, before entering the army.

I took the 11+ in March 1941, but the headmaster of the grammar school wouldn't permit evacuees to join in September, so we had a term off school (when I missed fractions work) before I was able to join in Jan 1942.

My father went into the army but was on leave at my barmitzvah in

April 1943. My father's name was Samuel Deitchman, (later pronounced Deetchman) which was changed to Delman in 1953.

After leaving the room in Lexham Gardens, in 1942, we moved to new accommodation – Little Orchard – a house at 25 Woodside Road near to where the Amersham synagogue was eventually put up. Little Orchard was next to, what is still, a pretty square of tiny workmen's cottages all joined up, called Amersham Court which had 1913, on the front of the building. CJ's Locksmiths' built around 1955/56 is now in front of Little Orchard. The old house's garden came right down to the pavement, and at the side of the house there was more land.

Our accommodation, even in the 1940's, was poor, with a tin bath brought into the kitchen when required. Miss Norris was the owner. In the 1952 Amersham Directory she is listed as a 'spinster'.

I spoke with the current owner of Little Orchard and he told me his wife was one quarter Jewish. He also owned Kingsley House School which was behind the current jeweller. When the shul [synagogue] was dismantled it was this man who used his big trailer to take the concrete blocks to the Baptist Church in Old Amersham. The shul was two blocks of concrete in height and the walls were screwed together through each end of the block – a real prefab.

The current owner of Little Orchard remembered that his father bought a glider in 1936. He told me he had fun making up the glider, during the war, with Oswald Mincovitch. I had a surprise to hear that name as he was my second or third cousin! Oswald lived near Amersham Cricket Ground. Being older than me, we didn't mix. He was a medical student on my mum's side.

In 1945/46, we moved from Little Orchard, 25 Woodside Road, which was already very near to the shul, to 1 Bellsome Cottage, which was next door to the synagogue! This home had two bedrooms upstairs, and a kitchen and living room downstairs. The house was attached to one other cottage, and to an upholsterer which had a shop frontage on to Woodside Road.

To map it out, walk from Iceland (the old cinema) to the crossroads and the corner where Ann Mays, another congregant, lived. Turn right into Woodside Road and continue toward Little Chalfont, heading out of town. The bowling green and hall were on the opposite side of the road,

Figure 2: Archway to Amersham Synagogue (shul).

both owned by the Free Church. Little Orchard, on the right, was followed by Amersham Court (and Kingsley House School), next came the shul (Woodside Hall). The archway that led to the shul is still there.

Under the wooden arch of Amersham Court you would walk up to the shul as the front door was set further back, a few yards from the road. After this came, the now demolished, Bellsome Cottages; 1 was fronted by the upholsterer and 2 was 'Elizabeth Ladies Clothes' which was owned, or rented, by the Jewish Rechand family.

Cheder was quite enjoyable and the whole group became friends. My barmitzvah portion was taught by Rev Sonnie Bloch, and he would officiate at services in Amersham. I was friends with his younger brother Leonard who was in my class at Amersham Grammar School (AGS). There were five Bloch siblings, Sonnie, Judith, Sidney (who went to the West Indies during the war and wrote a book *No Time for Tears*), Morris and Leonard. Their uncle was a prominent rabbi in New York. The Blochs were related on their mother's side to the Jung family who lived in Chesham. Sonnie would arrive, occasionally having come from performing a Brit Milah [circumcision]. I read from the Haftorah [a passage from the prophets following the main Torah reading] on April 3rd 1943.

I don't remember a lot about my barmitzvah, in Amersham, except having, embarrassingly, to kiss various ladies, and that my father was on leave for the occasion, and I can't remember a celebration party.

I believe the first communal seder I attended was in Chesham Bois, in a property which had some sort of veranda, but it is a vague memory.

For entertainment we went to the cinema – I can remember when, in about 1943, seeing Jane Russell in *The Outlaw*. We had fun with using balsa wood to make model aeroplanes. We used to go on rambles and the one that I remember was, probably with Sonnie Bloch, outside Wendover, up to the war memorial (Boer War) on Coombe Hill, where down below is Chequers – the Prime Minister's country home. We had a matzo ramble over Pesach. The memorial was covered in camouflage. One of the soldiers listed there may have been Jewish. Also, I recall going to Hemel Hempstead swimming pool, travelling by bicycle. There were also walks on Christmas Common and many other places.

Back in the shul there was the kitchen, where we once made tea for someone unwell whilst fasting on Yom Kippur [Day of Atonement]. The main hall followed with a stage and then room/s at the end. The walls were concrete slabs. As you looked out of the windows on Shabbos there would be a (Jewish) man working in the adjacent garden – on purpose I think. The man gardening must have been living there (at number 1) before we moved in. We stayed on until 1954.

My shammas [synagogue servant] duties, from which I was paid two shillings and six pence per week for, was tidying up after the service and on Yomtov. I would be there probably an hour after everyone else had left. I had to adjust the time switches for the lighting as required. Also I had to remember who "shnodered" and how much. When called up for a mitzvah it was customary to shnoder (donate). Years later, in Reading I believe, we did away with it as being 'old fashioned'.

One of the congregants was an old man who would bang all the walls when he prayed. I think he was related to the Rechtand family living in Amersham and they were related to Sidney Stanley who featured in a prominent court case after the war. Professor Cyril Domb (theoretical physics) was also a congregant, as were Walter Goehr, conductor, and his son Alexander, 2 years younger than me. He became Professor of Music at Cambridge. He was known as Sandy and a bit of a lobos! [Yiddish for mischievous] The father would come to a shiur [Lectures on Torah] given by Rabbi Indech.

When in Cheder [religious school] one Sunday morning, there was a loud thud/explosion which turned out to be a buzz bomb in the Chesham Bois area about a mile away. The table in Cheder shook. I think we took it all for granted and of course we were only in our teens.

I remember travelling to London on the train with Dirk Bogarde, the film star, who lived in Beel House, Little Chalfont.

I also travelled with the late Maurice Edelman, MP. In 1945 Labour won the General Election. Maurice Edelman, new MP for Bristol, came into the synagogue in a camel hair coat (very good looking) as he lived locally, in Clifton Road, Chesham Bois. Sometime, later on, I was invited to have tea at their house with his daughters but they were too young to be eligible! The Edelman family moved to Bristol as that was Maurice's constituency. But they later had a house on Woodside Road, Amersham, called Wendouree. Many years later (1981/2) my daughter, Susan, taught his granddaughter her Batmitzvah portion. She had never been in a house with so many books! They had a ceremony at Maidenhead and lunch at the old Disraeli house, Hughenden Manor, where Tilli Edelman had a grace-and-favour apartment, as her husband had written a book about Disraeli.

Other names were Maurice Sofier (later Gabicci Clothes), Jack Sofier, Norman Kornbluth (name changed to Kingsley), Reverend Izaac Rapaport (conducted my barmitzvah), the Richman family who owned the Green Park Hotel in Bournemouth and Mr. Ben Grossman – a prime mover in Social Events especially for US Airmen from Bovingdon and other forces. I cannot ever remember being hungry during the war. The USA servicemen, at the local club, opposite the synagogue, would give us confectionery.

My Mum rented a room for me to work in, for maybe 10 weeks, probably located somewhere on the main A413 near the end of Woodside Road. She rented it so I could study for my accountancy exams without the noise of the upholsterer who had a room in the front of Bellsome Cottage.

Later I became a synagogue trustee. As I was active in the community, the adult members knew me, and one of them introduced me to the person I was later articled to as a member of the Institute of Chartered Accountants.

JACK WOLCHOVER

I went to Dr Challoner's and lived in Highfield Close, cycling to school. I was taught by Sonnie Bloch and barmitzvahed at Woodside Road shul, April 1943. I stayed at cheder until sixteen, learning Modern Hebrew – Ivrit.

Dr David S Nachsen

I lived with my parents and two sisters in Little Chalfont, 1939 – 1945.

My father was a member of the synagogue in Amersham. We attended services there from time to time. My own barmitzvah was celebrated at this synagogue in June 1944 with Reverend Jonah Indech. Maybe he wore a green coat?

I attended the cheder in Chesham, where there was a thriving Federation Orthodox community, under the leadership of the late Rabbi Julius Yisroel Ehrentreu, the father of Dayan Chanoch Ehrentreu, who became Rosh bet Din [senior rabbi of a religious court for the United Synagogue]. Over four miles walk on Shabbat was a problem, hence my family's membership at the Amersham synagogue.

Judith Barnett (Nee Katz)

I went with the other children, on holiday, with Sonnie Bloch, who taught at cheder. He often took us for days out on Sundays. We were fortunate enough to have a happy and protected adolescence amongst beautiful countryside.

JOHN WEBER

I'm brother to Jill Weber and Anne (Wollf). Those who attended the same Amersham cheder with me in 1942, aged 8-13 were:

Della and Arthur Rosenberg

Nita Serchuk

Ronald Gold

Ivor Deitchman

Manfred Weidenfield

Ann Mays

Jack and Gerald Wolchover

Judith and Manfred Katz

Clive Stein

Anne Weber

Cyril Wick

Maurice Kershaw

Shena Gordon

David Marks.

Barbara Horwitz (nee Brent)

I was born on 29th December, 1944 at Ashridge House, near Berkhamsted, where Charing Cross Hospital was evacuated to. I was born there because my mother was in Amersham, 3 Hundred Acres Lane, while my father [Secret Listener Egon Brandt who became Ernest Brent] was stationed at Latimer House. My mother was disappointed that I didn't receive a teddy bear from the hospital as I arrived late – a few days after Christmas – apparently all those earlier babies received a teddy bear! My parents were very happy in the area. Amersham always held a special place in their hearts and was a favourite "Sunday outing" place throughout my childhood and teenage years and throughout my marriage to this day. We still love to visit Amersham for lunch or tea.

Tilli Edelman

I am the widow of Maurice Edleman. He was an MP.

My husband and I lived with our two daughters, Sonia and Natasha, in Clifton Road, Chesham Bois, during the war. We lived in the same road as the Nathans and the Kahans. My husband, Maurice, often wrote plays for the Amersham Repertory Theatre.

The one and only wedding that ever took place at the synagogue in Woodside Road, Amersham, was that of my daughter, Sonia. The officiating rabbi came from the West London Reform Synagogue of Upper Berkeley Street in London. That was in 1956. [Sonia married Philip Abrams, a Professor of Sociology, whose father was the social scientist Mark Abrams.]

My daughter, Sonia, got pneumonia. She was terribly ill for a month. These were the days before penicillin. There was no heating. I had to fill up boxes with coal. My husband was working away as a war correspondent.

My daughter Sonia is a professor and Natasha a psychiatrist.

Professor Sonia Jackson OBE (nee Edelman, formerly Abrams)

There was a flourishing amateur dramatic group called The Playgoers that we and our friends Lesley and Shirley Shaiman were involved in, and I suspect a lot of the members were Jewish though it wasn't much talked about during the war.

I remember George Marks [Founder of Amersham Playgoers] as my very first paid job was babysitting for their family. I was totally incompetent. The baby, whose name I don't remember, woke up and starting crying. I managed to settle him and spent the rest of the evening sitting on the edge of the sofa praying that he wouldn't wake again.

The director of the Playhouse was Sally Latimer and a good friend of my father. They used to put on marvellous pantomimes every Christmas in which I think Richard Briers appeared.

Lindisfarne in Clifton Road, Chesham Bois was a lovely house to grow up in. I remember Clemens Nathan quite well. He tried unsuccessfully to teach me Hebrew. I was very ungrateful and resistant, which I thoroughly regret now. He became Vice-President of the Anglo-Jewish Association.

Joe and Xenia Kahan were incredibly hospitable. They held open house on Sunday afternoons and I often used to go there with my parents and sister, Natasha. The house would be full of all kinds of writers, artists and musicians, mostly refugees I guess. The one I remember best is Vicky, the cartoonist. Walter Goehr, the composer, lived quite near, with his wife Laelia and son Sandy, who also became a famous composer, and three enormous poodles. My piano teacher was called Mr Ticciati. [The Canettis and Motesiczkys would visit the Amersham Music Studio, in Chestnut Lane, where non-Jewish Ticciati, concert pianist and composer, would play]. He lived in Chesham Bois village. I imagine he was in flight from Mussolini.

[Sonia married Philip Abrams in September 1956 at Amersham Synagogue. Coincidentally, Philip was a pupil at the Royal Grammar School, High Wycombe.] He attended RGS during the war years, when they lived in Kimble, until his parents split up and he mostly lived with his mother in Worthing.

LITTLE KIMBLE – DR MARK ABRAMS[78]

[Sonia and Philip's son, Dominic, interviewed his paternal grandfather, Mark Abrams in 1984].

A British born Jew with an illustrious career in social science, the late Dr Mark Abrams (1906-1994) made a significant input into the allied war effort. He established a methodology of analysis, and deeper understanding, of the rhetoric of Nazi propaganda, allowing prediction of Hitler's next moves and emotional state. Mark and his family evacuated to Little Kimble. His son, sociologist Professor Philip Abrams, married Sonia Edelman in the only wedding ever held at the Amersham Synagogue. Their son, Dominic, became Professor of Social Psychology (University of Kent at Canterbury).

Thanks to Mark's grandson, Dominic, and to John Hall for providing permission to reproduce parts of *An Interview with Mark Abrams*[79]. John worked with Mark from 1970 to 1976 at the SSRC Survey Unit and maintained a close professional relationship[80] until the late 1980s.

Mark Abrams conducted psychological warfare at the BBC where he ran the Overseas Propaganda Analysis Unit. In an interview, *Wartime at the BBC*, Mark Abrams explained that the unit 'produced each week an analysis of all overseas broadcasts, either originating in Germany or from occupied parts of Europe – occupied by Germans or the Italians later on.'

Mark stated he 'transferred to the Foreign Office ... and it became the Political Intelligence Department.' He also became 'the manager of the FO's Political Intelligence Department.'

Mark Abrams mentioned his son Philip went to board at Wycombe Grammar School, 'which he didn't find terribly stimulating except for one thing. For many years after the war there was a shortage of newsprint in this country. So not only did you have four-page newspapers, but you also had a shortage of comics. And, to young school boys in the first form and second form, this was a terrible handicap, to be without comics. So, Philip organised a Comics Exchange [laughs].'

Mark's grandson, Dominic, questioned:

DA: Where was he at school from say up to about 1940/50?

MA: Ah, well once the war broke out you see, we moved out to a cottage in the country, Buckinghamshire, to a village called Kimble. And he went to the village school for a bit and then they began dropping bombs on Kimble, because Kimble was very near – we were so stupid to pick Kimble – it was very near the headquarters of Bomber Command. We didn't know that but apparently the Germans did! [laughs] And when I heard bombs had been dropped on Kimble, I thought it was time we did something. So Philip was sent off to some progressive school in Scotland.

John Hall noticed the village name was used by Mark as a *nom de plume* for a published book by 'Philip Kimble.' John added there is 'a story about Mark once accompanying an officer to arrest a spy. A little girl answered the door and by the time they negotiated entry, there was a fire-grate full of burned papers.'

EVELYN ABRAMS

I was born 1938. I lived in cottage in Kimble with my older brother of five years Philip and my mother. My father Mark lived in London doing his important war work. My paternal grandparents were Russian Jews who escaped the murderous pogroms and came to England. My grandmother, whom we called 'Booba', took in washing to survive. She had thirteen children and my father, Mark, was the middle child. His dad, my grandfather, whom we called 'Zaida' had a horse and cart. He would travel around the country and gather people onto a green. He would declare there was no God and 'if you believe in God you are wrong.' He was never arrested! Yet, my dad was sent to Leeds to train up as a rabbi. He decided quite quickly that it was not for him!

My parents met in a grammar school in London. After that my father got a First at the London School of Economics. But for every university that he tried to secure a job he could never get one. Finally, he asked during a university interview, 'You're not going to give me this job are you?' The response was, 'No. We don't want Jews in England.' After this, my parents went to America and immediately found employment in a university. The British Government sent my father a letter asking him to come back to work for the war effort. People can be changeable regarding Jews. My parents went back as they were British and wanted to help.

In the Little Kimble cottage, I remember getting up at night, going down in the dark, as we weren't allowed to put on a light and sitting under a table with my brother. My mother would be at the window looking at the German planes on their way to London. [Evelyn's mother was Una Strugnell who was a French expert and teacher.]

I remember taking our gas masks everywhere. For children it was fun. I didn't connect it to anything more. We walked to the farm at Little Kimble. The farmer was lovely. He had huge Shire horses and he would pick us up and put us on them.

The general feeling from the war was anti-German.

One day all the children were gathered in the field and asked to sit down and listen to a talk from the army. The sergeant was telling us how lovely it was to go out and play, to enjoy nature; he was very pleased about that but we must not pick up shrapnel. As a two-year-old I simply nodded my head but Philip, who was always bright, put his hand up. The sergeant said as he was nice and polite what did he want to know? My brother stood up and said, 'Tell us why? People should always know why.' That was the sociologist in him! The sergeant told him that he hadn't intended to tell them but that he would now. 'If you pick things up you could get bits of a bomb which could kill or damage you.' Philip, replied, 'Thank you, Sir' and sat down. That was the nearest I came to a bomb in Little Kimble!

We were very well bought up. We had to stand up straight, sit properly and wait until our Mum finished before we could leave the table, that sort of thing. We spent time gardening and planting vegetables and we learnt to read before we started with school. I became a teacher and my brother, Philip a sociologist. He died very young. Every year an important conference for sociologists is held in honour of my brother. I went once. It was very emotional and I was invited to speak. All around the room they have his name written, 'Philip Abrams'.

I only discovered this year [2014] that my mother converted to Judaism when she was young. We didn't have a cultural or religious Jewish life when we were growing up. It was when I was thirteen, on a youth hosteling weekend, that I first became aware of being Jewish. My friend and I met two boys in the Lake District Youth Hostel on our first day. I never had a boyfriend before and I thought, 'This is nice'. In the morning the youth hostel designated jobs and people were called out by surname. 'Abrams' was called out and the boy who had liked me stood up and spat. He said, 'You never gave us your name. You're a Jew.' I hadn't really realised and I didn't know much. When I talked to my mother she told me that unless I changed my surname it would happen again. It has but never as open as that. I have had people turn around and walk away when they've heard my name. My Uncle Frank, the youngest of the thirteen children, changed his surname to Adams.

Recently, I went back to Kimble to find the cottage. We drove around and around but couldn't find it. It was a fine spring day and lots of people were working in their gardens. Just as we were about to give up a man working in his garden was able to direct us to 12 Kimble. In the place of the cottage was a huge house where the friendly owner was putting his horses away. He invited us in for tea and afterwards showed us one brick wall, on the exterior, which he had retained from the old cottage and indeed that was it!

Major Reuben Berman

Professor Ruth Berman, daughter of Major Dr Reuben Berman, published *Dear Poppa: The World War II Berman Family Letters.*[81] The following correspondence is between Major Berman, who was stationed with the US Army in Europe, his wife Isabel, and four children, David, Betsy, Sammy and Ruth the baby. Ruth Berman has generously allowed us to include both published and unpublished material (Note Sonya Edelman is actually spelt Sonia). Ruth Berman continues:

My father didn't really have any work in Buckinghamshire during the part of the war when he was in England. He was stationed at a base in East Anglia, where he was in charge of seeing to the medical problems of the soldiers there. But there weren't many medical problems among a group of healthy young men, and he was often able to take the train to London, where his second cousin, Dr. Joseph Naftalin, and his family lived. (Less often, he was able to travel to Glasgow, where most of the Naftalin family lived.) He met Maurice Edelman on the train that took Maurice home from travel to London, and continued on into East Anglia, and they got to be friends. It was get-togethers with the Edelmans that made up his visits to Bucks. In 1945, when my father was sent into Germany as part of the invasion force, he was no longer able to see much of them, but they remained friends by mail after. (It wasn't a frequent correspondence – and my father didn't save the few letters – but the feeling of friendship was still there.) The following are extracts from 'Dear Poppa':

June 8, 1944
Dearest Isabel,

...I met a new correspondent on the train last week, and our conversation ended in an invitation to dinner. I was there last night. They have a very fine house in the outer suburbs [in Chesham Bois] of London. The name is Morris [Maurice] Edelman. They were married by my friend Rabbi Rabinowitz. Sunday the Edelmans were here for dinner, which is just like old times.

July 2, 1944

Dearest Isabel,

...Tonight the Edelmans are coming to supper here. That is I think they are. This morning there was a loud noise from their neighbourhood so I can't be sure. If they do come, I'll hear how close it was. I have a picture of them and me.[82]

July 13, 1944

Dear Betsy,

...The place where I go to dinner often on Fridays is called "Lindisfarne," the home of the Edelmans. Their daughters are 7 and 10. Natasha is 7, Sonya is 10. They have a dog named Terrier Terry. They have a great big lawn on which they play croquet with a wonderful English set of mallets and balls. They have 20 chickens that lay 10 eggs a day. (Question: How many eggs per chicken?)

July 24, 1944

Dear David,

I am quite friendly with a family named Edelman with two children, girls, one your age and one Betsy's age. You might care to write to

Miss Sonya Edelman

Lindisfarne

Chesham Bois

Bucks

Lindisfarne is the name of the house. All houses have names in England, It's a quaint custom.

July 25, 1944

Dear Betsy,

...If you would like to write to a girl of your own age here you might care to write to

Natasha Edelman

Lindisfarne

Chesham Bois

Bucks, Eng.

September 15, 1944

Dear David,

…Sonia Edelman is having a birthday party tomorrow. I am invited and I will go if the press of military duties doesn't interfere. I hope you don't mind my reading your letter to Sonia. I haven't yet but I think she will show it to me. I am a particular friend to Sonia and she tells me all.

September 17, 1944

Dearest Isabel,

Even though I didn't go to Glasgow, all my plans for Rosh HaShonah didn't go awry. I was able to attend the birthday party for Sonia Edelman yesterday. 23 guests gathered around two tables. Rather foolishly Mrs. E. invited the children for 2:30. You can imagine how she felt around 7:00 when the children left. And then two adults including me stayed for dinner. Around 10:45 we left but by 9:30 Mrs. E. was making snippy remarks, something she never does! She must have been ready to drop.

But to return to the party. What went on before 4:30 I don't know because that is when I arrived. The children were gathered around two tables. The place of honor between Sonia and Natasha Edelman was reserved for me. I am the hero in uniform. To eat was the following simple fare: open sandwiches of lady finger size of egg salad, sardines, meat paste, and something else; tea for adults, lemonade (synthetic of course) for the children; about ten varieties of cookies (biscuits over here) all good; a trifle (raspberries, fresh peaches, and some other fruits in custard, very English and usually terrible but this one like everything Tilly Edelman puts her hand to in the kitchen was perfect and delicious); two kinds of pie, apple and cherry; and a peach flan. A flan is a fruit business on a crust. It is called a flan because the crust is usually like a flannel. Then there were all kinds of sweets. You might think the above are sweets but they're not. Sweets are candy. I brought some of the FF. After everybody ate themselves more or less sick we went out in the garden where I told them a story-the Foxes with the Bushy tails. Then we played Charades (In England Charades is pronounced to rhyme with ye Gods). Then we played run-sheep-run which I taught them. All in all as you can guess it was a very successful party. But it wasn't managed as to games and food with the practiced care of a momma with four children whom I know in Minneapolis who takes care to have the children assemble *late* in the afternoon, who serves the children just a few very good things to eat, and manages games that blow off the children's steam without breaking up the furniture. There was a treasure hunt. Then everybody got a prize. David's letter hasn't come yet. It is going to be more difficult for me to visit the Edelmans in the future but I must return at least to read that letter.

October 5, 1944

Dear Betsy,

...I have sent your request for a picture of Sonia and Natasha on to the Edelmans. If they have one I think they will send it and if they haven't, perhaps they will have one taken...

Natasha is just your age but she was brought up like an Englishman so she talks differently. When it's fall she says it's "Ohtum."

October 30, 1944

Dearest Isabel,

...I visited the Edelmen a few days ago. They showed me the letters that David and Betsy had sent and one of the answers. The other had been already mailed. David's letter shows his grown up attitude and his remarks about the bombs and the blitz really amazed the Edelmans. They wanted to know where he had found out about all those things. I off handedly remarked that he reads the newspapers. They thought his handwriting was better than mine but still not good enough for a ten year old.

October 31, 1944

Dear David,

What grade are you in school? Mrs. Edelman showed me your letter to Sonia and it said that you are in the sixth grade. I thought that was too high for a boy of ten going on eleven. Incidentally that was a very good letter and the Edelmans were quite surprised to see that you know quite a bit about what is going on in the war, especially in England. I told them that you kept informed by reading the newspapers. They sniffed a bit at your handwriting but who am I to complain? ...

Dear Betsy,

That was such a nice long letter that you wrote to Natasha Edelman. I was over there and they let me read it. Also I saw Natasha's answer to you but I won't tell you what's in that. I am fine.

November 6, 1944

Dear Betsy,

When I was over at the Edelmans last week, Natasha, that's the little girl who is just as old as you, was sick. She had a fever of 102 and was dizzy. They didn't call a doctor because I was there. I'll have to call back now to find out how she is. She had the flu. Did I ever tell you that the English children wear school uniforms? All the children who go to the same school wear the same clothes. The school uniform for boys is a tiny cap like a jockey cap, a blazer which is a striped coat, and a special tie. Girls wear a uniform hat and dress. Some schools have ridiculous uniforms like Eton where the boys wear cut-away coats and plug hats. Parents worry about all the clothing coupons they must spend to keep the children in school uniforms...

Your loving Poppa

The Unpublished Letters

June 19, 1944

Dearest Isabel,

...Saturday I was out to dinner again with the Edelmans. Morris Edelman is the War Correspondent I met a couple of weeks ago. After dinner we went to the local repertory theatre and saw Shaw's "You Never Can Tell." Sunday I listen to the stories of the P Plane as told by "I was der, Charlie." I can't tell you anything about that, but the guns in London make a terrific whorooomm-room-room as they open their mighty throats and snarl their defiance of the enemy.

June 19, 1944

... A lot of English people are a bit afraid of the Americans. Some of them think we eat too much, dress too much, talk too loud, and pay too much attention to their women. Every one of us is an American ambassador and we function as such every time we talk to a Britisher. I talk to everyone: on trains, trams, buses, tubes. To me British reserve is a myth. The average Englishman loves to talk and you can strike up a conversation with anyone anywhere. I think it is very important that the English and American people should understand each other. I'm thinking in terms of how to prevent another war when you and Sammy grow up. I don't mean between you and Sammy! I think the English speaking people COULD get together and prevent or indefinitely postpone the next war. I'm not saying we will.

In the meantime we are doing right well in Normandy and in Italy. I think soon Germany will be persuaded to adjourn the battling. We will persuade them by conquering the land, capturing their armies, and destroying their weapons...

Expatriated Poppa

June 19, 1944

Dear Betsy

Do you know what I like most of all? It's letters from home. From you and the boys and Momma...

I shall tell you how the English girls dress. They have to give coupons for everything. Over here the first thought is "how many coupons". They pronounce it Koopons, swallowing the n. So they like to get durable material like heavy tweed or worsted. When you see a well dressed person, you assume

a. It's an American
b. She got it before the war
c. She's not a nice person who gets gifts from not so nice Americans

The girls use a lot of lipstick. A hell of a lot if you ask me. Most girls wear no stockings; some paint their legs with brown barnpaint to look like stockings only it doesn't. More like jaundice. The lipstick is quite sticky and comes off on cigarettes, on beerglasses, coffeecups, and the boys tell me it smears up their lips when they kiss them which they do quite often over here in England I'm told. Especially in the cities. And also in the country. Shoes are also a problem. They have a wooden soled shoe that is quite the craze here. You know what I mean when I say "quite the craze": people are crazy to wear them.

The Edelmans have two daughters – one seven and one ten. The ten year old is Sonya and she walks on the piano. The seven year old is Natasha and she plays the piano not quite as well as you do but she is very good at croquet. Both of them speak with an English accent which really isn't surprising because they live in England. Still I must admit I was surprised.

I have a big staff car all for myself but mostly I ride the bicycle. We need the petrol, that's what they call gasoline over here, we need the petrol for airplanes over Germany.

June 19, 1944

Dear Sammy,

Yesternight had dinner with the Edelmans in A. I think they are rich people. They have a very fine home with a tremendous yard. And in the backyard what do you think? They have a croquet set. Not a little dinkystinky set like we have in the states. The wickets are of ½ inch steel. The mallets are beautifully finished. The set would cost about $100. They have a Poochie who is the same breed as Rafni only more of it. I forgot my pipe at the Edelmans' and when I got back after it I think I shall stay for dinner. Tilly Edelman is a very good cook. Not as good as Momma is but still a very good cook...

August 1, 1944

Dear Mom,

...I have become quite friendly with a Jewish family in the neighbourhood. Maurice Edelman has two daughters, 7 and 10, and two evacuee nephews, 5 and 7. I am a favourite of the children because I bring them gum, chum. I am generally there for dinner about once a week and always for tea Saturday afternoon. Edelman is a war correspondent for Picture Post.

...The war couldn't be going any better. Germany is thrashing around in her death agonies now. We haven't got long to wait now.

August 26, 1944

Dearest Isabel:

... I am invited to a birthday party by Sonia Edelman, the ten year old. I am going to get her a brooch for a present. The party is Saturday Sept 16. I expect to leave that night for Glasgow and spend Rosh Ha Shonah there. Mrs. Edelman has written to you she says. I am on my best behaviour over there so what she says doesn't signify. The Edelmans are wonderful people who would fit into the group we like naturally and easily.

October 2, 1944

Dearest Reuben

...I have sent you three packages. One had the makings of an apple pie. I had thought that Tillie Edelman might make you the pie. Now, I suppose you'll have to turn the package over to your camp cook. Another package had one two pound F sausage and a two pound Egeqvist fruit cake. The third package was for you and the Edelmen. For you, there were three rolls of 620 film. For the Edelmen, there were playing cards, candy and candy bars, nice rayon underpants and stockings, a can opener, etc. I hope you can get the things to them without too much trouble...

Love, Isabel

from Reuben Berman
0-297356 TE1 343 A
Major MC
1 CCRC Group APO 633 NYC
October 2, 1944

Dearest Isabel,

I was in London and Chesham on my 24 hour pass yesterday. Visited the Edelmans who reproached me for not sending you the piece of Sonia's birthday cake I was supposed to. Now, two weeks later, I am told I must be sure to send it. Due reflection convinces me that a piece of cake six weeks old is a menace to mankind so I won't send it. Now if you can search your soul and find there the means of telling a little lie, will you write to

Mrs. Maurice Edelman
Lindisfarne
Clifton Road
Chesham, Bucks

And thank her for the cake! Sonia hasn't received David's letter yet. I have some very good pictures I picked up at the Edelmans. The colored ones are to be carefully handled until I return home to mount them.

from Maj Reuben Berman
1CCCR Group APO 639 NYC
November 5, 1944
Dearest Isabel,

In the last few days two packages came from Minneapolis. From Dayton's came six pairs of nylon hose. Three went to Mrs. Joe Naftalin and three to Mrs. E. The ladies were speechless with delight especially Mrs. E. who couldn't understand how you knew her size. (She was being polite; her size was half a size smaller!) Her sister-in-law in Chicago had just sent her the unimaginative gift of six dishtowels and I heard her comment "Dishtowels from America! If she'd only sent stockings!"

November 19, 1944

Dearest Isabel,

Friday evening I was invited to dinner at the Joe Naftalins in London. Stayed over night there, and went to Natasha Edelman's birthday party (8ᵗʰ) Saturday. Your package of wonderful things for the Edelmen came just in time for me to bring the things with me. Mrs. Edelman you can imagine was thrilled with your selection. She showed me the letter you sent her. She was very pleased that you called her "Tilly" and dispensed with the Mrs. Edelman. She needed a can opener so she got that too. The children are very happy with their books.

I am fixing up a package to send home. Most of it is presents from the Edelmen. There will be things for everyone. I haven't sent packages home for two reasons

a.   You have so much better things in the stores in America
b.   I don't like to use up shipping space.

Neither a. or b. applies to the Edelmen with such force, so the presents. It's quite a battle between me and the Edelmen: I am continually trying to show my gratitude for their wonderful hospitality by bringing them little gifts, and they outdo themselves in generosity to me trying to repay me for these gifts.

The panties were very welcome. But the most appreciated gift of all are stockings. Suggest you get another six pair size 10. Formal request: Please send me six pairs of stockings.

The Natasha birthday party was a great success. There were fourteen guests ranging in age sharply from 8 to 10 with one exception aged 36 and very nearly now 37. Three boys and eleven girls. They played blindmans buff, Charades (rhymes with mar-odds), musical chairs, musical bumps, whispering, and treasure hunt. In the group competition games Maurice Edelman captained one team and I the other. With squeals of new found love, half the little girls attached themselves to me and half to Maurice. The little boys were bored. Musical bumps is a good non-furniture breaking variation of the chairs game. The little devils jump up and down while the music plays and drop to the floor when it stops. The last one down is out. Whispering is a good game when the grownups' nerves start going bad. The children sit in a circle and start a word or a message going around the circle by whispering. The last one tells the message or does what the message says. The food Mrs. E. Serves we would think would be enough for four parties.

November, 1944

...The Edelmans are having a party in a few weeks to celebrate Maurice Edelman's new book. I am instructed to bring my presence and no presents but I have yet to go there empty handed. I shall bring a can of Kosher meat loaf and some salad if it lasts. Also a censored item of liquid refreshment.

November 21, 1944

Dearest Isabel,

Yesterday was Natasha Edelman's birthday. I came with the stuff you sent which were received you know how. I'm a day off. The birthday was day before yesterday and I've written you all about it. Today the package of gifts from the Edelmen was dispatched to you. I'm not indicating who gets what because it will be quite obvious, I think. The gloves were handmade especially for you. The size was suggested from a picture I have of you. I read your letter to Tilly. Your thanks for the cake were beautifully done! But you nearly got me into hot water by detailing the contents of the package you sent! The lipstick went to Mrs. Joe Naftalin and some of the candy to Adrian Naftalin, her seven year old. Tilly observed that you must be a very imaginative and intelligent person to choose gifts so well. I agreed. I told them the story of poor Captain Loth. His wife wrote and asked what did he want sent in a package. He suggested a fruit cake. He comes from a big family. They all called his wife and asked for suggestions what to send him. Result: the 25th fruit cake was consumed this week. So geht es een Amerikeh. I hasten to add that you mustn't cut down on anything you intend to send me because of this story. Not that I need anything. Except a clarinet. I also want a half a dozen clarinet reeds Vibrator number 2 ½ or a reed of medium softness. Get them at Schmidts.

December 18, 1944

Dearest Isabel,

A crazy weekend. I was invited to the Edelman party celebrating the publication of his book on France. He spent a few weeks there during the early months of the invasion and together with his knowledge of North African France, Maurice wrote himself a book which in due time I shall send to you. The party was something terrific. The food in the opinion of those who know was definitely prewar: roast chicken, pickled tongue, both in profuse quantity and various other minor items I don't remember. You would have to be over here to appreciate what people mean when they say something is prewar. The drinks also flowed freely. Present were a scintillating company including symphony conductor (1) member of parliament (if he gets elected from Luton), writers, army officer (1 major) a member of the British Council. Several of the men including the council appeared in beards. They lent distinction and an old world air to the affair. I spent the night on the Edeldavenport with their pooch curled up at my head.

December 24, 1944

Dearest Isabel,

Yesterday came three wonderful V★mails from you mailed early in December. I particularly liked your story of the children's shopping at the dime store; and taking them all to dinner at the Rainbow… I showed most of all the letters to the Edelmans who came to the party here last night of which more infra…

Now about the party. I invited three people: the Edelmans, and Mrs. Dr. 1st Lt Pearl Ketcher from Colchester Military Hospital, a friend of the Edelmans…The Edelmans came from London and I met them at the station at B. Mrs. K came from the other direction and arrived by herself from C in the camp bus. We met in the lobby of the three large nissen huts which comprise our officers club. It may convey the wrong impression to you to speak of these three buildings as Nissen huts. They are, it is true, the shape of a barrel sawed in two sagitally but they each measure about 100x40 feet. First we have a drink at the bar. Then we take our drinks to the main lounge where they all comment that the ministry of Fuel ought to see the fire in the fireplace – it's eight times the size it ought to be.

After we warm our behinds for about five minutes we go into the dining room Nissen hut and there is a buffet supper. We march down the line taking cheese sandwiches, potato and fresh egg salad, salmon salad, coffee and cake. Back at the tables are platters of fruit and salad (right out of the fruit cocktail tins) pears and peaches. It doesn't sound like much but to the fruit starved British it is a terrific spread. Then we go out to inspect the kitchen and the smart mess sgt slips each of them a nice beautiful American Apple, I think it was a delicious apple, I mean Delicious. I think you know what I mean. The food always makes the party. We were invited to the colonel's quarters for a drink but we didn't go because the colonel never did leave the dance floor. Just what the colonel did I am not going to say because who knows? Should the censor stop this and want to call my COs attention to my censorious writing, he would simply buck this letter on to him. Anyhoo we next inspected the sick quarters where all comment on the ingenuity of my dentist who has rigged up all manner of rubegoldbergan ideas in lectricity doubling in brass. It was not the best of parties but everybody had a good time. I seem to bring married couples as my guests most of the time. I varied the routine this time because I didn't want to have Maurice E sit around bored if I were to ask Tilly for a dance. At midnite buses went off to the various towns and away go our guests and the party is done. Except for the station surgeon who must investigate the latrines and corners for stray inebriates. None last night.

Love

Reuben

January 20[?], 1945

Dearest Isabel,

I haven't seen much of this field the last week. Three days I spent at the RCP meeting. I took off for 48 hours; and I spent one day scrounging supplies. So in a week I was here one day. I came back to find your letters of early January telling me how you spent the New Year, David and Betsy's recital, etc. I also got another package from you – peanuts, shrimp and tomato, cigars, and lipstick. And candy. A very well chosen selection. But it wasn't packed well. The cigars were pretty badly ashed and one of the lipsticks unscrewed itself and painted some of the peanuts red. I was able to wipe the lipstick off its coating of peanut shell and it will never be suspected by Mrs Edelman that it was first used to paint peanuts. All these difficulties occurred because of slight motion in the interior of a package. The package must be firmly packed so there is no internal motion. I have decided to use one can of shrimps and tomatoes for a cocktail at the officers mess. It will make a sensation at our table. Most of us haven't tasted a shrimp in several years.

I brought in some grapefruit the last time I stayed with the Naftalins. Joe remarked that he hadn't eaten grapefruit in five years…

Saturday evening, I called on the Edelmans visiting Mrs. Edelman's parents. Her father is gravely ill with diabetes, diabetic retinitis, and diabetic gangrene of one foot. Whilst I was there (that is how they say it here) whilst I was there I was invited to give a curbstone consultation on the old man. They realised they couldn't pay me so they gave me a box of cigars for me and something for you. The cigars were magnificent specimens of the cigar makers arts: the kind that retail for about $1.00 apiece. I thanked them quite effusively for them and I glanced at the gift for you and said a rather cursory thanks for it too. It is a squarish metal dish for cigarettes. But I overlooked one little item in my first look at it: it is Sterling silver. And worth, I suppose $50. Anyway you will shortly receive a package containing a sterling silver cigarette dish and I want you to write a letter to the Yager family address 20 Wilverton Road, Brondesbury Park, London. The seven involved are Sol, Reuben, William and Sydney Yager and the daughters, Mathilda (Tilly Edelman), Debbie, and Mrs. Rosefield. I hope you understand all this. I have listed the names of Tilly's brothers and sisters all of whom combined to give you a gift and when you write you must diplomatically mention them all!

Love, Reuben

***

On September 8th, 1997, the long-widowed Tilli Edelman wrote from the old Disraeli home, Hughenden Manor, to Reuben Berman. She recalled Reuben's aid 'in getting penicillin for my father during the war & thus preventing his leg from amputation.' It would seem that Major Reuben played down his medical intervention in his letter home.

Lesley Filer (nee Shaiman)

I moved to Amersham at the age of two until I was married aged twenty-three. My boyfriend got so fed up of putting me on the Amersham train that he married me! All my family lived here – parents, sister, cousins, aunts and uncles. My father was in the Home Guard. One of my uncles, Ben Grossman, founded the Amersham Hebrew Congregation.

I went to chedar in Amersham. The Jewish community were so friendly and the families lovely. It was a happy time for the children but a hard life for the adults. There were blackouts in Amersham during the war. Food was rationed but because we lived in the country we managed to obtain fresh eggs and butter from the farms. There was a bartering system for this produce. I can also remember powdered milk and powdered eggs which were not so delicious!

Evacuees came from London and servicemen came to stay. I used to cycle down to the bridge and watch the doodlebugs coming down.

I remember the railway at the bottom of our garden. The trains used to stop at Rickmansworth where steam engines were attached.

Miss Berman

I used to travel frequently to Amersham to visit my friends, Simon Tabor and his wife, Jeanette. They bought a house on a housing estate in Amersham called High and Over, one of the first British Modernist houses, distinctive for its Y shape and camouflaged during the war, which was on top of a very steep hill. This was a disadvantage because they could not, for example, receive coal deliveries in bad weather conditions. The houses on the estate were unusual. They had big windows which also had to be blacked out during the war.

The Tabor's were highly educated people and were well travelled. They had no children. Mr Tabor was an art metal worker (antique metals). Mrs Tabor, who was the daughter of a rabbi, did voluntary work in the local hospital. They were strict vegetarians and grew their own vegetables.

Mr Tabor was a great bible scholar. He was not fanatically religious but very Jewish in outlook. He had just the right mentality to teach, and taught chedar children right through the war.

MARK BLAUG

Professor Mark Blaug was an eminent historian of economics. His wife Ruth is a renowned economist. Their sons Ricardo and Tristan are also academics. The Blaug/Toeman family were connected to the airmen Frank Samuel Day.

Mark Blaug's widow, Ruth Towse added:

Mark (then known as Norbert) and his elder brother George were sons of Sarah Toeman, sister of Bob and Joe Toeman. Joe had a wife called Rosa. [Their daughter is Zerka Toeman Moreno who was interviewed earlier]. They were evacuated to Amersham and attended Amersham College, which they apparently liked. Mark loved walking in the countryside there with his cousin's wife, Anne (married to Charles Toeman, the brother of Zerka).

Maurice Blaug recalled:

My brother Mark spent weekends at the home of Charles and Anne. Meanwhile, my other brother, George, stayed in the boarding school they both attended in Amersham. They may have both been fire wardens there during the Blitz. I and my parents never visited England at that time but stayed on the continent since my father was refused admission to England because he had fought in the Austro-Hungarian army during WW1. After the war, my parents and I returned to Europe, and we visited my uncle Bob in St. John's Wood, London several times. We also saw my uncles Joe and Colly who lived in London as well. The three Toeman brothers owned a stocking firm. I remember that Joe was described to me as the 'intellectual' one meaning that he read books! Both my brothers ultimately returned to England, one in the movie business, the other in academia. Both took up British citizenship.

Xenia Kahan (nee Kirschner)

I moved to Amersham at the age of thirty, in the summer of 1940 during Dunkirk, and lived there until I moved to London in 1960. My father had a timber business and money in England so we got visas. I was born in Vindau which was Russia, but the Tsar forced us out, and we only went back when it became a new country called Latvia. Then we had to leave again because of persecution. I learnt English only when I had to in England. I can speak many languages. My cousins and friends, who could not get out, did not survive.

First there was the 'phoney war' and we were in Wales. Then we came back to London and the dangers came so we all came to live in a huge house in Buckinghamshire.

My parents were Max and Mary Kirchner. I lived with them, my husband, Joseph, (a Lithuanian) and two sons, George and Richard, in a house named 'Whitehaven', Clifton Road, Chesham Bois. It was a huge corner house with four acres of land. For twenty years we were there. There are now four houses built on this land, which was our garden. There was a school on the opposite side. There was some anti-Semitism in Amersham. One school in Chesham Bois would not take in Jewish boys.

My father supplied timber for making guns and he was involved in secret building work to help win D-Day. He also supplied the timber for building the Amersham Synagogue. My son, George, had his barmitzvah there. The officiant was the Rev I Rapaport, who later became a rabbi and emigrated to Australia.

During the war people came to Amersham looking for accommodation. They bought big houses with large gardens, and they also bought flats. Everyone grew fruit and vegetables. All Dug for Victory. Some of these houses became central to the Jewish community. The enormous gardens are now gone and many houses built on the sites. Large families lived in the houses, for example, grandparents, parents and children. I think there could have been one-hundred-and-forty Jewish families living in Amersham at the time.

The members of the Amersham Jewish community were very well integrated with everyone in the district. They served in all committees in Jewish and other circles, and did a lot of good in the Amersham district as a whole. The Jewish people were a very close knit community. They worked very hard. The women looked after large families, belonged to the Women's Voluntary Service and made barrage balloons. I was a member of the WVS. They knitted balaclavas, knitted for WIZO, and knitted gloves and scarves for soldiers. Their husbands were often at war. The Jewish people took part in all local activities, always winning cake baking competitions.

Before the war, many of the Jewish families had servants and the ladies did not have to work so hard. During the war they suddenly had to learn to do everything for themselves – quite a major re-adjustment to their lives. Our German Jewish nanny was interned and the maid left for war work. The women had to run gardens with two hundred apple trees and half an acre for vegetables. There were bazaars and competitions for the best apples and jams, and "Make Do and Mend" competitions. Everyone learned how to pickle eggs and do practical things, such as how to make jam with less sugar, exchanging one pound of sugar for one pound of fruit to get two pounds of jam out of one pound of fruit!

Amongst so many other activities, I learned to ride a bike. Goods, like coal, were not delivered to us. I would go on my bike and collect them.

People were happy to exchange goods, for example three or four eggs for chicken food. There was a good bartering system, no black market dealing, but always a good trade going on. When I needed a new bicycle pump, I put a notice in a shop window saying I would give six eggs for a bike pump. It worked! There was no shortage of anything. There were enough pickles, jams, bottled fruit, etc. to last families from one year to another. Everyone learned to bake, bottle, and pickle.

I remember mushrooming. In particular, on one such occasion, I had picked a basketful. Unfortunately, I had an accident with my bicycle. My head was hit and I was taken off to Amersham Hospital with suspected concussion. The staff were amazed to see the big basket with mushrooms, and wanted to know where they were picked. I would not tell! The hospital had a kosher food department. I was given the choice of kosher or non-kosher meals. I was not particularly fussy, but thought it would seem better if I did eat kosher. I was then given pilchards, and ate them, whilst other patients ate roast beef and Yorkshire pudding!

My family were in daily contact with about forty Jewish families, through communities and groups. The Tabors were well known to us, and I liked them very much. My family did not go regularly to services, but contributed a lot to the Jewish community in many ways. Our large garden was used for garden parties.

I remember the Levys. Mrs Levy re-married and became Mrs Marx. One of their daughters became Mayoress of London. I also knew the Hirschfields, Kleiners, Blochs, Stamlers, Tabors, Nathans, Rosenbergs, Zanders, Goehrs, Mrs Lissack and Professor Lewis. Mrs Lissack was prominent in WVS work. Walter Goehr conducted the BBC Symphony Orchestra. Apart from living in Amersham, there were Jewish families living in all the surrounding areas, Chesham, Beaconsfield, Hyde Heath etc. The children played with each other, parties and dances were organised for them, there was a strong Jewish youth group.

DIANE CLEMENTS

Shardeloes was converted into a maternity unit for mothers from London. I was evacuated from the Elizabeth Garrett Anderson Hospital, London. I gave birth to a baby girl. So many births left babies lying in the corridors. My mother and step-father were evacuated to Chesham, which is where I went to stay for a while, with the baby, until our return to London.

GERALD FINESILVER

I was born in 1941, in Amersham, at Shardeloes, the Tyrwhitt Drake mansion, which was requisitioned. My uncle, Harry Goldberg, lived in Amersham Old Town, next to a pub, 'The Wheatsheaf', which has since been pulled down. Lord Haw Haw, who made Nazi anti-British propaganda radio broadcasts during the war, lived in Amersham.

MR GOLDSTEIN

My mother lived in Amersham during the war. When the synagogue was closed she collected the Sifrei Torah. There were three scrolls lent to the wartime congregation. One belonged to the Cricklewood synagogue, which was taken back by Rabbi Landy. The other two were returned to the United Synagogue Head Office.

Cyril Lassman

I lived in Amersham Old Town from 1942-1945. There were five or six Jewish families living there at the time. I remember the reverend in the green jacket!

Interviews and Nine Memoirs – Anne Zeto Kaye[82]

At the age of four (in 1940) I found myself in Little Missenden, and after a few months went to live in Old Amersham. I was there until 1945, and my dearest friend who died remained in the area.

I lived in Old Amersham from 1940-1945 at The Bungalow, High Street, Old Amersham. The Bungalow was a terrible tin shack that was once the canteen for the bus crews, but it was home. It was between the bus station and the fire station, in the shadows of the gasometers.

My evacuated mother shared it with another evacuated family and made a cosy home whilst my father was away in the army. There was a wood yard where wood was cut up. Opposite, in the High Street, was Thompson's, a shop which sold cigarettes and wonderful books. The owner was a fierce woman, but she always placed a few cigs in my Dad's newspaper when he came in her shop. He didn't smoke, but was too polite to tell her! My mother used to buy me Enid Blyton and Odhams Press Albums which were beautiful. Wilsons was my very favourite shop. It was on the corner (on the same side as the bungalow, and I passed it each day on my way to St Mary's School in School Lane. A lovely old lady ran it. The windows were filled with treasures, toys, cards, even then wonderfully old world. I wish I had some of them now! Sweets and chocolates were rationed, but occasionally something would come in that was not rationed, liquorice pipes, and chocolate milk bottles. It was a treasure trove. The large house with pillars on the same side as Thompsons was Dr Starky's surgery, and further down was dear Dr Johns. He was brilliant and let me watch him make up his medicines with a mortar and various powders.

SCHOOL LANE

Starting school at the age of four years old was a glorious event. My mother held my hand firmly as we left the Bungalow and started off down the High Street. I was squirming, trying to evade her hand, and walk alone, like the big girl I felt myself to be.

We arrived at School Lane, and Wilson's, the corner shop beckoned as usual for me to linger and gaze at the treasures in its windows. Postcards, toys and objects from decades ago – a treasure trove which usually held my attention. Today, however, I was off to school, and Wilson's would have to wait until the end of the school day.

School Lane, on one side filled with cottages and a few brick houses, but opposite were the hedgerows – far more interesting. A whole world existed amongst the bushes and trees, hazel nuts in season, and springtime the nests filled with eggs, and the constant chirping of baby birds. I especially loved the dog roses, far sweeter than any carefully tended prize blooms in manicured gardens, the soft pink petals and black peppercorn centres delighted me.

At last we reached St Mary's School, and I was left in the Mixed Infants class, in the care of Mrs Wilson. Yes, another Wilson! It seems that all the nicest things were associated with ladies of this name. There were forty children seated at little tables, each containing four chairs, on which the mixed infants sat, ten tables in all. Mrs Wilson, an ancient lady, dressed in a long grey dress, and wearing a coral necklace was the kindest and most gentle person I had ever encountered. She never had to raise her voice, and just lowering her glasses, and sadly shaking her head at a noisy pupil would immediatly result in improved behaviour. She never lost her temper, and when a new lad wet himself because he was too shy to ask to 'be excused' she silenced the laughter of the other children by sighing and shaking her head. She ruled by kindness and did her best to install it in the children in her care.

Kindness and the urge to learn, alas how quickly the year passed, and it was now time for me to move into Miss Harrison's class. There were four classes at St Mary's, and due to Mrs Wilson's excellent teaching, I was jumping a class and going straight into the third class with children who were older than myself. Miss Harrison knew nothing of kindness and ruled her classroom with a spiteful wooden ruler and an even more spiteful tongue. She demanded that we all recite our 'times tables' each morning, and fortunately, I was gifted with an excellent memory and so never fell foul of her. Whilst we recited, she slowly walked around the classroom, suddenly crashing her ruler down on the hands of any child who made mistakes or was not reciting loud enough.

Miss Harrison was of an indeterminate age, with a long horse-face and wattles like a turkey which reddened as she grew angrier. She always wore dresses with 'V' necklines which showed off her wattles, and her iron-grey hair was screwed back into a hard bun. The only positive thing I ever found about Miss Harrison was that every afternoon she gave out books for us to silently read. They were not the usual Beacon books, which we used and which were graded in difficulty by the colours on their covers, but rather lovely volumes, published by Palgrave, bound in blue and with gold edging to the pages. How I loved the tales from Ancient Greece, but when I asked Miss Harrison how to pronounce a name, I believe that of Persephone, she shouted at me for asking foolish questions and hit me over the head with her ruler. I never asked a question again.

In actual fact, my school grades were going down. From being first in the class, I dropped to third, and then swiftly joined the simpletons at the bottom of the class. I would gaze out of the window, watch the clouds and be drawn by the sun beams chasing dust motes. Miss Harrison would demand that I go and stand in the corner, which I did, but as soon as her back was turned, I would run out of the classroom and go down to the 'Rec' where the swings and slide awaited. I would ignore these amusements and instead would go down to the river and paddle whilst seeking sticklebacks and other small fish.

Things finally came to a head at Easter Time. Miss Harrison was telling the Bible story, or rather her version of it. "The Jews killed Jesus" she said not once, but continually. Angrily, she pointed a bony finger in my direction, "This girl is a Christ Killer," she shouted, spittle foaming around her thin lips. "The Jews killed our Lord, and today they sit amongst us"! I

110

stood up, with tears in my eyes. I went to Hebrew class and loved my Bible studies, and I also loved Jesus, the gentle baby born in a stable. At that age I loved so easily. "What are you saying"? "Jesus was a Jew." Miss Harrison became even a redder shade of crimson, not only her wattles and neck, but her arms and very eyeballs. "Wicked child," she shrieked, "How could our Lord be a JEW"? She seized her ruler and started to beat me, whilst half the class cheered and a few others wept. I raised my head and grabbed her ruler, with strength unknown to me then and still today, I snapped it in half, and walked out of the classroom.

My emotions when I left the classroom that day expressed the strong sense of never wanting to go back to St Mary's, and I never thought I would. My mother had spoken to Mrs Kelly, the headmistress, and found her a very sympathetic Londoner who was doing her best with so many children and a very limited staff. Miss Harrison was past retirement age, and whatever her faults, she had taught for many years, and her services were urgently needed.

At that time, my mother had found a job as cook at the Imp Café, later the Willow Café, on Amersham High Street. She had never worked professionally in this field before, but delighted the owner Mrs Paget by producing the finest dishes with the limited supplies available.

Mother took time off to sort out my problems, and finally got me into St Michael's School in New Amersham. This too was a Church school, but very different from St. Mary's. It was run with a strong sense of tolerance, the children following the example of the school ethos, and the bullying and prejudice found at my old school were happily absent.

My mother found it very difficult getting me to New Amersham and back since the buses ran at infrequent hours, and I had to spend an hour at the end of each day sitting in the offices of the WVS until my mother arrived to collect me. I don't think the women at this office were over-delighted to have a small child hanging about, and they put me in an empty room at the top of the building, where I could watch for my mother from the window. There was an ancient typewriter on the table, and I recall learning by heart the letters on the faded keyboard.

New Amersham seemed a different world to the old town, and I missed the centuries old buildings and most of all the rural landscape which blended with the heart of the town. So despite the kind teachers and warm atmosphere, with winter approaching and the bus journeys becoming ever more difficult, I returned to St Mary's.

Miss Harrison received me back without comment, I was as important to her as a fly on the window. Now, I was a changed pupil. I no longer found learning a joy, and hardly bothered to listen to the lessons. I read whatever books I could lay my hands on, and Miss Harrison and I seemed to have a mutual agreement of each going our own way. The bad habits of indifference were formed, and for the rest of my school career the damage of those early years took its toll.

The War ended, and we returned to London. I was thrilled by the city streets, the Woolworth stores, the museums and cinemas, and yet I sorely missed the fields and the river where tiny fish darted amongst the weeds. All my life, wherever fate took me, I would remember the smell of fields where mushrooms grew, and the magical azure carpets of bluebells growing in the beech woods. Time could not diminish the harshness of life as an evacuee, but neither did the deep love of nature ever become lost in the excitement of new experiences.

BURNING THE MIDNIGHT OIL

Although she wasn't an evacuee, Aunt Kate was such a frequent visitor, that she was almost an honorary resident. She would arrive, after a smart walk from Amersham train station, her cheeks red and her curly short hair in a halo around her face. A small woman, in cold weather she always wore a camel coat, and sensible brogue shoes, whilst in milder weather she would be dressed in slacks with a mannish shirt. Her springy step and vigorous appearance did not advertise that she had been up most of the previous night, driving an ambulance through the darkened streets in London's Blitz. Kate was my mother's younger sister and she was the son my grandfather had longed for after three daughters. A cricketer par excellence, she had worked for Reuters and could hold her own with the most hard-bitten men. She had a huge collection of books, and as a very small girl, I found her Penguin series fascinating, especially as different colour covers denoted the subjects. She was a member of the Left Book Club, and had done service in Spain, but she always had time for her small niece, and I adored her. Kate always kept her promises, no matter what, and she had promised me a rabbit. One day, after an especially rough night, she appeared marching down the dirt road to our iron shack, the place we called on our postal address as the 'bungalow' and which I simply called 'home'. She was carrying a cage covered by a cloth, and when the cover was removed a tiny grey and white rabbit was revealed. A home was found for Whiskers at the end of the 'garden' and carrots, cabbage and other treats were laid before him. I was in heaven – at last I had my very own rabbit. I fed him and petted him, whilst Kate watched with a cigarette placed firmly between her smiling lips. After she returned to London, I would rush home each day to play with my pet, until the awful day when I came home and found an empty cage. "The rats got him" was the dreadful explanation. I never forgot Whiskers, and as I grew up I never forgot the kindness and consideration of a wonderful

113

aunt. That kindness and love carried her onwards through the terrible ruin of Europe, when peace was declared. Through Germany and into Belsen, driving an UNRWA ambulance, to care for the starving remnants of humanity who remained as terrible evidence of mans' cruelty. Kate was a heroine, but never a prude. She smoked, she swore, she was impatient, often intolerant of fools or those whom she considered so, but she never forgot to keep a promise.

Bits and Bobs

Cyril Lassman was a schoolboy when I lived in Old Amersham. He was at St Mary's for a while. All I can remember was that he wore glasses and was a few years older than me!

I remember a Cheder teacher in Old Amersham who took our class once a week at St Mary's School. His name was Mr Isaacs and he was a lovely and patient man. We were wicked kids! I never knew his first name, but he wore glasses. The Hebrew lessons I attended were in a concrete outbuilding beside St Mary's School. It grew quite cold, but we all sat around a long table and sang songs. The Hebrew Classes in Old Amersham were a much more informal arrangement, and we actually received lovely Valentine Press books as prizes for just attending.

I recall a cow having its head blown off by a bomb. I never saw it just heard the shocking news in the area. Local legend!

There was a saying in Amersham that when the River Misbourne dried up it meant it was a time of war, when full a time of peace. Whilst I was there it was nearly dry.

There was an awful lot of illness about. I was in hospital twice, once with Scarlet Fever and once with Rheumatic Fever. Residents believed it must be something in the water.

Shardeloes was the place where during the summer cricket matches took place. My Grandfather (maternal) used to like to take time off from his ARP duties and come and sit in the pavilion and watch the players.

I visited the Little Theatre (Amersham Rep) with my mother. There were also two cinemas in Chesham and one in Amersham. The majority of the Jewish evacuees experienced theatre at the Musical or Empire (actually great stuff) and found my mother odd as we attended the opera in Watford and enjoyed classical music. The Music Halls and Empires were actually a chain of theatres. There was the Hackney Empire, the Shepherds Bush Empire and many more. They had variety shows which changed weekly. The Music Halls were also theatres, such as the old Gaiety in the Strand to name one. Stars such as Jessie Mathews and George Robey were stars of the old Musicals. But it was hard to get into London. The trains could take three hours, arriving late or being cancelled for troop trains.

Other Jewish families included a lovely family called Vilinsky, with a son Alan and a daughter. There was a Doreen Courts born 1936 who lived half-way up the hill. [Doreen's son, Marc Levine, added that his grandmother was Rebecca and that Doreen had a brother, Louis. They evacuated to 10 First Avenue with their Uncle Alex Simons, or Simmons, and Auntie Cis]. I also recall Renee Sofier, her husband, and sons Morris and Jack.

Funny thing, I went to school after the war in Golders Green at the Hasmonean Grammar. There was a girl in my class called Hannah Ehrentreu. Now I see that she lived in Chesham when I was in Amersham. Small world!

My mother worked for a short period as a nurse's aide at the Amersham Hospital. She worked with wounded soldiers, and they were based in prefabs in the grounds of the hospital. She said the ward sister was Jewish and of German origin, so I wonder if it was Katie Krone?

AN ENEMY ALIEN

We finished up living in Old Amersham by a strange series of events. My mother and I stayed for a while with a lovely family called Armstrong, really "upper crust", but Mrs Armstrong couldn't give a damn about appearances and wore pyjamas with wellington boots if it was cold. She had a son named Brian and we rode ponies together to the rage of the Nanny, who was antisemitic and a fearful snob. The Armstrongs got too fond of me and wanted to adopt me, so my mother left (she was working as the cook, but we were treated as family). In 1940, my mother and I were living as evacuees in Little Missenden, in the house of a Mrs. Stone. Never has a woman been so aptly named, stone for a heart, and stony of countenance.

My father, remained in London, living and working in our West End apartment, and it was planned that he would come and visit us at the weekend. Late one evening he arrived, tired and hungry, after a difficult journey in which the train was crowded and seemed to stop every few minutes. Hearing a man's voice, Mrs. Stone rushed out of her living room and gasped with horror. "I have let the woman and the child stay under my roof because I am a good Christian woman, let it not be said that there was no room at the inn!' She stopped for breath, her face reddening and her bulging cold eyes filled with hate, "But a Jew Man! Never! You will not enter my house. I am a widow woman and must protect my honour." My parents were naturally very upset, and agreed that my father would seek a room at the local pub, and we would find new lodgings the next morning.

Suddenly there was another knock at the door, and Mrs Stone still trembling opened it. The local police constable stood there, together with a plain clothes man and two military police. "We have information that you have an enemy alien staying under your roof." This was bluntly stated.

I must now interrupt and explain what had happened. My grandfather came from an early Zionist family, his sister Deborah had gone to Palestine, and was the mother of Moshe Dayan, who later became a famous Israeli. My grandfather was married to a lady from Vilna in Lithuania, and with their two children, born in London, and my father expected in a few months, rather than travelling to Palestine, went to a Zionist Settlement, The Baron Hirsh in the Argentine. My grandmother suffered badly from the heat and begged that they return to England. Life was hard in the Settlement, and grandfather agreed. Back in London the six month old baby who had been born in the Argentine (my father) was registered as newly born. The years passed, and eight more children were born, altogether nine boys and two girls. All were British and my father's original history was forgotten.

Suddenly War came and in the turmoil, four of my uncles enlisted for the British Army. Afraid of losing his eldest surviving son, my grandfather went to the authorities and confessed what he had done. The police were decent men and on the spot made my father an offer, enlist and all will be forgotten and forgiven. My father was now 35, soon to be 36, the same age as Guy Crouchback in Evelyn Waugh's "Sword of Honour". He shared much of that character's heroic spirit, indeed was quite thrilled at becoming a soldier. Cheerfully, he kissed us goodbye and off he went.

The next day, my mother found me a temporary home on a farm run by plain farming folk, the Dwight family, with a no nonsense approach, but the the kindest and warmest-hearted people imaginable. I boarded alone. They had three daughters, Pat, Janet and Pauline. They lived opposite Mrs Stone and loathed her. They took me in because life with Mrs Stone (who lived opposite) was like a horror movie!

Although they were so homely, I fretted badly for my mother, who had returned to London, being only just four years old. Every evening I stood at the end of the lane waiting for the bus and see if she was on it. I cried each night at the end of the lane. Eventually, my mother came for me and we went together to Amersham, and agreed to move into the Bungalow, just so that we could be a family once again.

Booba

Animals played a greater role in rural life. They were not just living meat, milk or egg factories, but were fellow workers in the daily life of farms and small holdings.

The inside walls of our 'Bungalow' were lined with yellowish wood, and when the rain fell it made an almighty noise, whilst the wind shook the flimsy window frames, and the fire flared up menacingly in the main room. The place had been divided into several smaller rooms and two families (one extended) shared the kitchen, scullery and lavatory. Naturally there was no bathroom, but for those days this was quite normal.

My mother and I lived in two rooms, which were kept immaculately clean. Mum dusted and swept each morning, polishing the dining room suite and did her best to create a normal home. We shared this hovel with a mother, father and their small girl and baby, and the wife's mother and teenage daughter. The old lady could not have been more than sixty. She was in that working-class widow's wasteland between fifty and sixty where social life ended and senility had not yet claimed her senses. We thought her ancient, with her long black dresses, grey hair screwed into a bun, and a permanent dew drop at the end of her sharp nose. Everybody called her Booba (grandmother) and her birth name had long been forgotten. Dragged out of the tenements of the old East End, she stoically accepted the transfer as she had done when she was shipped out of the Polish shtetl [Yiddish, a small Jewish town or village] and arrived one day at an English port.

For Booba, Amersham could have almost been the shtetl. There was a very shabby hovel to call home, fellow Jews to converse with, and Gentile neighbours to be wary of and avoid contact with. Most of all there was land. The Bungalow was surrounded by stony earth, filled with bits of iron, and old bus parts. A few lovely trees stood at the bottom of the garden, and lilac bushes and dog roses clamoured for space in season. Booba at once set about growing vegetables, soft fruit and above all, tomatoes. Only cabbages flourished, at least those not devoured by the wretched green caterpillars which were a source of terror for me. The soft fruit never materialised, but the tomatoes, well they grew and grew, wondrous globes, first green then yellow, and finally bursting forth in wonderful shades of red. These were used in omelettes, with the field mushrooms we gathered from the cow pastures, in borsht, the tomato soup from Eastern Europe, fried with meat, and eaten between slices of bread as sandwiches. And why did the tomatoes grow so promiscuously? What was Booba's secret? Very simple, it was manure.

How my friend, her granddaughter, hated the very mention of manure. The smell and texture of it made us shudder, watching as it rose steaming from the discharge dropped by the passing cart horses. It was our horrible and dreaded task to follow the horses, holding shovels and buckets and gather the smelly manure. As we bent to pick it up we heard the mocking voice of the local children "Here come the Yids. Here come the Yid Shit Gatherers!" Sometimes Annette would weep, whereas I, a different type of child altogether, would gather up a shovel of manure and hurl it at our oppressors.

Above all, we dreaded market days when cattle would be herded into the market square, and the cobbled stones were rich with manure. Sent by Booba into service, for years I could never eat a tomato with real appetite.

GRANDFATHER'S CABIN

My grandfather and his long-suffering wife, my step grandmother, came as London evacuees to Old Amersham. Actually, they finished up in Ley Hill. We took a bus to Chesham, and then another (small green coach-type bus) to where my Grandfather lived although to a small child, it was almost another country. Grandfather had refused to be evacuated, but when he emerged one morning from the shelter and found his East End home was just a mound of rubble, he arrived on the doorstep of the Bungalow, glaring angrily at the world, while his wife huffed and puffed as she straggled up the dirt road dragging what remained of their possessions. Fortunately, they had two large suitcases, as each night Grandfather ordered The Aunt to fill them with essentials. I must tell you here, that Grandfather was from an educated Russian family, and used the term Tante for his second wife. This was rather crudely, translated into The Aunt, by which the unfortunate woman was forever afterwards known. At the premature death of his first wife, whose death certificate gave the cause of death as Exhaustion, he was left with six boys and a daughter still at home, so quickly remarried. Unlike his first wife, The Aunt was a Polish born, uneducated woman, a widow with five children of her own. The poor woman must have been desperate to have taken on my dictator of a grandfather, but those were hard times, and any husband was considered better than none.

Their stay at the Bungalow was a short one, Grandfather found his demands going unanswered, and only the poor old Booba, for some reason developed a passion for him. She started to steal rouge from her youngest daughter's cosmetic box, and wore a bright artificial flower in her black hat. She even forgot to send us children out to collect horse manure, and the tomatoes hung their heavy heads in disapproval. This passion did not go unnoticed. The Aunt was furious, and laid secret articles in Booba's bed. She carried a dried up old clove of garlic attached to a red string and waved it whenever Booba passed by, and caused great mirth by spitting three times through her second and third fingers every time she saw The

121

Aunt's ample form disappearing from view. Grandfather could bear it no longer. He applied hair oil on his thick white wavy hair, stiffened his back, and packed their cases.

Evil Eye is believed to be a curse put by jealous, evil people on those whom they envy. New babies should never be called, 'beautiful' as disaster will befall them. If a mother is out with her newborn, and someone says, "How lovely this child is." The mother will reply "Fah! She/He is a miserable wretch." When the person departs, the mother should spit three times through two fingers. A valuable amulet is garlic, tied to a red string or ribbon, to ward off the Evil Eye – East European superstitions, whilst the red string has roots in the Kabalah of Jewish spiritual lore.

The elderly couple found two rooms in Ley Hill, in a house owned by a tolerant, if not exactly friendly countrywoman. They had no complaints about the bedroom, or the living room, the problems arose with the shared kitchen. The Aunt kept a strictly kosher kitchen, milk and meat completely separate, including storage and cutlery and all cooking utensils. The landlady was an extremely clean and neat person, whilst The Aunt was the worst housewife imaginable.

Grandfather grew tired of the fighting, and offered to build a wooden storage hut for the landlady, Mrs Brown. His father had been the manager of the forestry in a large estate outside Kiev, and he assured Mrs Brown he knew exactly what to do. My grandfather toiled as he hadn't for years, and a wonderful chalet arose in the garden, well away from the main house, a wooden chalet in the Russian style, with every home comfort.

Mrs Brown never got to store anything in her 'storage hut' since Grandfather moved himself and The Aunt there for the duration. Mrs Brown wasn't exactly pleased, but she saw the advantages. She was no more bothered by The Aunt's untidy habits, nor the weird religious practices of the old folk. Above all, as the war drew to a close, she knew she had a quite valuable piece of property on her land. Indeed, when her son was demobbed and came home with a new bride, a most unpleasant girl, according to Mrs Brown, they were able to set up home in Grandfather's Cabin.

EAST IS EAST AND WEST IS WEST

My mother was born in Soho, in the West End of London, as were her parents, and she had her first contact with EastEnders when we moved to Old Amersham. True my father had grown up in the East End, but he had left it at seventeen and lived, and worked near his future wife. Most of the evacuees who moved to New Amersham were not from the East End, in contrast to those who settled for the 'duration' in the Old town. New Amersham had much in common with a suburban way of life. Neat little houses, everybody pretending to mind their own business, and Japanese Cherry trees blooming in the tidy front gardens.

Old Amersham was a complete culture shock for my mother. Not only were the natives divided into strict social classes – the upper class who occupied residences half way up the hill, and a few professionals who dwelt in lovely stone mansions in the High Street, towards Shardeloes, a stately home, used as a maternity hospital. Then there were the trade people, a solid class of Yeomen types who owned small holdings and who had run the butchers, the bakers, and the candlestick makers for generations. Finally, there were the 'working class', consisting of farm labourers, casual workers, and a core of ne'er do wells, who existed hand to mouth by poaching and other non-social activities. Used to the cosmopolitan world of Soho, Mother found these country folk strange, and she must have appeared an exotic bird to them, with her well-tailored suits (made by my master tailor father), or smart dresses always with stockings and good shoes. Even strangers to her, however, were the Jewish evacuees from the East End. The ties of a shared religion were tightly strained, and only the antagonism of most of the Gentiles towards the newcomers forced my mother into relationships with the EastEnders. At first, she was shocked at their vulgarity, crude language, and loud voices, but she soon became endeared to their good heartedness, generosity, and zest for life. When she returned to London after the war, many remained life-long friends, whereas in contrast, the Gentiles, who had, after condemning the Jewish evacuees, shown amazement that Mother was a Jew, were not included in visits to Old Amersham. Mother found it especially hurtful that the amazement was depicted by saying, when they realised she was Jewish, "But of course, you are different."

Living in Old Amersham, the squalor of the Bungalow, and the harshness of much of wartime life, was made bearable by the sheer beauty of the countryside. Those evacuees in New Amersham could have remained in a sterile outer London suburb. Nature was not allowed to infiltrate the neat villas and tidy gardens. In Old Amersham, the shrill cries of the vixen calling out for a mate broke the stillness which descended as night fell. The hooting of owls as they flitted over the ramshackle roofs of The Wheatsheaf, a collection of vermin-ridden cottages, which housed the East End Jewish evacuees and the poorest natives was an integral part of life, and made me shiver in my bed. They were a wonderful, warm crowd, and brought a whole new perspective to my life (I was from the West End).

The hedgerows were a world apart, in spring and summer filled with greenery, Dog-roses, nests of birds with eggs of wonderous colour. Autumn was perhaps the best of all, hazelnuts clothed in little leafy cups and ready to crack, berries of all descriptions, elderberries and berries I never named. The fields where the cows trod summer and winter, revealed white patches which were wild mushrooms. Strangely, the natives never bothered or even knew about these gifts, but my mother and I delighted in picking baskets of the wonderful fungi. Fried quickly and eaten on toast, no mushroom has ever tasted so good.

The chalk hill where blue butterflies flew in season, and the bluebells in the beech woods were images that I carried all my life in nostalgia of a true country childhood. These special sights sustained me through much of the bitter reality of being an evacuee.

THE LITTLE BLUE BANTAM

A flock of chickens strutted around the Bungalow, muttering contentedly, and adding to the general untidiness of the grounds by shedding feathers and splattering their mess wherever they passed. They were fed household scraps, and there was a continual battle between the fowl and the rats as to whom got the choicest bits. The best thing about them, in my childhood mind, was that the chickens ate the caterpillars which for some unknown reason terrified me, even more than the evil-eyed rats which boldly crouched waiting for victims. My mother loathed the chickens and wanted them out, but she was pacified by the eggs which we received after hunting them down in unlikely hedges. Eggs were rationed, so however much my mother hated the dirt, she was happy to give me a fresh boiled egg for breakfast, or even egg and chips as a teatime treat.

My friend Annette's father, a bearer of wonderful gifts, returned one day from Club Row, an East End street market famous for cats, dogs and all livestock with a seventh birthday gift for me. 1942 was a hard year, and this was a gift beyond belief. No chicken fashioned by the greatest artist could ever compare with my little blue Bantam. Small, but perfectly formed, his feathers shimmered even more brilliantly than the wings of a dragonfly. He seemed to sense he was mine, and followed me around like a baby. Many times I smuggled him into the bedroom I shared with my mother, and hid him beneath the bedclothes. No sissy, he was the fiercest cock bird imaginable. He violently attacked any cockerel that crossed his path, and lived for fighting.

Scarlet Fever, a nasty condition those days, came to Amersham, and I was brought down with what was then a dangerous disease. Dear old Dr Johns in the High Street persuaded me to agree to go to Stoke Mandeville (the Fever) Hospital, and so after seeing my books and toys taken away to be destroyed or fumigated, I left in a closed dark green ambulance. I spent a horrific three weeks in Stoke Mandeville Hospital – all my toys were burned! [German Jewish Refugee Dr Lutwig Guttmann established the

125

National Spinal Injuries Centre there and after the war, he developed the Paralympics to rebuild the confidence and physical strength of the injured military patients.]

I have dreadful memories of the place. There was a really vicious Sister, who made my three weeks there a misery. No visitors, and once a week my mother, and my father (who received leave from the army) looked at me and blew kisses through the window.

At last, the day arrived when I could go home. My father had to carry me as I was so weak and had lost so much weight due to refusing to eat the dreadful food. Back home, a royal welcome awaited me. Annette was overjoyed to see me, and every little old familiar thing seemed blessed.

I sat eating my lockshen soup, real Jewish chicken soup, with globules of golden fat adorning the steaming aromatic dish. At last satisfied after the first proper meal in three weeks, I leaned back and asked to see my Bantam.

Annette, who was usually a gentle and kind child, had suffered by being neglected and completely out of the limelight whilst I was so sick. My father had sent gifts of sweets and butterscotch and even American comics which American servicemen had donated for his ill child. With a slight smirk she raised her black eyes and stared amazed at me. "Didn't you know, you have just eaten him?"

Black GIs in Town

I was only a small child, between the ages of 6 or 7 when the GIs came to England. With the other children, I ran after those handsome soldiers, each looking like a film star, squealing, "Any gum, chum"? They were so tall, so healthy looking, such smart uniforms, a complete difference to the mainly pasty-faced, ill-nourished British Army boys in their badly tailored uniforms and prison-style haircuts. I envied the girls who were old enough to meet them at the weekly dances, and prayed that they would be there long enough so I could marry one!

At that age I knew nothing about the racial segregation policies that America so willingly enacted, and as far as I was concerned, the black GIs now arriving, were just 'sun-tanned' versions of the earlier influx. The American authorities had arranged for the local councils and public house to be aware of the segregation policies, and certain pubs became 'coloured' whilst others admitted whoever could pay for his drink. The dances too did not welcome 'coloureds', although many of the girls found the black servicemen attractive and definitely exotic.

A well frequented pub opposite The Bungalow, did not welcome my father, when he arrived in British Army uniform, because they recognised him as a Jew. Neither would they receive Goldberg, his good friend from the regiment. So the 'coloureds' certainly had no chance there! Rather they patronised a pub on Whielden Street (previously Union St) where the landlord was friendly and the drinks good.

One day, I invited a couple of GIs to The Bungalow, fascinated with their stories of America, and delighted with the comic books they gave me. My mother, surprised, but ever hospitable welcomed them into our corrugated shack of a home. She was, after all born in Soho, and was no stranger to different races, and didn't have any hang-ups about race or religion. A pleasant time was spent hearing about their lives in The States, and one GI from the Deep South said our humble home resembled his back home, right to the ramshackle veranda with its two steps.

Over the next few weeks, more black GIs visited, and I learned to jitterbug, and listened with delight to many of the songs they knew by heart. The wonderful Quaker paid a visit one evening, and soon the GIs were met with a warm welcome whenever they visited their homes. So what with us London Jews and the established Old Amersham Quakers, the black GIs were no longer outsiders.

Unfortunately, prejudice was not restricted to the narrow minded villagers, some of the wealthier London Jews came to hear of our visitors, and whilst not condemning them outright, quietly suggested that we were doing ourselves, and above all the London Jewish community, no favours, and would stir up the anti-Semitism which forever simmered. The Old Amersham London Jewish evacuees, however, dismissed these concerns, and mocked the (dare not write what they named them)! New Amersham snobs, and came along to drink coffee or tea and listen to the best jazz this side of the Atlantic!

Pheobe Isaacs

I lived in Amersham from 1940-1945. My brother, Lucien, helped to obtain a building for the synagogue. He was Secretary, Ben Grossman was Chairman and the minister was Rev. Rapaport. The congregation was an active one.

I know the Nathans, the Lissacks and the Richmans. The Richmans later owned the Green Park Hotel in Bournemouth. I used to go to look for accommodation for evacuees with Mrs Lissack as she was quite important in the WVS which I also belonged to. I was also in the Civil Defence Corps and was on duty one night a week 8pm to 8am at the Report Centre and we knew where all the bombs fell. We had a map and had to stick black pins where they fell.

One particular incident from the war years is the night my father died. Mr Nathan (senior) rode his bike in the blackout to go to our home and comfort my family. I will never forget his kindness.

I worked for R.F Equipment, a radar factory, in Amersham. A colleague of mine told me her son arrived home from school very indignant. A boy had called him a JEW. He replied I am not a Jew I am an EVACUEE. My boss was Michael Sobell. I visited the Sobell family, first in Beaconsfield then in Fulmer. I had various jobs including Welfare Officer and Canteen Manageress. Sir Michael Sobell died aged 101 in 1993.

Lucien Isaacs

I am the brother of Pheobe Isaacs. I was a member and secretary of the congregation from 1939-1942. After I left in 1942 I became their solicitor. My ex-wife was very involved with the theatre in Amersham.

I was the First Secretary of the Amersham and District Congregation, but I had to resign in about November 1942, when as an officer in the RAF I was posted overseas, and did not return to Amersham until 1945. When I resigned, the congregation presented me with a Dunhill pipe and a beautiful leather tobacco pouch.

Sonnie Bloch became a chaplain to the Forces in the RAF, was never ordained as a member of religion, "Reverend" being a courtesy title.

Initially there were only a few Jewish families in Amersham. It was only after the Blitz started around the latter part of 1941 that families moved out of London to escape the bombing.

Mr Levy, of Highlands Road, established the first minyan.

I recall initially services were held at his house, and later possibly at houses of other members. The majority of the Amersham residents were members of constituent synagogues of the United Synagogue. I recall attending meetings with Sir Robert Whaley-Cohen, who was then President of the United Synagogue. As a result, it was arranged that the Amersham and District Congregation became [loosely] affiliated to the United Synagogue, which provided funds for the congregation whilst the members maintained their membership of the constituent synagogue of which they were a member.

By 1942, there were possibly around two hundred families who were in Amersham. Services for the High Holydays were in a church hall. I think it was St Leonard's Hall in Chesham Bois. There must have been over two hundred people who attended. The bricks in one of the walls had been removed to leave the sign of the cross, which we covered up by placing a board over it, but one of the members, a Mr Rechtand, who was extremely orthodox, objected and refused to attend.

Mr Rechtand was the grandfather of Mr Domb, who became Professor Domb. He was also, I believe, the father of Sidney Stanley, who achieved great notoriety in or about 1942, when proceedings were taken against him and Mr Belcher (a Cabinet minister who resigned as a result of the scandal), for substantial commercial transactions in breach of the wartime regulations.

REV IZAAK RAPAPORT

(Information provided by his son Dennis)

My father came to London by himself in the mid-1930's from Poland (some of his family made it to Palestine, but most remained behind) to do a doctorate at Kings College.

My parents, Minnie and Izaak, were married in London the year after the war. Minnie was the sister of Harold (who was in the Forces) and had a slightly younger sister, Millicent.

My father would have been actively involved in youth activities, as he later was in subsequent years. My mother used to work in London at her father's wholesale food business (Wolf Brand, known for their horseradish, among other things), riding the train every day, never knowing if their East End premises had survived the nightly bombings.

The son of my father's older brother, Jack, (who was in the army) recalled from childhood visits to Amersham that Grandpa [Wolf Simons] had a seat in the front row of the synagogue.

Figure 3: Rev/Captain (later Rabbi) Izaak Rapaport (Army Chaplain).

132

HAROLD SIMONS

My family evacuated to Amersham shortly after the war was declared in 1939. Various friends and acquaintances joined together to hold weekly Sabbath services. Eventually, a hall on the fringe of Chesham Bois was used to hold services and social activities. The community grew in numbers and at a later date the hut was erected. During the war years three ministers were appointed.

When I joined the RAF in 1941 the incumbent minister was Reverend, later Rabbi, Izaak Rapaport. My visits to Amersham became restricted to occasional leaves.

I left England in June 1943 and spent a year flying around North Africa and Italy. My operational activities ended in April 1944. Whilst relaxing in a transit camp in Taranto, Southern Italy, awaiting transport to Palestine for operational rest and to train future air crews, I was called to the phone. A low slightly accented voice said, 'Hello, Harold.' It was Captain Rapaport, Army Chaplain. He had arrived in Algiers a few days previously and traced my whereabouts. The following morning we sat overlooking Taranto Harbour sharing a small bottle of whisky and kichels [Yiddish for traditional sweet biscuits] baked by one of the Amersham congregants. He bought me up to date with Amersham activities. Two years later he married my sister. They spent the next twenty-five years in Australia, he as Rabbi to the Melbourne Hebrew Congregation. On retirement they moved with their family to Israel.

One or two bombs dropped during the war. When the shul was opened at the end of 1939 an elderly gentleman came, who said he was Jewish and had lived in Amersham all his life. He was so delighted to discover that so many Jewish people had been evacuated to his locality. He joined the congregation and they made him a warden.

MALKA DAWSON (WAS MILLICENT SIMONS)

Dear Amersham Dwellers,

I lived with my parents and family in South Road, Amersham from December 1939 until the end of the war.

My late brother-in-law became the minister and also taught in the cheder. He was there until he became Chaplain in the army. His name was Rev. Izaak Rapaport.

Rev. S. M. Bloch was also a teacher at the cheder until he became R.A.F chaplain.

The community ran a social club for members of the armed forces who were stationed in the area. This was attended by British, Polish, the Palestine and U.S.A armies and other men. Families would invite them home for Shabbat or Yom Tov.

As there was no TV and almost no cars we had to make our own entertainment. Motzei Shabbat [Saturday night end of Sabbath] quite a number of people went to the Amersham Repertory Company performances. For some people, it was their first taste of living in the country, and we enjoyed peaceful walks thro' farmland, down to Old Amersham, or the other direction to Chesham. Some of us had bikes and would cycle to neighbouring towns and villages. I for one was unhappy (after the war) at the thought of leaving the country. However, once the war was over, my two brothers, and future husband were duly released from the army and air force, and living in London became normal.

Many families had come from the area around Stamford Hill, Stoke Newington and Willseden. New small communities started in Chorleywood, and in Chesham, where the Ehrentreu family lived.

Kosher meat, challot, [singular is challah, a plaited bread for Friday night Sabbath] and other food had to be brought from London.

For the people who worked in London, and travelled daily, any train leaving before 7.30a.m cost 1/6d for a return ticket – so those trains were well used. Travelling could be quite unpleasant as often there was no heating.

Some of the women did voluntary work with the hospitals, or the WVS etc. I used to cycle to the Amersham hospital once a week. Others became active in other fields of Air-Raid-Precautions. My sister and I did fire-watching duty once a week.

My husband and I came on Aliyah over eight years ago. Our children and grandchildren live here in Hevron.

Affectionately

Malka Dawson

Paula Bright (nee Indech)

We lived in "Bramley" Station Road, Amersham during the war years. My father Reverend Jonah Indech officiated at many services. He later qualified as a rabbi. He had very much to do with Jewish/Christian relations, and was minister of the Amersham congregation from 1st April 1944 until 31st December 1945. It was an active community with many young evacuee families. There were regular Friday night and Shabbat morning services as well as Yom Tovim. On Shabbat afternoons my father would give talks and have discussions on various topics. One active participant he remembers clearly was Cyril Domb. Cheder took place in the shul on Sundays and one evening in the week. There was an assistant teacher, Mr Sonnie Bloch, who became a chaplain to the Forces. The children were taught in mixed groups arond large tables. I remember one occasion when a flying bomb came overhead and landed in Weedon Hill Wood. My father, who was teaching chumash at the time, called out, 'Under the tables!' Down he went books and all. No one was hurt. The only other bomb we remember was when the church was hit.

My father did not meet the Reverend Rapaport, who left to be a chaplain before we came to Amersham.

I went to Heatherton House School with several other Jewish girls, including Liese Feuchtwanger, who was my closest friend. My father taught the Jewish girls there on Friday mornings. [Harold Slutzkin added, 'My late wife Liese Feuchtwanger, born 1933, sister of Frank, lived in Amersham for most of the duration with her parents Jakob and Vera, who came to London from Munich in 1935.]

Della Rosenberg married Fred Worms. She is famous for all her charity work. I remember Ivor Deichman (now Delman).

With regard to Kashrut, everything needed such as meat etc. came from London and was brought mainly by men working there.

My own memories as a ten-year-old, was of a happy time with my two brothers [Michael and Asher] and then my baby sister Judy was born in

Shardeloes. My mother was transferred. My father walked all the way to Chesham Cottage Hospital from Amersham during Shabbat to his wife (Sarah), who remained in hospital for some time. Judy was brought home to be looked after by our family.

Figure 4: Reverend (later Rabbi) Jonah Indech.

Devora Wolkenfeld (nee Doris Rabbinowitz)

After Rabbi Indech left Amersham, the community invited my husband to conduct all the religious services until 1947. My mother lived at 'Cosy Nook', Station Road. We well remember the Blochs and Stamlers amongst other walking over, come rain or shine, to all the services as there were no longer a sufficient number of congregants in Chesham to form a minyan. The reference written by the warden, Ben Grossmann, for my husband, stated, 'He conducts our Services to the fullest satisfaction of our members. He has an excellent tenor voice and a great knowledge of the traditional Chazonus. We are confident that Rev Wolkenfeld is able to reach the highest expectations.'

Shirley Samuel (Daughter of Rose Israel)

My family came to Amersham in 1944. We lived in the house that the Nathans lived in. I was aged twelve when I left Amersham. I recall what life was like during the war years. The Jewish community was very strong. A Forces Canteen was held in the shul every Saturday night. Bovingdon Air-Force base was nearby. The Rev. Saul Amias was the chaplain to the army camp. Every Pesach each Jewish family would invite two servicemen to their seder.

The Bloch family lived in Chesham. Dr Maurice Bloch moved to London. His mother used to get the bus from Chesham to buy fish from a shop in Amersham. Every Pesach she would take her own knife along to the fishmongers, to make sure the fish was cut with a kosher-for-Pesach utensil.

There were few telephones, in those days news was passed on by word of mouth.

The Jewish community in Chesham held orthodox services but came socially to Amersham. The Auction Room in Amersham was originally a theatre. Next to it stood a school, where some pupils were from Jewish families in the town.

Audrey Marks (nee Samson)

My parents Rueben and Anne Samson lived in Amersham with my sister, Betty and I, from 1939-45 at Linden, Lea Long Park, Chesham Bois.

My father travelled to London each day doing vital war work. My mother looked after a big and extended family, and many soldiers who were entertained in our house – British, American, Polish, and Free French etc.

My sister was a cook at Amersham hospital and I was involved with Amersham Rep Theatre. A great friend was a <u>very</u> young Dirk Bogarde (very young and poor at the time – extremely charming and talented).

My aunt, who lived with us, made uniforms. I entertained with songs and piano at the camps where the troops were waiting to go for D Day, also at hospitals where wounded civilians from London were treated. We also at times had about sixteen people (mostly from London) sleeping in our cottage!

We knew the Edelmans, Hirschfelds, Kleiners, Goehrs, George Marks, Phoebe and Lucien Isaacs.

My father was an Air Raid Warden and I became a musician in broadcasting.

Figure 5: Some Jewish Children of Amersham and Chesham having fun.

DELLA WORMS (NEE ROSENBERG)

I was 8 or 9 when my family first went to Amersham in 1940 until 1946. We lived at 18 Highfield Gardens. My brother Arthur Rosenberg (now Arthur Harverd) was about 6 years old. I'm afraid neither of us can remember a rabbi who wore a green jacket!

Sonnie Bloch was my Hebrew class teacher and he took shul services. I attended Habonim[83] and B'nei Akivah.[84] I believe we bought kosher meat from High Wycombe.

I first went to St. Michael's Preparatory School, then Turret School and finally to the Grammar school, Dr Challoner's, where we had excellent tuition. I was in Milton House.

I remember a fire bomb dropping at the bottom of Highfield Gardens about 1941. It caused a fairly large crater but in later years it filled with water, plants, and insects and the nature class from Dr Challoner's used to come to study it.

I remember Mrs Rosa Israel, a friend of my parents Mick and Esther Rosenberg. Also, I recall Ivor Deichman, Manfred Wolkovitch, Cyril Wicks, Alan and Sylvia Webber and Rene Levy.

A favourite walk was to Old Amersham to the 'Golden Hind Tea Room'. We visited Champneys Health Spa at Tring.

RENE LEW (NEE LEVY)

I lived in Highfield Close, Amersham-on-the-Hill, during the war years. The hut which the congregation bought was a pre-fab. Before services were held at people's homes. I taught Hebrew in a voluntary capacity. I was Arthur Harverd's teacher, and only eighteen. There was an American Air Force base nearby and a forces club. My family were instrumental in forming the Amersham Hebrew Congregation.

Arthur Harverd (formerly Rosenberg)

(Brother to Della)

Rene Lew was my Hebrew teacher when she was eighteen years old. I changed my name from Rosenberg to Harverd. Har is Hebrew for mountain or berg and verd is Hebrew for Rose.

I remember the Bloch family. I have always regarded the late, dear Sonnie Bloch as the greatest teacher I have ever had. In the early days of the Jewish community services were held in the church hall in Chesham Bois.

My daughter married Gill Lewin's son!

Gill Lewin (nee Weber)

My son married Arthur Harverd's daughter.

At the age of four and a half I caught measles, and then contracted a measles-related disease. There were no antibiotics in those days. I went to a special isolation ward at Stoke Mandeville Hospital where I lay in a coma. The doctors did not expect me to live. After a week I woke up. I swear, to this day, that it was because of the services that were held in the shul to pray for me.

After being discharged from the isolation ward, my mother went to see the matron. She was told to be careful when combing my hair – my head was itchy. It turned out I had caught chicken pox whilst in the hospital! Much to my embarrassment, due to my weakness, after being so desperately ill, my mother bought me a pushchair. It was awful having to be wheeled about at the age of four and a half. As a result I had to go to my headmistress's study every day where I was given a hot meal.

I remember fetes being held in our garden, and especially the jam tarts my mother baked and sold at these events. We also kept chickens during the war years.

The Battle of Britain planes flew overhead. My brother, John was always finding bullets. My father was in the ARP. When there was an air raid warning he would don his hat and patrol the street. We had a tiny cupboard under the stairs in which our family sheltered in during an air raid. My mother wrapped me in a blanket and put me in the cupboard. My brother would stand on one side and my sister on the other. We had a big jar of boiled sweets which were eaten on those occasions, and the jar is still in the Weber family!

Susan Lewin (nee Morris)

(Married to Nachum Marks)

I was born on the 31st May 1941. I had always been told that I had been born in Chesham Hospital but when I just checked this on my birth certificate it gives my place of birth as Tenterden, South Road, Amersham. At that time, an invasion of the Nazis was expected imminently. My mother said that in the hospital, the nurses had milk bottles filled with cyanide all round the room and the nurses said to her, 'When they walk up the path, we'll be ready for them.' It was not a very calm place to spend the first ten days of my life.

There is a big connection with Michael Lewin. [Michael and his second wife, Gill attended the reunion for the Amersham Hebrew Congregation in 1994.] Michael was my former husband and the father of my two daughters, Julia and Deborah. Michael and Gill (née Weber) are good friends and we see them regularly. Gill's sister is Anne Wolff, who is a few years older. The ties to Buckinghamshire are extraordinary and my sister married Richard Toeman. We all spent time in Buckinghamshire, and later met, and married!

My father, David Morris, (a solicitor) was in the RAF and we followed him around the country for a while to be near where he was stationed. Our family evacuated from London to Amersham at the beginning of the war – probably the end of 1939. After that we followed my father to Doncaster and York and when he went overseas in 1942, we moved to Bovingdon and then Little Gaddesdon. My father came back in August 1945. As far as I can gather, people knew others who had moved to Bucks, so a community developed.

My mother was Dorothy Morris (née Jackson). Her parents (my grandparents) were in Amersham for a while with us – Bernard and Johanna Jackson, formally from Dublin. They emigrated from Dublin to London in 1927. Also, my mother's brothers, Walter and Douglas Jackson, and my mother's sister Gladys Selwyn, with her husband Maurice and their daughter Barbara. My sister Diana Morris (now Toeman) is four years older than me. The male relatives I have mentioned above; my grandfather Bernard and my uncles, Walter, Douglas and Maurice were all dentists and used to commute to London during the war to work.

In Amersham we lived in Orchard View, Orchard Lane. I think that as a family we did adjust well to the country and I have longed to live in the country ever since. My family didn't attend shul and didn't appear to play any part in religious life. I think the war was the single most defining event of my life and of my family. I had moved home seven times before my fourth birthday. My father was abroad and therefore apart from my mother, my sister and me, for two and a half years. There was fear of invasion and constant fear of bombs. I don't think our family really recovered from the disruption, separation, fear and insecurity. The British attitude of keeping a stiff upper lip kept everyone going, but had its psychological costs in shutting off emotions. I expect this has something to do with my career choice as a psychotherapist.

We moved back to London when I was three and a half so my memories are vague but I do remember asking my mother why the sky was red and she said that it was London burning.

DIANA TOEMAN MBE (NEE MORRIS)

(Susan's sister)

I discovered after I met Richard Toeman that his parents, Iris and Bob, actually lived a few streets away from us in Amersham at that time. Richard was four years older than I was. His elder brother, Edward, must also have been living with the family then. Richard went to a prep school whilst living in Amersham, called Little Abbey, in Great Missenden. I believe it became a health spa after the war. I also know that Iris joined the M.T.C. (Motor Transport Corps) whilst living in Amersham and became 'Bomber' Harris's driver.

[Sir Arthur Harris, Commander-in-Chief of Bomber Command. From 1942 – 1945 lived at Springfields, Great Kingshill, opposite the aptly named, 'Cockpit Road', prior to his residency. This was a drive away to Bomber Command HQ, an underground bunker hidden in the woods of Walters Ash. The RAF is still there. Imagine the surprise of the authors of this book, that the only two people we should bump into whilst wandering around Great Kingshill were two life-long local residents who shed some light on WW2 in the village. Springfields, was called Springfield, without the 's' at the end. The mansion would have been a place of gathering for high-ranking officials, such as French President De Gaulle and American General Eisenhower, who was to become president of the USA. Everyone knew when 'Bomber Harris' was coming as his driver never switched off the headlights in a blackout. Perhaps the position of authority gave him insight into when the air raids were coming!]

The three Toeman brothers, who had a wholesale stocking company in London, were Bob, Joe and Colly and there was also a sister, Sarah. Bob and Iris's children were Edward, Cecile (known as Bobby) and Richard. Joe and Rosa's children were Charles and Rudy. Colly had no children. Sarah's children were George, Marc and another, younger son.

147

Putting myself in my family's shoes, I believe the war must have had a profound effect; my mother Dorothy and her sister Gladys (both in their early thirties) had only been married just over four years when war broke out (they had had a double wedding in 1935). They moved into what must have been a fairly small bungalow with their husbands, two small daughters, two brothers and their parents. Each couple had had a very pleasant house in the Hampstead Garden Suburb, so the lack of space and privacy must have tested their patience to the limit.

I had a long talk to one of my late husband's best friends, Adrian Davis, who was living in Amersham at the same time as we and the Toemans were. It seems that most of the Jewish population of north-west London ended up in Amersham and surrounding towns at the outbreak of war!

Adrian Davis

My parents were Caroline from Liverpool and Cyril Davis from London. Before the war they had acquired a bungalow in Lye Green Road, Chesham before moving to Chenies, Copperkins Grove, and then to Stubbs Wood in Chesham Bois. We lived there variously from 1939 until we moved back to London in 1944. Eventually my parents released the bungalow to Jewish German refugees called Gruenbeg. We went back before the war ended, buzz bombs or not, to return to London, because my parents were not happy with my education in Great Missenden. In 1938, I had started my schooling in The Hall School, boy's prep, in Swiss Cottage, and returned there in 1944. I was born in Hampstead.

For a very short time I went to Heatherton House School. I failed to get into Beacon School and ended up going to the combined school. I would ride my bike to Amersham Station, leave it there and take the Aylesbury bus. The school in Great Missenden was originally called Shortenills prior to amalgamation with a Kent based school called Boarzell, and formed 'Little Abbey'. Miss Brosonovitch taught me with impeccable English. The Headmaster was called Ferrier. It was there that I met Richard Toeman, who came from the Tunbridge Wells School. Richard and I became lifelong friends. He died suddenly. I was his best man, and he was mine at my wedding.

We wore blazers, and I recall Richard Toeman's evacuated school wore pink hats, when they temporarily amalgamated with us. In 1946 we went to Clifton College in Bristol together. Richard's parents were Bob and Iris. His older siblings were Bobby and Edward. Their house was in South Road, Amersham. I was always made welcome there, and at their house in London.

I had one anti-Semitic experience at Little Abbey. I did nothing about it but my mother blew up. It was in the summer term. On the back of my shirt, in which I had played cricket, someone had stuck a swastika and the words 'Dirty Jew'. The boy put his hand up to it eventually and wrote an apology to my parents. I didn't think that much about it, I was more upset when my mother tore up my fine collection of bus tickets when we moved to Stubbs Wood. They were Greenline tickets with different colours and all the stops printed out. When we paid the fare the conductor punched the declared destination.

A boy, not Jewish, lived near the Town Hall in an old house, 63 The High Street, Old Amersham, on the way to Great Missenden. His mum was a nurse and his dad a civil servant who could speak eight different languages. The boy was bad at getting ready for school. When the bus came, his mum would often rush out and wave it down. Out came the boy, half dressed, carrying the rest of his clothes, and would finish dressing on the bus.

We used to do silly schoolboy pranks. We got off in Old Amersham. There used to be a shop at the end where we would buy cherries and throw the stones at people through the open top windows of the houses.

The arts performance centred on Amersham Playhouse Theatre. Friends of my parents were very much involved with it. Sophie Isaacs lived in a big close nearby. She was a pianist. I went to see her play in Brighton once. Sophie had two sons. Carol Jenner was not Jewish but she was the other moving force for the Playhouse and this work led to the formation of the Unicorn Theatre. I smoked my first cigarette in the Playhouse and I enjoyed it! My parents knew about it. I was only ten years old. Carol Jenner allowed us to come back stage. Someone asked me 'Would you like a cigarette?' I replied 'Yes', just for the hell of it. Sophie Isaacs would give our family complimentary tickets. The theatre was plain inside and not highly decorated. We used to go every Christmas for the pantomime.

We went to Amersham Synagogue for High Days and Holy Days. When I lived in Stubbs Wood I had private Hebrew lessons in someone's house where we read text.

I recall a family seder in Chenies Cottage, with my mother's eldest brother and his wife. Dad hid the Afikoman in a glass decanter. I found it a year later. Another time it had been hidden in the piano.

I did lots of walking and cycling. I would ride my bike right to the other end of Copperkins Lane to Old Amersham. I remember walking through a dried up lake outside of Shardeloes, the maternity home. At the house in Chenies Cottage, there was an air raid shelter down there with beds in. I was very flexible at that age. When the siren went we went there. In retrospect it was a big shelter. In the garden there was a wonderful Victoria plum tree and an orchard with crab apples.

My father built an air raid shelter in our next house in Copperkins Grove, which is still there, covered with grass and used as a store. I remember picking wonderful bluebells in the back road down from Amersham to Old Amersham.

Our house in Chenies was nice, but not quite as big as the one in Chesham Bois. At Stubbs Wood we had lots of land and four bedrooms. There was a very large lounge adjacent to a room with nothing in it but the family piano, which I still have. It belonged to my maternal grandmother and has been in the family since 1920. We had a very large garden with a tennis court, but being wartime it was not in use. It had a large orchard. The garden was overlooked by the Chalfont to Chesham line, and you could always see the train. The line was on the embankment above. This time of my life fostered an interest in steam trains. I was once offered a ride on the footplate from Amersham to Rickmansworth. In those days we didn't have mobile phones, and I wasn't able to tell my mum, so I couldn't go. I made up for it in later life, when I got a ride on the footplate of a steam train. My father took down a few trees, which gave access to the line. Then I would stick pennies onto chewing gum and put them on the railway line. The steam engines would flatten them and put the pennies out of shape. It was possibly with Richard Toeman that I did that.

We were very lucky. A stray flying bomb only just passed over our house and landed in the next road, at the home of a master from Great Missenden School. The bomb killed his only adopted daughter.

Very close friends of my parents had a young baby lying on a bed under a big window. It blew in and covered the baby in glass, but there wasn't a scratch anywhere. This was the Green family, best friends to my father, and they were staying in a house called Trees, but the family did not live in Bucks. I remember visiting their grandfather in Croxley Green, when my toy submarine dropped in the canal.

We were not affected unduly by rationing. On the food front, I do remember lunchtime meals at school, where rabbit was served with amazing frequency. I remember the little bones. Our family were mid-way between kosher and not. We did not eat pork or shellfish, and my mother patronised the kosher butcher when in London.

My parents adopted a German refugee. She was a member of our family but may not have been officially adopted, as I never saw any paperwork. Her name was Cecily Orenstein. She lived with us until she married Eric Nabarro. He was part of the important firm of solicitors called Nabarro Nathanson. Her brother-in-law Felix lived in Amersham and was a part-time fireman. Cecily's sister was my governess. She was a clever woman. She left us when she was in her twenties, which was before our move to Amersham and became the first lady member of the New York Stock Exchange.

The family electric cable making business was manufacturing (in Leyton, London) certain strategic items for the war effort. As a protection against bombing, the Ministry of War requisitioned a Royal Bucks Laundry building to create a duplicate facility in High Wycombe.

One of my maiden great aunts, Sarah Davis, while remaining resident in Ealing, and at the age of 70, commuted daily to help manage the High Wycombe factory – as far as I know for the duration.

My father was a part-time fireman. He was exempt from military Service. He was a sub officer in an important fire station, Long Acre, Covent Garden. He was on duty when St Pauls was on fire. My dad lived in a top floor flat during the week, in Albany Street, by Great Portland Street Station. He came home weekends. He had a car fitted with a tow bar for an auxiliary water pump. He served for the greater duration of the war. He and a colleague were called to Holcroft, Cricklewood to make a magnetic mine safe. They had to blow it up. My dad was decorated with the British Empire Medal.

LITTLE KINGSHILL – NACHUM MARKS (WAS NORMAN MARKS)

My wife, Susan Lewin was born in Amersham whilst I lived in Little Kingshill but we didn't know each other until recent years. I was evacuated to Little Kingshill in October 1940, without my parents, on the night the bomb obliterated my home, and lived without them from that day until the end of the war in May 1945.

I was an only child. My father was a professional musician who played at music halls and my parents lived with my mother's family in Chevening Road in Kensal Rise.

I went alone, not with family, to Little Kingshill. I lived with foster parents, Mr and Mrs Brown, and their son Horace, in a house called 'Restcott'(?). My foster family were not Jewish. There was no religion in the house. They may have been atheists or agnostics with a mild recognition at Christmas. I arrived in Little Kingshill a fortnight before my fourth birthday in October 1940. We were bombed out in London. I don't remember that house but I do remember the shelter and I can smell the dampness of it still. We didn't have an air raid shelter in Little Kingshill. We had to hope and pray that nothing would happen. I still find the sound of the sirens a frightening sound.

I remember barrage balloons like great big fish in the sky held up with cables and gas to prevent German planes flying beneath, making it more difficult to hit their targets with accuracy. There were barrage balloons and searchlights everywhere. The home guard practiced about two hundred yards from the Little Kingshill house.

The front garden had flowers in it and was beautifully kept. We grew vegetables for Victory; peas, beans, potatoes, carrots and rhubarb. In autumn we acquired apples. To preserve them, through winter, each one was wrapped in newspaper and we only took out what we needed.

The house was not connected to the main sewer. There was a big cesspit in the front garden. The council would send someone out from Amersham to empty it.

We had no running hot water. It had to be boiled. In the bathroom we had what we called 'a copper' which we filled with water, and when the water came to the boil, we ladled it into the bath. Once a week we would have a bath.

To make the pillowcases whiter there was a blue dolly bag to put into the washing machine. My foster mother would have to wring the clothes through the mangle. She had to cook on a paraffin burning stove. It was only a two-burner and very hard work. She made lots of homemade jam – strawberry, raspberry and blackberry which we picked from the hedgerows.

I loved the family I lived with. They were a marvellous family. I went back there, after the war, three times a year, Easter, summer and Christmas until they died. My foster father was a gardener. He would take me to work and introduce me as 'his little evacuee'. He worked opposite Little Kingshill Common at Ashwell Court. It was a huge house and grounds belonging to the Bradford family. I would push the wheelbarrow and be pushed in it! I met the servants who lived in the servant's quarters there. The owners of the house had two cars. One was a Rolls Royce with the old 'RR' on the front of the bonnet in red. Later it was changed to black when one died. The number plate of the second car was GBH 11. My foster father cycled to work and I sat on the cross bar. It was hard on the bottom!

Our family doctor was Dr Wilson from Amersham. He drove a black and yellow car. We didn't go to a practice. If we were ill he came out to us. When I had mumps I had to spend a long time in bed.

We played outdoor games like football on the village common. There was a game called 'Tracking'. A group of children set off in one direction. They would leave clues for the others to follow such as chalk marks or a mark on a tree.

For a walk we would go to Little Missenden over a field, over a little minor road, to a stream in a field. The River Misbourne widened out. There were cows, and crab apples, and we'd mess about in the river. In winter we would go tobogganing with a toboggan the family made with wood from the local woods.

We went to the cinema in High Wycombe. I remember one film in particular about war in the Far East, men going through the jungle and being ambushed by the Japanese.

The name of my optician was Theador Hamdlin. The number 27 bus took us to High Wycombe though we did our shopping in Little Kingshill. In the village there were two pubs, The Prince of Wales and the Full Moon but I was too little to go in! There were two schools and two shops. One was the post office that sold general groceries, household stuff, food stamps and postal orders. I don't remember going into the other shop, or what it was.

It remains a mystery to me why some ration books were marked with a pencil and some with a pair of scissors. We never went hungry. We shot rabbits and pigeons. My foster father would hide in the hedges and wait for them to come. Our main meal was at lunchtime at 12.30 on weekdays and 1pm on weekends. Tea and biscuits was at 4pm and afternoon tea at 5pm. There was a cold supper before bed. Bedtime was still in daylight in summer. I shared a bedroom with their son Horace, but he played tricks and bullied me sometimes. He made model airplanes out of balsa wood but they were too complicated for me.

I started school aged five in 1941/2. I still have the reference written in Little Kingshill, on my departure in 1945, for Kilburn Council. It said something like I would have been the best pupil in the school if it weren't for a truly outstanding pupil who beat me. That outstanding pupil was Stefan Cang. He was a Jewish boy from London. Stephan Cang, and his Polish parents, lived in a lovely house in Little Kingshill. I went to see him after the war, in London. He went to Cambridge. His father wrote for the *Jewish Chronicle*.

The headteacher, Mrs Kempster, was a wonderful woman and I owe to her my love of the countryside. Every morning we would have to practice putting on our gas masks the right way. We had training in the times tables so that I became fluent. My two children are amazed at my ability to handle numbers. My son, Saul, is a genealogist who appears on the BBC programmes 'Heir Hunters'.

The school had two rooms and took children from aged five to scholarship age at eleven. There were three different age groups taught together so we had to get on. Unlike my foster home which had indoor plumbing, the school had outside, non-flushing, toilets. The school used

Lifebuoy Soap. There was running water but it was freezing cold. Each school room had a wood burning stove. Our teacher would announce, 'Playtime! Go and play.' She would then call us back in at the end of the break. I was impressed with the stories of Jesus. We did reading, writing and arithmetic. We wrote on slate with chalk and graduated to pens. We made the ink up from powder and had ink wells in our desks. We had to suck the new nibs before we could use them. We would plant beans in a glass jar and watch them grow and we also grew sunflowers. We had some lessons in the headteacher's garden. We would sit under the trees when it was sunny and warm. Mrs Kempster would take us on nature rambles and point out the plants and wildflowers in the hedgerows.

The doodlebugs were scary. The engine would cut out and they would just drop. One fell one to two miles away on a Sunday morning. What frightened me most were the V2 rockets, cigar-shaped things, which had a better guidance system.

Infrequently, I would see my parents on a Sunday. They would come from Baker Street and arrive at Great Missenden station at ten past eleven. They left on the same day at 4pm. The train was hauled by electric to Rickmansworth where it was changed to a steam locomotive.

The American troops came through the village with their tanks and armoured personnel, leaving caterpillar marks behind on the road. They threw tins of food at us and handed out gum. Their arrival brought the war nearer. The Americans set up a camp nearby and established an airstrip for light aircraft.

The day after the Germans surrendered I left Little Kingshill. My mother was keen to have me back. My parents were not observant. I didn't know I was Jewish until I was about nine years old when I went back home. It came as a shock!

Seer Green, Beaconsfield and Denise Levertov

Cautious for the well-being of their talented protégées, the Legat School evacuated to the countryside in 1939. Who would have thought it – a classic Russian ballet school, in the little village of Seer Green near Beaconsfield?

One pupil was Denise Levertov. By the age of sixteen, Denise was not quite a ballerina and not yet an established poet. Her father was a descendent of a great rabbinical family, from Hassidic Belarus. He converted to Christianity and became an Anglican priest. His beliefs were the fore-runner to Messianic Judaism.

Denise and her older sister, Olga, were raised with Celtic, Jewish and Christian influences, which all manifest in Levertov's poetry, as in 'Illustrious Ancestors' which includes a rabbi and a Christian Welshman.[85]

Professor Hollenberg in, *A Poet's Revolution: The Life of Denise Levertov* writes of Legat students night-walking in Seer Green:

In Denise's exuberance at its beauty, even the black-out seems like a lark. When she goes walking with friends in the evening, the moon shines so brightly that they don't need a torch.[86]

On the ever increasing dangers posed by the war, Hollenberg observed:

Denise focused on her studies, assuring her parents that she was as safe in Buckinghamshire as she would be anywhere. There was an air-raid shelter at the school, she wrote, urging them not to worry, as well as "a refuge room" that is "Sand-bagged, blanketed, and medicine-chested."[87]

Denise inadvertently became the principal dancer for the Dying Swan, after avoiding falling victim to an outbreak of mumps. The after-party was celebrated next door in the house of Margaret and Herbert Reed, the man who was to become influential to the poet. The normally weight-conscious dancers enjoyed the feast. Denise referred to the "most marvellous *creamy meringues.*" [88]

Denise Levertov's first published poem was written whilst evacuated to Buckinghamshire. In *Listening to Distant Guns,* she layered her thoughts of war and invasion onto the Seer Green countryside.[89]

Dana Greene the author of *Denise Levertov: A Poet's Life*[90], kindly gave permission to reproduce information from her book. Greene summarised the content of Denise's letters to her parents:

> ...regaling them with tales of the crowded dormitories with their curtained windows and the motley group of characters living at the school – dancers, refugees, Russian exiles, and misfits of various kinds – all under the watchful eye of Madame, the eccentric Russian teacher who ran the place.

She wrote of the weather; the places she visited during her free time; her lessons in French, German, and Russian; and the long hours of ballet practice. Apparently the air raids never bothered her. She worried about Olga and lamented that her sister never wrote. She insisted that she was not looking for a mate...[91]

Dana Greene continued:

> Denise's year at the ballet school was a strange experience, but it did provide the opportunity to be away from her parents.[92] She wandered freely and had time to read and write poetry. She had the good fortune to be able to visit the Herbert Read household, [Broom House] which was right next to the school and filled with paintings and books. Read, curator of the Victoria and Albert Museum was an art critic and poet. Their brief encounter would lead to greater engagement in years to come.[93]

Denise walked about four miles to Burnham Beeches after she was shouted at by her ballet teacher:

Curiously, it was not fear of the bombing or war or missing her family that Denise remembered from that year in Buckinghamshire. Rather it was the day she walked out of ballet class. In early spring of 1940, she spontaneously and resolutely gave up on ballet. She left the practice room, shed her ballet clothes, dressed, and knowing full well that there would be consequences for her actions, took to the road, singing and kicking up stones. She realized that even after five years of practice she did not want to be a ballerina. That was Olga's aspiration for her. She walked for miles, free and happy, returning to the dormitory after dark, aware that Madame would be furious. Although she remained at the school through the summer before returning to Ilford, the die had been cast.[94]

In her twenties Levertov moved to America and became recognised as a highly respected poet whose work was often concerned with political and environmental subjects. Dana Greene added, 'She had a very ambivalent attitude toward her Jewish heritage, although I think it definitely influenced her language and her social justice commitments.'

GISELA PRESSBURGER (NEE SPITZER)

(By daughter, Suzanne Freedman, and Gisela's grandson, Paul)

After Kristallnacht in Vienna when many synagogues were burned down, Jews no longer had any rights at all. In fact, the non-Jewish neighbours upstairs from my mother decided they wanted her family's flat, so just made them swap and go upstairs to their much inferior and smaller one. Once, my mother was even hauled into the police station for questioning. She then said to herself, "That's it. I have to get out of here". That was in November 1938. Her friend had put an advert in an English newspaper offering her services and received three replies. My mother replied to one of them, the famous children's author Enid Blyton. By March of the following year she left Vienna. She came over to England on a Domestic Service visa. You could only get the visa with a domestic service job to go to, but it was a proper organised scheme. The visa gave you permission to enter Britain for that purpose; at that time the Nazis were glad for Jews to leave. She remembers her father and little sister seeing her off (her mother felt too emotional to come to the station). Her little sister of 12 was crying as she left, not really knowing – or did she – that they would never see one another again?

My father Oscar followed a week later. The equivalent to the Domestic Service visa as a means of escape for young women was for young men (18-40) to come to the Kitchener Camp, near Sandwich. That option only happened for a few months, until war broke out. At that point almost all those at Kitchener were declared 'friendly aliens' and a large proportion, including my father, immediately joined the Pioneer Corps of the British Army, still based in Sandwich.

I hadn't quite realised that when they left Austria, they actually thought they would eventually be going back. However, when war then broke out, it meant that her two sisters left in Vienna, aged 12 and 16, were not able to come on the last Kindertransport. They, together with all the rest of her family, were deported and subsequently murdered in the concentration camps.

So my mother arrived in March 1939 at Liverpool Street with instructions on where to go, with little luggage and no English. (It was after hours and she thought the shop signs saying 'closed' meant there was a toilet – Water Closet!) She moved in at Green Hedges, Beaconsfield; Enid Blyton's home. She hated the countryside, the quiet, the spookiness, and the Alsatian dog. She hated calling Enid Blyton "Madam" – she had pride and didn't feel like being considered a servant (which of course she was). I believe her pay was 15 shillings a week with a half day off. In Vienna she had been a qualified bookkeeper. "Madam" was actually Mrs Pollock (Enid Blyton's married name) but she told them they were all supposed to address her as "Madam." Although, years later, she told us more about Enid Blyton because she was the famous one, she also spoke of Major Pollock though he probably wasn't around much. The class structure was very rigid. All the deliveries had to come to the back door and any visitors to the front. Her friend Mary, the parlour maid, had to open the front door with a silver platter and put the post on it. They all wore uniforms, very Upstairs Downstairs.

Enid Blyton actually employed three refugee girls from Vienna as cook (my mother), parlour maid and (probably) nanny, although none of them spoke much English at the time. As has been reported, Enid Blyton was not really interested in her children, and they came in at the end of the day to say 'good night'. She had just enough time for this, before returning to her little portable typewriter, which was balanced on her knees. She did not approve of my mother reading German books apparently from the local library and said scathingly that she should be reading English. I remember my mother recalling one day venturing into town and into Woolworths. She overheard a girl asking for Nivea face cream but pronounced in the German way (accent on the 'e') and she immediately recognised another refugee girl like herself. They became friends as a result.

My mother told us she could not actually cook and so at that time, *before* war broke out, she was able to correspond with her mother asking for recipes and cooking tips. Some of those recipes, including Liptauer cheese and a particular Viennese strudel have since been handed down to a second and third generation (who obviously never knew Vienna). Things like rabbit pie and a full English breakfast were definitely beyond her repertoire! For her own meals she was relegated to the kitchen quarters where there was a huge house dog, an Alsatian, drooling and hoping for some scraps. She was a city girl, not used to dogs, in fact terrified of them. She didn't like Alsatians because of a bad experience of them in Vienna. I always pictured Nazis with Alsatians when Austria was annexed, but I actually think it was that she had to walk past some very scary Alsatians that always barked at her from behind a fence on her way to school, when she was little, and it stemmed from that.

Enid Blyton was not a pleasant employer but I am not sure whether she was anti-Semitic as some have suggested. Why would she have had three Jewish girls in her employment? Certainly she was not happy that my mother wanted a couple of days leave to get married (Enid Blyton's opinion was that it was "irresponsible to get married during the war") and said she would dock the lost days off work from her salary! I think my mother proudly gave in her notice at that point. Once married, she would no longer have the restrictions of only working as a domestic. She joined Oscar (her Ossy as she called him) in Kent, where they married at the Ramsgate Synagogue and subsequently enjoyed over fifty years of marriage. When she eventually passed away aged 89, some 67 years after arriving in Beaconsfield, she had lived to see her small family grow to include a daughter, grandchildren and great-grandchildren, all of whom she adored. She never met her most recent grandson who is named after her husband Oscar.

THE WEDDING RING –
OSCAR PRESSBURGER[95]

…The Viennese girl who was to become my wife had landed on these shores, the only member of her family to escape the Nazi horror, one week before me, having obtained a permit which enabled her to work, but only as a domestic servant. She was employed by the well-known writer of children's books, Enid Blyton, who lived in Beaconsfield…

We soon decided to get married – I wanted so much to give my bride a gold wedding ring, but I simply hadn't enough money to buy one. I was so upset that I couldn't keep my disappointment to myself and confided in my army pals – all refugees like myself. They evidently held a summit conference and informed me they would give me a gold wedding ring as a wedding present. I was moved beyond words and not a little embarrassed – they told me to ask my fiancée to send a pattern, the size of her finger, and leave the rest to them.

Amongst the men was a goldsmith by trade and he would make the ring, assuming of course he could be provided with sufficient gold. Little scraps came to him, bit by bit, a few links from someone's precious watch-chain, a piece from a ring that was not found when the Nazis searched each man on leaving Austria, one man donated the end of a tie pin that belonged to his father, and so on. Even a couple of gold teeth were handed in – in those days one could always depend on a Continental having a gold tooth in his head. The goldsmith melted the gold – there was enough for two wedding rings! This was even more wonderful as it was customary on the continent of Europe for the bridegroom to wear a wedding ring too.

Our names were engraved on the insides of the rings and the date of our forthcoming marriage. So my bride had a gold ring after all… I will never forget those men whose kindness remains with us – a memory forged in an endless band of gold.

THE CHALFONTS –
UPSTAIRS, DOWNSTAIRS –
HENRY WERTH[96]

I had two aunts who came to this country in 1938 to work as domestics. Both were appalled by the treatment meted out to household staff and each, in their own way, decided to rewrite the rule books and make their employers feel pretentious and decadent in the most charming manner. Upper middle-class wives were easy to manipulate: they felt insular compared to my aunts, who were used to moving in Viennese high society and frequently travelled abroad.

My father's sister was married to a lawyer and was entitled, in accordance with Austria's unwritten law, to call herself 'Frau Doktor'. She expected instant service – and got it. She was an excellent cook and anyone invited to her magnificent flat considered themselves very fortunate. She had two daughters who went to Vienna's finest lyceum. Alas, the Anschluss forced changes in her household.

Through her ongoing connections she was appointed a cook in one of Britain's finest ladies' boarding schools. She made it a condition of her employment that her daughters received a free education in the establishment. On her arrival, she immediately announced to management and staff that she was 'Frau Doktor' and wished to be addressed by her full title. The school considered itself honoured by her presence and was sad to lose her at the end of the war when she returned to Vienna.

My mother's youngest sister was an astute businesswoman; men were visually stimulated by her and easily manipulated. She held soirées in her flat in the Innere Stadt and politicians and businesspeople vied for an invitation. She received an early warning from friends that Austria's days were numbered and was advised to cut and run. But she was a patriotic citizen and her husband was an officer in the reserve. However, the

Anschluss changed everything and a few weeks later she obtained a visa and found a position in an upper-class English household as a cook. I don't think she had any idea what the job entailed and she certainly couldn't cook. Her husband, a spit image of the Hungarian-Jewish comedy actor 'Cuddles', Szöke Szakáll, was installed as the butler.

In late 1938 I was invited to spend Christmas with her family and new friends. She forgot to state her address on the invitation but, checking the cancellation on the envelope, I discovered it was posted in Gerrards Cross. She included a postal order to cover my Green Line Coach fare, adding that I could spend the night with friends in Chalfont St Peter – or Chalfont St Giles! – who'd be waiting for me at the bus stop.

That December England was covered in snow and travelling was hazardous. The coach stopped in Finchley Road and that's where the fun began. The conductor asked for my destination and I said Chalfont St Peter – or, maybe, Chalfont St Giles. I explained in my best Viennese dialect that my invitation didn't say which. I produced my letter and he was mystified by the mishmash of English and German. He called for assistance from other passengers and the letter was passed from hand to hand. I was looked upon as an alien object, my elegant Austrian ensemble causing much mirth. The letter was passed on to the driver, who looked as bewildered as the passengers. Eventually we stopped at the first Chalfont, but no one seemed to be waiting for me. When we got to the next stop, with no one in sight, I bravely got off the coach – profusely thanking everybody for their assistance.

I trudged around the village, glancing through windows into rooms decorated with mistletoe and cards hanging from the ceiling – so different from a Viennese Christmas Eve. I was cold, hungry and lost. Before long, I spotted my old friend the bus driver on his return to London. The conductor beckoned me to get on and they dropped me off at the local bobby's house-cum-police station. I questioned the constable whether there were any foreigners in the area, but he couldn't say and suggested I return to London. He telephoned his superior and arranged transport for me, and in no time I was back in Lancaster Grove. Welcoming me were more police – my aunt had reported me missing. I was whisked back to Gerrards Cross. When we got there, the ever-resourceful constable popped in at the local nick and established there was only one foreign couple in the village – it had to be my aunt and uncle. They delivered me at the house safely.

My aunt, whom I hadn't seen for months, welcomed me with the inspiring words 'I'm glad you've finally arrived but I have a problem. I'm making a strudel and I need 1 kg of Topfen. Be a good boy and run down the road and speak to Herr Sainsbury. He has a grocer's shop in the village.' I found the shop but couldn't find the mysterious Herr Sainsbury. The staff searched the shop for Topfen. Everybody was consulted, customers included. The net was widened and neighbouring shopkeepers were questioned. But what on earth was Topfen? Fruit, vegetable, washing-up powder? Or more foreign muck!

I insisted that my aunt had said 'Everybody knows Topfen', but it was no use. It was a rare comedy: a foreigner dressed in funny clothes, speaking a guttural language, and demanding something no respectable English shop would sell! It confirmed the English attitude that all foreigners were mad.

Crestfallen, I returned to my aunt, only to be chided 'You are totally useless!' I'd got back just in time for tea and joined family and friends in the lounge. Everyone was given a saucer and a cup of hot water, but there was no teapot. Tea without a pot – whatever next?

The lady of the house announced pompously that since the Viennese cook – 'a much-travelled, health-conscious woman' – had arrived, the family had been made aware that tea brewed in a teapot was unhealthy, insular and … unfashionable! We were seated balancing our cups of boiling water on our laps as my aunt went from one to another dipping a Continental 'tea egg' on a chain in the water and mumbling 'Very good for you!'

My uncle the butler, who could just about tell the difference between red and white wine, served refreshments. He wouldn't disclose the contents of the glasses – it was a traditional healthy Austrian drink. I noticed he abstained from tasting the liquid he served. He was a model of patience, forbearance and loyalty, but occasionally he bravely refreshed himself with a glass of French brandy which he kept for medicinal purposes!

Christmas Day was the big day in the house. An enormous turkey was prepared, mounted on a large serving plate, and wheeled into the dining room by the butler. The assembled guests eyed the bird hungrily.

The cook was congratulated on presentation. The master of the house sharpened his carving knives ever so professionally and carved up the bird to great applause. He forced his fork into the wobbly carcass and began slicing but, to everybody's horror, the bird disintegrated. Tears rolled down the hostess's face. Silence prevailed during the entire meal. My aunt, unaware she had spiked an old tradition, cheerily informed everybody who cared to listen that in a civilised society people shouldn't be expected to chew meat from a bone in the company of others. Instead of bemoaning her ill-fortune, the lady of the house heartily agreed with my aunt that meat and poultry should always be carved in the kitchen and that the old tradition would be laid to rest. This incident became the talking point in the upper echelon of local society and crossed the Atlantic, there to be immortalised in the Hollywood production of Mrs Miniver.

Aunt and uncle left service during the war and set up home in the area. They were universally liked and obsessively dedicated to taking the stuffiness out of the old English society. Near the end of the war they bought a small house in Berkshire. After the war they were invited by Viennese friends to return home but informed their friends that if they wished to see them they would be welcome in England at any time. They would never ever cross the Austrian border again. Their friends regularly came to England to visit them. My aunt and uncle loved the English and the local countryside passionately. Both are buried in Berkshire. In their own way they punctured away the pretensions of middle-class England – a breath of fresh air in a stuffy society.

HENRY AMAR

My family moved to Amersham the day war broke out. We also lived in Great Missenden and Little Chalfont at 'The Rafters', Cherries Avenue. There were my parents, Raoul and Essie, grandparents Sam and Jeanne Franses, my sister Maureen (born March 1944) and myself. My other sister, Jane, was born November 1945.

I remember the Levy family, who lived, during the war, in Chenies Avenue and Burtons Lane, Little Chalfont. Violet Levy went on to live in London. Her husband was Lewis, who was a firefighter during the war. Her children, my friends, are Brian, Rosemary and Sheila. When we moved to Little Chalfont the village was tiny, inhabited by approximately three hundred people and served by about half a dozen shops. My home was situated on an unmade road. In order to get to the railway station I had to walk through fields.

I can still visualise the gliders flying over Chalfont on their way to Arnheim, and the flying bombs. The latter were in fact guided missiles, and most frightening. The noise of the planes would cut out mid-air, and everyone knew that the bombs would come down. This would be followed by a terrifying explosion. One such flying bomb, a V1 rocket, went over our house, and the bombs fell on Chesham Bois, just two miles from where we lived. My uncle, home on leave, shouted at me to get indoors. My father built a brick shelter in the garden and I remember them all laughing at my Granddad running to the shelter with a metal pudding bowl on his head

My father, Raoul, served in the ARP as an air raid warden throughout the war. He did night-watching with Mr Jack Maymon. They sat in the entrance to the bungalow, next to Statters Switchgear, which made parts for the RAF. It was in Little Chalfont but has been demolished. Amersham International stood in its place. [Now GE Healthcare] A German aeroplane dropped silver paper, all over the area, probably to target Statters. Teachers sent out children to collect the paper. My own contribution to the War

Effort was also some very poor knitting for the Navy and pity the poor sailor who got my effort.

The bungalow was owned by Mr Hines, the Managing Director and Chief Engineer of Statters. Raoul was awarded a Long Service Medal for his work. After the war he was involved with Civil Defence for many years. [Raoul established RH Amar distributors and importers of fine foods in 1945. It continues as a thriving family business, with warehouses in High Wycombe]

Other families were the Lelyvelds, Conquys and the Maizel family who lived in Copperkins Lane. Nathan and Nadia Maizel had four children. One son is married to my cousin. My grandparents, Sam and Jane Franses, also lived in Little Chalfont. Miss Moos used to come to Amersham after the war and gave Hebrew lessons to me and Anthony Duparc. Anthony's father was the secretary of the Liberal Jewish Synagogue in St John's Wood, London.

ESSIE AMAR

(Henry's mother)

I was always involved in fundraising, and my work was well recognised. I was even invited to a Garden Party at Buckingham Palace for my work.

[Essie raised money for charity including for the National Savings Committee. £425 was made at a flag day for the United Aid to China. £76 was raised with Mrs Hine, for Warship Week in 1942.]

Ruth Lelyveld

Free to walk the country lane
Miles from nowhere, I'll not complain
Sad and alone, but memories remain
My thoughts return when first I came.

Twas September the first '39 I remember
When the course of our lives was changed forever.
The war was upon us and survive we must
Accepting the hardships, for the struggle was just.

Looking back, I often think
The choice we had to swim or sink
Remained for each of us to decide
Do all we can, and hope to survive.

I have lived at the same address in Chalfont St Giles for well over fifty years. I arrived in the district together with my husband Eddie, our young son Anthony, my parents Kitty and William Gold and brother Gerald. This was on 1st September 1939, the Friday preceding the day war broke out. Eddie was drafted into the army.

I remember the rabbi in the green jacket!

In the year 1940, on one of my walks, I met a man working in the field. I said to him, 'You are foreign, aren't you, and Jewish?' I have never forgotten the terrible fear written on his face. I quickly told him that I am also Jewish. After that, he often came to my home for coffee. His name is Ernie Halberstadt. He met his wife Frieda in Amersham, also a German Jewish refugee. They had a daughter Judith and a son, Melvyn.

There was a hut in Woodside Road, which was used as a shul, and demolished after the war. There was a bungalow attached to the hut. A refugee from Germany, who was shammas for the shul, lived there. He had been on his way to Israel, but was delayed by the war. He married in 1941. His wife was also from Germany.

Ernie Halberstadt had asked the shul if he could be shammas and live in the bungalow next door to the synagogue. He got the job!

During the war, my mother, Kitty, had a stroke. She was looked after by Sister Katie Krone at Amersham Hospital.

My son, Anthony, was taught his Torah portion in Amersham by Rev. S. Bloch, and his barmitzvah was held in London.

In 1939 Anthony could not be found a place in Chenies School because of overcrowding by wartime evacuees. He was, therefore, sent to Belle Vue School for girls, which was situated, in a large house, in Burtons Lane. The school itself was evacuated from Brondesbury in London.

Mr Golodetz was Jewish. [He owned the house, *Burtons Hollow*, and Burtons Wood. He had a patent to do with cattle feed and lived, from before the war, in Little Chalfont].

I remember a plane coming down in a field and a buzz bomb that came down in Amersham, smashing all the windows. I had been out walking during the daytime and heard the terrible noise. On another occasion, I was sitting down with my family to a meal, when we heard a terrific bang. A bomb had come down in the field opposite.

Here is another poem I wrote, this time about one of our local fields:

Walking through the field of snow
I chanced to glance at the sunset glow.
The sky was clear, a delight to behold
The sun in its glory, like a crock of gold.
At that moment, I paused to stare
Admiring nature, with time to spare
If only I could paint that scene
Of beauty, joy, and heavenly serene
Such pleasure I'd give to the busy few
Who find no time to stand and view.

B. S. Henes

I was born 6th August 1939.

When we were evacuated we lived with my aunty and her family – Rose and Harry Gold, with their two children, Ronald and Hilary. Hilary, who became Hilary Rueben, moved to Nairobi, Kenya. During wartime they lived in Chesham Bois, just off the Chesham Road, quite near a Catholic school, run by nuns. Harry Gold dealt with caravans and a site somewhere in Amersham.

At some point in time we must have left the Golds and moved to Chestnut Close in Amersham new town. The family consisted of my parents, Saul and Gertie Henes, my sister, Sonya, and me. My sister became Sonya Cole and lived almost all her life in Amersham, first in Chestnut Close, and then in Grimsdell's Lane.

I do not have any memories of shortages in any period of my life in England, from 1939 until 1957 when I came to Israel. I am aware there was a black market, from people called, 'The Boys'. Local farmers supplied us with eggs. There was no local kosher butcher, so meat and poultry was bought in from London.

Most of my memories are based around the shul a horrible pre-fabricated building, consisting of an entrance room, with cloakroom and toilet facilities, followed by the main hall and ending with a room for the cheder. During the good years the succah [temporary hut decorated with harvest fruits to celebrate Sukkot, a harvest festival] used to be built at the end of the building. In front of the shul was a large area of 'garden' (real overgrown weeds). On one side of the building was a primary school and on the other a Jewish family lived who looked after the building. They had a son my own age whose name may have been Melvin? [Melvyn Halberstadt]

The main hall consisted of a number of rows of chairs for the women, a small gap and a few rows of benches for the men. Each bench had room for perhaps five to six men. The front of the main room had a one-step high stage with an Ark right at the front, with a bench at each side, and a table in front of it.

There might have been a minister during the war. After the war no such creature existed, all the services were conducted by the congregants themselves. My father used to daven with other men. The 'laynim' [prayers led by lay readers] was performed by a Chesham father and two sons, who were the 'foremost' people in the congregation. A Mr Tabor was also involved in conducting the services. He lived in a large, futuristic white house on the hill between the New and Old Town. [High and Over]

If my calculations are right there could never have been more than forty to fifty men in shul at any one time. By the time of my Bar-mitzvah in 1952, it was almost impossible to get a minyan and I had to go to Harrow to study with the Rabbi there.

Of the congregants there was not a shortage of Cohens and Levis, but the actual names I don't remember. One name I do remember was Angyalfi – a diamond merchant, with a son called Michael and a daughter. They lived in the centre of Amersham.

Ann Lowry (nee Mays)

I can remember doodlebugs coming down on my way to cheder. On my arrival I announced what had happened and that thank goodness there had been no injuries. Rev. Bloch replied, 'Thank you for panicking us all!'

Egon Brandt (became Ernest Brent)

I was in British Army Intelligence based in Latimer. My wife lived in Amersham. This was from the end of 1942 – May 1945. Our daughter was born near Amersham in December 1944, at Berkhamsted Hospital. My wife had to be admitted to the hospital early because of all the snow and ice and fear that the ambulance wouldn't get there on time.

My wife and I fondly remember the theatre in Amersham, which we loved. This was based where the auctioneers are today. The theatre was in fact a converted little shop. I also remember the Odeon Cinema at Amersham-on-the-Hill.

Every Saturday evening, dances were held at the Millstream Restaurant, which became a dress shop. Many Jewish people, who were in Intelligence, attended these dances.

The hut in Woodside Road, where services were held, was always full during Rosh Hashanah and Yom Kippur. It was attended by many soldiers and their wives. There were indeed many Jewish people serving in Intelligence. There were fifteen to twenty Jewish people in my department alone.

WILTON PARK: A VERY SPECIAL PoW CAMP

(Permission from Howard Spier of AJR, and the author, Fritz Lustig)[97]

Before May 1945, it was a very special prisoner-of-war camp, where prisoners from whom it was hoped to obtain important information were sent. Wilton Park was one of three camps forming the intelligence unit CSDIC (UK) – Combined Services Detailed Interrogation Centre – as not only army, but also navy and RAF intelligence personnel were serving there.

The other two camps were at Trent Park near Cockfosters in north London, which housed German generals and other senior officers (...the subject of a Radio 4 Afternoon Play, which was written by the son of an ex-refugee who served there), and at Latimer House in Buckinghamshire, where lower-ranking officers and other ranks were held, which was also the case at Wilton Park. At the latter camp, there was a Palladian mansion called 'The White House', originally built in 1779, in which a few Italian generals were housed and which also served as the mess of the British intelligence officers. It was demolished in 1968 (the prisoners' cells had disappeared a few years earlier) and now there are no buildings of the old camp left – instead, a 15-storey-high structure has been erected, which is claimed to be the highest building in Buckinghamshire. The camp is now the Defence School of Languages.

CSDIC was a highly secret unit; anybody working there had to sign the Official Secrets Act. I had been serving in the Pioneer Corps since September 1940 and, like most of my contemporaries, was very keen to be transferred to a more active unit. In early 1943 CSDIC was expanding and, although until then only commissioned officers had been working there, the War Office had decided to allow sergeants and warrant officers to do the same job. At that stage, recruitment was by recommendation from people already working at CSDIC and, through a relative who was friendly with an officer serving there, I was recommended for transfer. After waiting about two months and having passed a day-long interview in London, I found myself at Latimer House, where I was at once promoted from private to sergeant. After further promotion to WOII (company sergeant major) a few months later I was transferred to Wilton Park.

What were we all doing? Listening to the conversations of the prisoners! The POWs' cells were 'bugged' – a microphone was concealed in the light fitting – and we listened to their conversations, in the hope that they would discuss something that might be of interest to British intelligence. There were only two prisoners to a cell, as far as possible from different services or units, which made it likely that they would talk to each other about their experiences. We had to identify who was who by their voices and accents.

The monitors operated in teams of about six, each in a separate room with an officer in charge. Sitting at tables which were fitted with record-cutting equipment (this was before electronic tapes were invented!), we had a kind of old-fashioned telephone switchboard facing us, where we put plugs into numbered sockets in order to listen to the PoWs through our headphones. Each operator had to monitor two or three cells, switching from one to the other to see whether something 'interesting' was being discussed. As soon as the conversation touched on a subject we thought might be 'valuable', we pushed a switch which started a turntable revolving, and pulled a small lever to lower the recording head onto the record. We had to keep a log in which we noted what our 'charges' had been doing or talking about, and specified at what times and about what subjects we had recorded their conversations.

As soon as a record had been cut, another operator had to take over the monitoring, and the person who had been listening went to a different room to transcribe what he had just recorded – not every word that was spoken, of course, but only those bits of the conversation which were important. After that, the officer in charge of the team (or later a sergeant major) had to check the transcription: correct errors (i.e. mis-hearings), fill in gaps if possible (often prisoners were 'security-conscious' and – suspecting a hidden microphone – started to whisper when talking about something important), and do some judicious editing, i.e. cutting out superfluous material.

There were a number of SPs ('stool pigeons'), i.e. prisoners who from political conviction or possibly practical considerations had decided to work for us. They were briefed on the subjects about whom their cell-mate would be knowledgeable so that they could steer the conversation around to them. Of course, they did not know about the hidden microphones and were left in the belief that whatever information they managed to extract they would have to report to their 'handler'. One SP, however, was an ex-refugee officer, and we were full of admiration for him, for what he was doing clearly required exceptional nerve, courage and presence of mind, let alone acting ability. As far as I know, he never gave himself away or aroused the suspicion of any of his cell-mates. He posed as a (German) officer and was always paired with some particularly valuable officer-prisoner.

All PoWs were, of course, interrogated several times (always by officers not working in our 'monitoring' section called 'M-Room' – we operators never dealt with any of them face-to-face), and their reaction to the interrogation was often particularly 'fruitful'. They would tell their cell-mate what they had been asked about, what they had managed to conceal from the interrogating officer, how much we (the British) already knew, etc.

We recorded not only military intelligence, but also any atrocities the prisoners might have witnessed or taken part in (and those records were kept in an archive, whereas others were scrapped after use); also stories about the German home front, when prisoners related what they had heard or experienced while on leave. Such material was useful for 'psychological warfare' purposes: there were several Allied radio stations purporting to be illegal German ones which broadcast stories calculated to undermine the morale of soldiers.

Until D-Day (6 June 1944) most of our prisoners were either shot-down Luftwaffe pilots or members of U-boat crews who had been rescued after their U-boat was sunk. After the Allied invasion of the Continent, a steady stream of army prisoners arrived, and we got busy listening to them. The material we obtained was, of course, very different from what we had recorded until then, and we felt that what we were doing had suddenly assumed a far greater importance than before. The success of the invasion depended to a great extent on good intelligence, and the existence of the decoding centre at Bletchley Park and its successes was then completely unknown, even in intelligence circles.

Fritz Lustig – Secret Listener

When I arrived at Chalfont & Latimer rail station I wasn't scared, I was looking forward to joining Intelligence. I had been waiting three years to join, and it was a joy and relief. When on the Isle of Man they were terrified of a German invasion, because all the Nazis had to do was just replace the Tommies with the SS, so it would have gone from Internment Camp to Concentration Camp. They asked people in the camp to volunteer to go to Canada or Australia. I did volunteer, as I was afraid of a German invasion, but around that time a U – Boat to Canada sank, and so they stopped shipping people out, and in retrospect, I'm glad that I didn't go. By 1943 there was no longer a risk of German invasion, so I wasn't scared anymore.

There were no Nazis in the Internment Camp where I was – the great majority were refugees from Germany and Austria. There were two German men who had been living in the UK for many years but had never got round to applying for naturalisation (or perhaps wanted to retain their German nationality). They were not Jewish and always stuck together and did not mix with us, but as far as we could tell, they were not Nazis.

The only unit that as a German Jewish Refugee I was allowed to join was the Auxiliary and Pioneer Corps. I am a musician, and was able to join the orchestra as a cellist at the training centre. I was not effective at fighting the Germans by playing the cello! It was my joy and relief to be accepted into Intelligence as a Listener.

I arrived as the lowest rank of Private, and was immediately promoted by two ranks, and this was gratifying. I was promoted to Sergeant Major.

I was stationed at Latimer House and Wilton Park, but I spent my days off in London as there was more to do there than in Latimer! I have been back since. The billets have gone, and the house is now a hotel. I lived in the stable block, which I think I recognise as still being there. I never entered the manor house, as this was the Officers Mess, and the rest of us were not allowed into the building. There were a hundred people there, and I knew a few, a small number. We were divided into three squads of ten or so. The others I knew by sight. I recognise the name Egon Brent, but I didn't know him. I was not a religious Jew, so I didn't know about any synagogue in Amersham or Beaconsfield.

I was a Secret Listener after the war in Germany, near Hanover. I did not do interrogating, that was done by the officers. We wouldn't have been able to carry on our secret listening if those Nazis had been tried for war crimes, as it would have become publicly disclosed. There were no air raids over Latimer House.

The Chilterns is a very pretty area. Wilton Park was surrounded by rhododendrons. When they were in blossom I would pick some and take them to my friends.

I was promoted – the lowest rank in our unit was Sergeant, and I was first promoted to CSM (Company Sergeant Major) or WO II (Warrant Officer Class 2) in November 1943, and then further, to RSM (Regimental Sergeant Major) or WO I (Warrant Officer Class 1), which is the most senior non-commissioned rank, in July 1944. Before we, ex-"enemy aliens", were recruited (i.e. in late 1942, 1943 and later), the listening was done only by officers, who had to be British.

We were housed in so-called Nissen Huts, which consisted of corrugated metal. As far as I remember we were about 6-8 people in one hut. The girls, of course, had separate huts, which presumably were in a different area of the Camp, but I'm afraid I cannot remember where either the men's or the women's huts were situated in relation to Latimer House. We were quite comfortable in the Nissen Huts.

We had no contact with civilians in either Latimer or Wilton Park. I can't really say anything about my colleagues who had family members left behind in Germany or Austria – I cannot recall that we discussed such matters. All my family (3 siblings and our parents) did get out in time, to Great Britain, USA, and Portugal.

I don't think there were any Jewish religious services at either Camp, but as I am not religious, I would not have been interested. But I think I would have been aware had there been any.

We ate in a wooden hut, the "I-Sergeants Mess", which was strictly separate from the Sergeants Mess of the soldiers who were running the

Figure 6: Fritz Lustig 1945/46.

Camp and were in charge of the POWs. We were served by ATS-girls, who also did the cooking. The food was quite good, by army standards. No kosher food was provided.

Our uniform was standard army issue: battle blouse, trousers, and beret. As an RSM I was entitled to have a bought beret (at the time, much smarter than the army issue), and an officer-style raincoat (the latter caused some soldiers in London to salute me, but I could not return the salute, as I was not an officer – which was quite embarrassing). We had the normal rank insignia on our uniforms, and the Intelligence Corps badge on the headgear.

On 4 July 1943 I was transferred from Latimer House to Wilton Park, and back again in November 1944.

In Wilton Park there was a small band, which I was persuaded to join. That was only for one concert. The other players were not very good, and I gave a detailed description of that concert in a letter to my parents in November 1943:

I had allowed myself to be persuaded to play in the "Band" as well as doing my solos (the Saint-Saens "Swan" and the Bach Gounod ("Ave Maria"). The band consists of two trumpets, which (when they are lucky) play correctly and in tune, one clarinet, guitar or banjo, piano, double bass, percussion and one violin, which later in reality only sits there to be seen. The concert consisted of 80% popular hits, which are shrieked for a microphone by girls who imagine they can sing, one or two "comedy turns", a few numbers played by the band only (one a waltz-medley, one something "jazzy"), and a clarinet solo of a similar standard. Although my girl-accompanist (who was one of the Camp switchboard-operators with whom I often went for walks or bicycle-rides) got a bit mixed-up with her part, (which is really not that difficult to play), the audience seemed to like my solos. Unfortunately she took the "Swan" much too slowly, so that I had to change bows much more frequently than planned in order not to "run out of breath", and when we played the "Ave Maria", she temporarily lost me in the middle, where the modulation gets a little more complicated. I continued playing as unconcerned as I could, and after a little while we celebrated a happy reunion. Anyway, I was better off than the clarinettist (a terribly funny oldish little man), whose accompanist got mixed up with the repetitions, and therefore did not even manage to finish at the same time as his soloist. But I really received hearty applause (by the way, I was the only performer with enough stage experience to acknowledge it!), and the Commanding Officer specially approached me at the end in order to thank me. Even as a little boy he had been singing the "Ave Maria" with great passion, etc. Next week we are to repeat the whole affair in the other camp.

I also played one or two solo pieces. But here I must repeat what my late wife claimed was the beginning of our "romance" – we met at Wilton Park in 1944 and married in June 1945. I met my wife Susan at a dance there. We married in London, because I had a sister living in Hampstead, and my wife had a cousin living there too.

I had to accompany an ATS-girl who thought she could sing, which was not the case. She sang "I'll walk beside you", and apparently I looked very miserable while accompanying her on the cello, so that Susan said to her fellow-ATS "that chap looks so unhappy – let's take him out for a drink

Figure 7: Susan probably in 1943, as she is still a Sergeant (she was promoted later).

afterwards". That's what happened. The other girl had a boyfriend with whom she soon disappeared, leaving Susan and I by ourselves and that was, she claimed, how it all started. I cannot remember any of this, but it is quite possible…

Normally cello-playing gives me great pleasure, but certainly not on that occasion!

There were no rules about "relationships", which naturally were formed very frequently. Apart from ours, which resulted in marriage, there were several others which had the same outcome. However, there was a stupid army rule: married couples were not allowed to serve in the same Camp. By the time we married I had been posted back to Latimer, so no action was necessary.

While we were "courting" at Wilton Park, we often went on bicycle rides into the surrounding countryside, and Susan later claimed that frequently I made her lift her bicycle over barbed wire fences, which she found difficult, but I suspect she exaggerated…

We became engaged on our second holiday together, at Carbis Bay near St. Ives in Cornwall. That we were "boyfriend and girlfriend" was pretty obvious to anybody who was around… "First kisses in Buckinghamshire" – yes, definitely.

On days off we had to walk to Chalfont and Latimer Station, unless there was just some military vehicle leaving on which we could hitch a lift.

The only event that sticks in my mind, from listening, was the sinking of the German battleship Scharnhorst off Norway in December 1943. It was a huge ship, crew of (I think) about 2000 sailors, of whom only about 40 were rescued. We listened to those, and of course whatever they said about life on the ship or its sinking was of great interest to the Admiralty.

I met Colonel Kendrick on only two occasions: when I arrived at the place in May 1943, he gave me an initial interview, at the end of which I had to sign the Official Secrets Act. He explained to me what my duties were going to be – I had no idea before I saw him. He also remarked that what I would be doing was more important for the war effort than driving a tank or firing a machine gun, which I was very glad to hear. The second time was when I had to ask him for permission to marry Susan, which apparently I had to do as we were both serving on the same unit.

We had several dances in the I-Sergeants Messes in both Camps, and also Christmas parties. I described the latter in 1943, when I was the senior rank at Wilton Park (i.e. "PSM", which stands for "President Sergeants Mess") in some detail in a letter to my parents. There were, of course, drinks and nibbles on such occasions.

At Christmas several parties were held in the two camps. In my camp I had been very active in Christmas preparations. I had managed to find some coloured paper strips in London (any paper products were in extremely short supply) which I proceeded to stick together in the form of paper chains. I reported to the parents that I had spent one afternoon and evening doing just that! The chains were then strung up across the room in all directions. I had also bought a small Christmas tree which I decorated with a few paper chains and some cotton wool balls. Holly branches were nailed to the walls and fastened to the tablecloth with pins. We also got a dozen candles which we stuck into potatoes cut in half – the flat side down, with a hole for the candle cut into the upper side, and the whole covered in coloured paper.

It was an army custom that the officers visited the Sergeants Mess on Christmas morning in order to wish its occupants the "compliments of the season", and vice versa. They did not all call at the same time, but singly or in small groups, and as I was officially the host it was my duty to offer them drinks, and of course drink with them. So by the end of the morning I must have been just a little bit tipsy…

The Christmas dinners were very good, and I had enjoyed the various festivities. One party in our Mess had finished at 5.a.m., and as we felt it prudent to clear up the resulting chaos ourselves it was 6.a.m. before we were able to retire, which did not leave much time for sleep, with duty starting at 9.a.m! I wrote in the first post-Christmas-letter, January 1944, to the parents that this had been my best Christmas since joining the army, if not since leaving home.

CHESHAM BOIS PAVILION

In wartime Chesham the cricket pavilion became an orthodox synagogue. It was not the only clubhouse to be adapted into something new and unexpected. A somewhat strenuous uphill walk leads into Chesham Bois. On Weedon Lane there is an ordinary appearing rugby pavilion, Chiltern Rugby Club. Who would have thought that it provided a Catholic/Jewish family with a place of safety from the Luftwaffe? Hartwig Meyerhof and his wife, Yvonne Muriel, rented the pavilion and made it into a charming space. The rugby pavilion became the first home for their Shardeloes born baby, Carolyn.

The Meyerhof Family – Carolyn Williams (nee Meyerhof)

My father died young. He had only really spoken about his childhood in Kassel, Germany. In the Wilhelmsoehe, my father was taken in his pram, and his mother met the Kaiser!

My father, Hartwig, worked for my grandfather who had a pharmaceutical instrument factory, and it was in this capacity that he came to England in the early 1930s. Later he brought other relations over to England. He and they were forced to sell their art collections, presumably in order to live, though we still had some wonderful items in my childhood home.

During the war he lived in digs, in Belsize Avenue, where he met and eventually married my mother, Yvonne. They married in Amersham. She was Roman Catholic, half French, a quarter Scots, a quarter Italo-Spanish! Being Catholic, she had to bring her children up in that faith, and I believe my father was okay with that.

They were evacuated from Hampstead, and went to live in the pavilion in Chesham Bois! My parents first had me in 1945, my sister, Rosemary Anne in 1948, at Tenterden, Bois Lane. They had a house built in Stubbs Wood. My father worked as sales manager, first for local firms, then in the City. As such, he travelled around the world. The only bomb my mother mentioned was a V2 that fell locally when my father was coming home from work.

Our home was very "continental", full of books, paintings, music. We travelled around Europe at holiday times, went to the theatre, ballet, opera, art galleries etc. We would visit my father's cousin – he had changed his name from Kurt Wertheim to Ken Wilson, as he had joined the army and been present at one of the German surrender points. We regularly went to see Kurt's elderly mother and aunt who would fill us with strange cakes and talk excitedly and simultaneously in German!

We were very close to friends of my father who lived in Hampstead. He was a very promising writer in Germany, and I remember seeing a book of his with a glowing review by Thomas Mann. They were then called Illa and Fritz Walter, and Illa came from Kassel. In the 50s, Fritz was the cultural correspondent in London of Radio Baden Baden.

Apart from that, our lives were not particularly different from anyone else's. My mother would try to mark the Jewish festivals, but I don't remember my father going to the synagogue. We lived with our German name, Meyerhof, and never once did anyone ever make any remark about it, never was there the slightest hint of racism. I felt different, but it did not bother me. My father would shop for delicatessen at Schmidt's in Charlotte Street, and I thought everyone ate rollmops, liver sausage, sauerkraut, etc!

Strangely, one of my grandsons looks very Jewish, with black curly hair! I never thought my father did, though both my sister and I apparently do. He spoke seven languages, but only sounded "foreign" on the phone!

I was not born in the Pavilion, but at Shardeloes, which was a nursing home during the war.

Figure 8: Inside the pavilion. Artwork by Yvonne Meyerhof.

Figure 9: Hartwig Meyerhof at the cricket pavilion in Weedon Lane, Chesham Bois, 1944.

Notes from the Diary of Yvonne Meyerhof

Including comments by her husband, Hartwig, 1944-1946: [ ] = notes, by their daughter, Carolyn.

20th September 1944. Rosh Hashanah. We lunched at the small British Restaurant in Chesham and then went up to the blind man's workshop (near the station). Do you remember that scene, my beloved? [This diary was being written for Hartwig, as a future surprise.] We felt like players in the "Dreigroschen Oper". The blind man sitting on the left, the bench in front with the girl and her Scottie dog, the comic opera policeman, and the little comedian, Goss, who owns the café…

28th September 1944. Yesterday was Yom Kippur…sunny but cold…

2nd October 1944…went to Wells to fetch paper and some of the sweet ration…Returned home to find milkman had left three eggs (!) which we promptly ate for lunch, the third being carefully divided, I beginning it and Hartwig finishing it…

Friday, 29th December 1944… On Friday, Mannie [Hartwig] arrived home at four o'clock, with a happy face (£21 bonus in pocket and Oatine cream for me from J.F)…it was bitterly cold.

5th January 1945… shops full of oranges – the first for many months…

26th January 1945 [the day before I was born]… For the last week or two it has been bitterly cold – shall not be surprised if this winter goes down in history as the worst of the war. Snow and ice everywhere; it looks perfectly sweet and romantic round our little home – the boughs of the trees heavily laden with ice and the little birds hopping hopefully under the kitchen window…There has been another orange distribution; lovely Jaffas this time…

2.3.45 (we shall not be able to write the date like this for 100 years!) Spring has come, the sun is shining, the sky is blue…I am glad you registered her [me!] as Carolyn…she now has her very own ration book, clothing coupons, identity card and what-not…

4th March 1945… On Saturday we went into Amersham and opened a Savings Account in her name…

[Hartwig has been given the diary and writes the following:]

8th May 1945 – VE Day…

Today – Victory in Europe Day – Winston Churchill announced on the Radio the end of the German war. What a triumph for the good cause and what a relief to us all, the first day I am spending with my adored with in times of peace…And our Child, born in wartime, will now, God willing, enjoy the blessings of peace…

Tuesday 5th June…We've had nothing but rain, rain, rain, for weeks on end…

1st July 1945…Carolyn started lunch for the first time with two teaspoonfuls of Brands Meat and Vegetable Broth…

[Hartwig:] Sunday 29th July 1945… Baby's cot and playpen arrived, freshly painted in a lovely cream by Rust and Ratcliff in Chesham. The cot was new "Utility" and therefore somewhat wobbly, and the pen second-hand and pre-war…

[Hartwig:] 16/8/45. Yesterday was VJ Day – the war is over and Japan has given in. No more fighting now anywhere, for how long everybody wonders. People are glad it's all over but rather apprehensive of the future. The world is in such a mess and the sum total of human misery cannot be measured. Even here in England, Churchill has lost his job as Prime Minister, after winning the war, the Socialists are in and there is no end of strikes everywhere. People are tired and on edge and scared of the implications of the atomic bomb.

Peace was proclaimed at midnight on the 14th and 2 days, the 15th and today, were public holidays.

[Yvonne added:] Our first day of peace. Oh, please God have mercy on the world and help us preserve peace on earth. Spare our little children the horrors of war – and bless my dear family – please dear Lord keep an eye on us that we may continue in our love; that our beloved baby girl will have a happy life and always love us!

Ivan Jakar

Aged five, I was living in Stoke Newington with parents, Grandfather Reverend Azriel Katz, Grandmother and several aunts and uncles of varying ages.

We were evacuated by train, did not understand anything; I just remember lots of other children with little suitcases or brown wrapped parcels, with clothes and a packet of sandwiches. We were met at Amersham station, put into cars driven by WVS ladies, who drove us to the houses of people who had agreed to take an evacuee. I remember when we stopped a lady came out, looked into the car and pointed at me. So began my evacuee adventure.

Evacuation came along and I was "delivered" to a house in Green Lane, Amersham-On-The-Hill, where I spent the next five years with a couple and an ancient parent of the man. Frank and Eve Ross were not Jewish but looked after me as their own son, wonderful loving, caring people who gave me a marvellous childhood in the country – as it was then.

My father was in the army. I saw him just twice when he was on leave. He and my mother came to see me in Amersham on those occasions, with Mum managing to come a few times more. She was in London looking after parents and my young sister (who was evacuated but was so unhappy, Mum took her home).

I cannot remember meeting Jewish people whilst I was there. I don't remember the synagogue hall, but almost on the same corner was a bowling green where I would stop after school, peer over the hedge and watch "The old ladies and gentlemen" play. Even now if I see a bowling green I will watch for a short while, reflecting on when and where I first saw it being played.

The school I attended in Amersham was an overflow class held in the church hall opposite the Regent Cinema, where Mrs Fairgreaves taught forty of us.

A young lad's impression of the Regent is of a large single story building devoid of anything but seats. No balcony. In those days you could go into the cinema anytime during film shows, so it was not unusual to go half way through and then stay on for the next performance, when you saw the beginning or the whole film again. If it was an "A" film you would ask an adult in the queue if they would "Take me in?" If you got a yes you would hand over your ninepence, go with them. If you got a no, you asked someone else. Another "wheeze" one lad would pay, go in, then when the lights went out he would open the side exit behind the blackout curtain and in would sneak your friend. I think if Uncle Frank had ever found us out we would have been banned from going for quite some time!! Films that come to mind, Will Hay, who was very popular before and during the war, Abbott and Costello, Tommy Handley, Tommy Trinder who both, although music hall guys, made some pictures during the war, plus of course cowboy and Indian films, which were enacted on Amersham Common next day with homemade bows, arrows and a clenched fist with a pointing finger for a pistol.

I never went into the shelter near the cinema. The siren was on the cinema. I had heard sirens in London prior to evacuation, so did understand it meant an air raid, and I did get frightened. I think a couple of bombs fell into the bluebell wood on the road going down to Old Amersham. This was the road the little theatre was in where I saw a couple of pantomimes. I believe Dirk Bogarde and Jean Simmons appeared there in their very early days. Later in the war a stray V2 demolished a house near the common. I was on my little bike, heard the bang, wobbled and ended up in the hedge.

Leaving school one day I noticed a lot of people walking down the high street. Being a nosy eight to nine year old I followed them, eventually arriving at Amersham Station where a large crowd had gathered, looking toward the entrance. Wanting to know what was going on, and being only a little lad, I made my way to the front where I climbed onto a window ledge. After a while a group of sailors came out who were greeted by much applause, cheering. Not sure how long after, Auntie Eve showed me a copy of *Illustrated News*, July 1943, in which was an article "Amersham Welcomes the Jolly Roger". On the page was a picture of the sailors marching from the station and perched up on a window ledge, yes you've guessed it, little Ivan. From my young memory I believe Amersham "adopted" a submarine, the visiting sailors being members of the crew. I should imagine it was the latter part of the war.

After the war, my sister, brother and I spent many summer holidays with "Auntie Eve and Uncle Frank", they in turn coming to barmitzvahs, weddings etc. always made most welcome by my entire family.

Altogether we were in each other's lives for thirty-five years, until their deaths. They were not church people, but to me and my family they were perfect Christians, caring, kind and above all, loving. I was so very lucky. In 1945 we went back to wonderful seders and Friday night family meals, with the same Aunts and Uncles, who after war service in various fields left, one by one, to make their own family lives.

I grew to love the country, but never imagined I would end up living in the New Forest, which is a beautiful area. Coming from London, at age five, the countryside was a magical place. I was given a small bike which after learning to ride, I, together with a boy who lived two doors away, after school would cycle to the common and just roam around on "adventures". We had a large side garden where Uncle Frank taught me to play cricket, together with the Taylor twins who lived next door. They grew up to become professional players, one with Surrey the other Nottingham. The difficult part was not seeing my parents and little sister. I think living a non-Jewish life for those five years gave me the basis for future understanding that, apart from worshipping G-d in different ways, human beings all had the same thoughts and worries about family life, work and the day to day living of their lives.

MR ELLEN

(Letter received 1994 from Mrs M Rodgers of Chesham Bois)

During the Second World War, my mother helped all she could. At one time during the war we had a Mr Ellen living with us, he had a room upstairs and was, I'm told, a German Jew. Of the people who lodged with us, he was my favourite, very quiet and sweet. I was a little girl at the time, and he saved me his stamps from Palestine. Also, he let us try his kosher margarine, etc. and gave the kosher things he could spare. I thought all the food beautiful, and can still remember the taste! He had meetings with his friends in his room, all quiet, polite people.

My mother always liked Jewish people, and I had one Jewish friend in particular. E Freeman, she came towards the end of the war from London with her family, and her mother made me beautiful dresses. I can still remember their East London address. They lived in a wooden bungalow in a field opposite us. We lived at 28 White Lion Road, Amersham Common. Our house is demolished now, to be replaced by two detached houses (next door to Recreation Hall).

I shall never forget dear Mr Ellen and the quiet peace when he was near. I haven't felt like that with other people (except my family and dear friends of course).

The LNER Train to Nowhere! – Harvey Millan

(Contributor Rina Silverman on behalf of her cousin.)

Well, it was shortly after the start of World War Two and it wasn't the whole train, but one buffet-car coach of a brown liveried LNER [London and North Eastern Railway] Pullman steam train that lay in a field behind a pub near the town of Amersham. An early morning observer with good hearing could hear the sound of davening, praying and Shacharis – the morning service, being said enthusiastically. To the landlord of the pub all this seemed very weird. When he looked out of his bedroom window above the pub he could see the buffet car full of men who were all standing in the same direction and bending and swaying with muted monotones emanating from the open windows of the railway coach mixing with the sounds of nature around – like the early morning blackbirds, wood pigeons, and sparrows. Our landlord found all this, a trifle upsetting, not quite what he had expected when he agreed to let my father and uncle rent a space in his field. There were two horses in the field when we arrived and a condition of residence was that we did not upset the horses, whose owners were also paying rent for use of the field.

I was just five when my mother and my younger sister of two years, were joined by my aunt and her five children on the evacuation from London. This was our third attempt to find a safe and suitable place to stay. First we were billeted with a family in Northampton, but that was short lived because the house owner's wife thought her husband was being over friendly to my mother and she became jealous and my mother uncomfortable, so we left and returned briefly to London. This was in the thick of the blitz and it was too unsafe to sleep in our Stamford Hill

London Home, so we were allocated three bunks on Arsenal underground station on the Piccadilly line. Underground trains were stopped around 9.30 pm and the bunks were then laid out on the station platform. Each one was numbered and blankets were provided. Trains restarted around 6.30am (as far as I can remember). Anyhow, after two weeks of this my mother, together with her sister, applied again for evacuation from London.

This time the two sisters, with a combined total of seven children, were allocated one room in a three room cottage in Amersham. This was at that time considered to be a place in the country safe from German bombing. I remember as a child being fascinated by the gas lighting, because we had electricity at our London home, whilst here the gas mantles had to be changed frequently and they had to be lit by a flame. This stay at the cottage was a nightmare. There was only one double bed in the room and we seven children slept on the floor in very cramped conditions. My mother always wanted all the windows open but her sister did not, and two of the children suffered from asthma.

The men of course were involved in the war effort and did not know too much of the conditions in Amersham. My father went to see for himself. He was shocked and immediately contacted his brother-in-law who was a minister of religion and was working at the London Schechita Board to provide kosher meat for Jews still living in London. When he heard what his wife and children were enduring he searched around for a solution, my father having to return to duty could not do so.

The solution was to find the railway coach. How my uncle managed to obtain such an item and install it for us to live in is one of those special things that people seem to do at times of crisis. Through his contacts at the London Beth Din he mentioned his problem to a visiting member from Manchester Beth Din who happened to know that there were many disused railway carriages at Crewe. Buffet and restaurant car services were mostly abandoned and were sitting targets for enemy aircraft, so apparently there was not too much difficulty in buying one. The wheels had to be removed and then the whole coach was lifted by crane onto a special type of lorry and driven down from Crewe to Amersham. Before this took place my uncle had to find a site and again this took some ingenuity because water for washing and toilet facilities had to be found on or close to the site as well. He found this pub with a field at the back, but what was special about this place was that there was a separate toilet and washroom facility behind the pub. You did not have to go into the pub to use the facilities and in those days not many Jews went into pubs. The coach itself consisted of one half set out as a buffet area with tables so it became our kitchen/dining room (and davening room), and the other half of the coach was divided into separate compartments much like those described in Agatha Christies books. This latter half we used as family bedrooms, giving some measure of privacy to both families.

A small number of the Jewish community were evacuated around Amersham and word spread that my uncle the reverend and schechita man [animal slaughterer] had left London to stay with his family. He would daven regularly at the railway carriage and soon there were enough people for a minyan, some services were held there, and he provided kosher poultry.

One of the humorous things about the place was that the horses loved attention and my mother hated animals, but loved fresh air. She would sleep with the carriage door window fully lowered and it was not uncommon for me to be woken up by a small scream and shouting because the horses head would be fully inside our narrow carriage section – and it was a big horse!! There was a ditch around the field and I can remember playing with my cousins in that ditch, pretending we were in a mountain gorge and we would climb up into the daylight of the field with some difficulty. I went back to visit the site with one of my cousins who was there with me. Amersham was still just about recognisable as a country area at that time and we went to the field and to the ditch and to my utter amazement the ditch I loved so much was only as high as my knees – and then I remembered with a shock I was only five years old at the time!

GERRARDS CROSS –
THE ZANDER FAMILY[98]

Dr Walter Zander had been a successful lawyer in Berlin. He was a German Jewish refugee who came to Buckinghamshire in 1937 with his wife Gretl Magnus, and three children – Michael, Luke and Angelica. Their fourth child, Benjamin, was born in England.

From 1944, for twenty-seven years, Dr Zander was Secretary of the British Friends of the Hebrew University in Jerusalem.

Gerrards Cross was a hive of wartime activity. Denham aerodrome was close by to the village. Bulstrode Park was the RAF Staff College and the WAAF (Women's Auxiliary Air Force) also trained there. Walter Zander's son, Professor Michael Zander, recalled, 'He loved walking in Gerrards Cross on the Sunday morning two hour walk around the Bulstrode Park, often with one or other of his children'.

The Zander family home was full of music. A reflection perhaps of optimism, despite persecution and then imprisonment as an 'enemy alien', first in Prees Heath then the Isle of Man. Subsequently, Walter's Slough printing business was confiscated.

Walter was an experienced musician. All four members of his Berlin string quartet came to England and sometimes continued to play together. In this wartime home, the youngest child, Benjamin, developed his love for music, notably becoming conductor of The Boston Philharmonic Orchestra.

Michael Zander said, of his father, 'He was a serious gardener in Gerrards Cross in wartime, gardening for the first time in his life, producing vegetables and fruit for family consumption'.

Michael recalled, 'There was usually a twinkle in his eye or a smile on his face. He saw the best in people and brought out the best in them. He was gracious and courtly in manner, in the formal continental style.'

Walter Zander lived to the grand age of ninety-four. After release from internment on the Isle of Man, Walter Zander 'was engaged by the Ministry of Information to lecture British troops on aspects of 'the Jewish question'. Dr Walter Zander would focus on goodness during difficult times, preferring 'to dwell on the kindness of his neighbours in Gerrards Cross. His wife took in lodgers, traders gave her extended credit, and the headmaster of the local preparatory school waived his fees. His experience of those years made him an inveterate Anglophile.'[99]

Professor Michael Zander

We lived in Gerrards Cross. We were not members of Amersham (or any other) shul. My father was Jewish. My mother, though of a Jewish background, had been brought up as a child in Holland as a member of the Dutch Reform Church.

My father was arrested in Gerrards Cross – believe it or not, by a police officer to whom he was at the time giving German lessons!

I can only imagine what he felt about being arrested and taken away from his wife and four small children, aged at the time eight (me) to just over a year (Ben).

However, his attitude to internment was very measured. He wrote about it in an article called, "Strength through suffering", which can be found on the website we established for all his English language publications.[100]

He was not bitter about internment – or indeed about anything.

As to music, there was plenty of that in our house. Mostly it was us children practising our instruments, especially of course Ben who went on to be a fine cellist before he became a conductor. But by the end of the war he was only just beginning his musical career. My parents were active in running the Gerrards Cross Music Society, and sometimes the visiting soloists would stay with us and play a separate small concert in our tiny house. I recall that Colin Davis played once, accompanying his then wife April Cantelo – but have no idea whether that was during or after the war. My father played quartet which often took place in our house.

I do not recall seeing any dogfights but we often saw the bombers heading for Germany. I recall noticing the mass of planes heading for France on D-Day – and when I got to school that day I remember saying that I thought it was the beginning of the invasion of Europe. We also occasionally heard and occasionally saw Doodlebugs. At school the senior boys took turns to stand on the air raid shelter by the swimming pool to watch for them and to ring a bell if one was heard, upon which everyone was supposed to take cover under their desks. During the Blitz we often slept in the Anderson shelter in our garden – which we children thought was a great lark. There was a parked railway carriage close to the railway bridge a few hundred yards from our house, over which we walked to get to the station. We only discovered after the war that that nondescript railway carriage had been an important railway control centre. If it had been a bomb target the houses in our street would probably have been hit. Fortunately that did not happen.

The Common remained a common, used only for recreation. It was not turned over to growing food.

I and my two brothers, Luke (then Lucas or Luki), and Ben (then Benjie), attended Gayhurst, a prep school only five minutes cycle ride from our home – an outstandingly good experience. It was a wonderful school – academically, and for sport. The headmaster took me in without charging fees as a gesture of support for a German Jewish refugee family. There was once an incident in which I was jeered at as a Jew – I don't recall in what exact terms. But I do remember what happened then – the boy in question, a bully who I detested, was expelled for the rest of the term. An amazing event.

I passed the Common Entrance Exam to get into Merchant Taylor's School but went instead to the Royal Grammar School in High Wycombe. I was in fact the first boy ever to have gone to the local grammar school from Gayhurst – a rather extraordinary fact. Everyone had always gone to a Public School. Luke went to St Paul's and Ben went first to St Paul's, then to Uppingham and then at the age of 16 left school to go to study with the great Spanish cellist, Gaspar Cassado, first in Florence and then in Cologne.

My sister, Angelica, went as a day girl to High March, a girl's school in Beaconsfield, and then as a boarder to Piper's Corner near High Wycombe. I believe I am correct in saying that she was the first person from that school to go to Oxford.

Norman Franklin – The Franklins at Chartridge

Arthur Franklin (1857-1938) was a banker and the eldest child of Ellis Abraham Franklin and Adelaide Samuel. He bought four small cottages in a terrace, and employed the architect Aston Webb (the builder of the front of Buckingham Palace) to build a large house, Chartridge House. He originally moved into his country retreat in 1899. His main home was in Porchester Terrace London W2. When he retired in 1926 Chartridge Lodge became his main home.

Arthur married Caroline in 1883 and they had six children: Jack, who married out, Alice, who never married, but was for years secretary of the Townswomens' Guild and then the Fawcett Society (a feminist group),

Figure 10: Chartridge Lodge, as seen from the main road, 1938.

Cecil, my father a publisher, Hugh, an ardent male fighter before the Great War for women's suffrage, who went to prison three times for his pains, and married twice, the second time out. Hugh attempted to horse-whip Winston Churchill in a train carriage (six weeks in prison), threw a stone through a window of Churchill's house (two months imprisonment) and set fire to a first class coach between Marylebone and Harrow (six months). He went on hunger strikes and was repeatedly force fed. Helen Bentwich became Chairman of the London County Council (LCC). Ellis joined his father in the family bank after the First World War. Jack served in the first war, and so did Ellis (who was invalided out). Ellis had five children, including Rosalind, the crystallographer, who contributed to the unravelling of the chemistry of DNA. Also, Eva Hubback *née* Spielman was my suffragist cousin on both sides of the family and another, Netta Franklin *née* Montagu who helped form the Jewish League for Woman Suffrage and whose sister, Lily founded the first Liberal Jewish movement in England. My great-uncle was Herbert Louis Samuel, 1st Viscount Samuel.

My father Cecil was the oldest son to marry in and have a family. He inherited the house and the estate, (which was about 250 acres, including Newlands Farm) on Arthur's death in 1938. Cecil could not afford to keep the house on, and sold it with half the four acre garden to Stewarts and Lloyds of Corby for £5,000 who wanted it as office premises to use during the anticipated war.

Before the War my family used to visit my grandparents a lot of weekends usually driving down from London, and we stayed for longer periods in the school holidays. Arthur was very frum; so frum that he utterly suppressed my grandmother's middle names, Ann Mary, and also disinherited his two sons who married out. I remember Shabbat morning services which he held in the hall at Chartridge Lodge, where he read the prayers from Singer's Siddur, partly in English but also in Hebrew. My grandfather employed a schochet, Lemuel Philips, to slaughter his chickens. He was also the estate carpenter but very unpopular with the other staff.

Arthur built the coach house, Broadway House, (which became a triple garage with accommodation over) 300 metres from his home. This was deliberately done so that the building was just inside three miles from Chesham Station and he would get free deliveries of freight. My grandfather had a Daimler driven by the chauffeur, Wilson who never drove faster than 20 mph.

Arthur set up a small charity Adelaide House, in Ballinger Bottom in memory of his mother who died in 1902. This was a holiday home for working women, within striking distance of London. The building has since been demolished, as the need for the charity disappeared after the Second World War. Ellis Cottage still remains there (the residence of the caretaker).

There was an indoor staff of about six, dominated by Cater, a formidable lady who ran the establishment. My grandfather would not have male servants in the house, because he believed they all drank. Two pubs in the village were Portobello Arms, which sold wine and The Bell, which sold beer. The second establishment is still trading. There were ten workers on the farm. Three gardeners were employed throughout the war.

The nursery, a room next to the dining room, was ruled by *Dadsnanna*, the nanny of my parents, who lived there in her retirement. She was a dour nanny and we went in fear and trembling of her.

In addition to the pleasure garden which extended from the house there was a walled garden which was the kitchen garden, supplying produce,

Figure 11: The dining room, Chartridge Lodge, 1938.

Figure 12: The living room Chartridge Lodge, 1938.

with three heated glasshouses, which grew peaches, grapes and cucumbers – all a luxury in those days. It had a large number of apple trees, mainly espalier, and the crop was stored in a thatched apple house on special trays, which could keep the apples in good condition until March.

There is a story that a zebra was found walking around the woods. The Rothschilds were known to keep zebras, at their house, Halton (near Wendover). My grandfather telephoned to advise them about an escaped zebra. The response from the Rothschild butler was "How do you know it is Lord Rothschild's zebra?"

We kept the bailiff's house Little Hawkshard as a weekend retreat, and were living there at the outbreak of war in September 1939. I was eleven. There was a fear of heavy bombing raids, and part of my father's publishing company, Routledge, was moved down to the garage, which after a few days was renamed "Broadway House" after the name of the office building in the City. We returned to London and lived there until the blitz started, when we promptly moved to Chartridge permanently. I was at boarding school, and so I was only at Chartridge during the holidays. My father commuted every day from Chesham to the City on the 8.05 through train to Farringdon. He always travelled with the same group of people.

My mother, Kathleen Franklin *née* Jessel, known as Kaye, threw herself into the life of the community, was chair of the Women's Institute, and became a councillor of Amersham Rural District Council, and a JP (Justice of the Peace). At her first time at Quarter Sessions in Aylesbury a whisper went round the Bench "Three or five". She thought the question was whether she wanted a three shilling lunch or a five shilling lunch and answered accordingly. The question really was how many years the convicted prisoner should serve. My mother wanted a light lunch and chose 3 shillings.

On one occasion my mother was looking out of the window. It was dawn. She watched the smoke trail of a V2 leaving Holland. Five minutes later it landed in Berkhamstead.

Pre-war refugee from the Nazis, composer Arthur Willner, stayed in Chartridge Lodge. I was ten at the time and remember him sitting in the Morning [music] Room composing a piece called "Bagpipes". [He also wrote the *English Concerto for Chamber Orchestra (Op. 98)* at Chartridge].

Before the war my father and his children used to go to the West London Synagogue in Upper Berkeley Street, and my principal memories of that period were the children's services, which I attended, and later, the adult services, where I sat with my father, to the left of the Ark.

I remember being taken in during the war to Amersham for the High Holy Days where there was a temporary shul, in what I now think of as a church hall, but other than the crowded room, I can remember very little about it. Amersham being five miles away, and petrol rationed, we went there only occasionally, and did not play any part in the community life. I was bar mitzvah in London, in the spring holiday so Chesham or the train to Baker Street was the extent of my local knowledge.

The bus service was good, two buses an hour to Chartridge from Chesham, one of which, the 394, went through to Great Missenden. It was in Little Missenden that my grandfather fished but he never caught anything! Further on, above Wendover, lived relations, the Langdon/Castello family.

My sister Irene was a student at Kings College London (evacuated to Bristol) where she met a Czech medical student, who was completing his degree at the Charles University Prague (also in Bristol). After graduating, she lived in our Putney house with her cousin Rosalind (who was working for the Coal Utilisation Research Association) while she was working with Anglo American Oil Company. After Hanus Neuner got his medical qualifications, and was called up into the RAMC as a lieutenant, Irene married him at the West London Synagogue. In 1943 Hanus was sent to Malta and then Italy. Their first child was born in 1944 at Shardeloes which was then a maternity home for officers' wives. Irene lived then at Broadway House in the flat above the garage. Hanus was demobilised in 1946 and their second son was born, also at Shardeloes in 1947. After he had trained as a psychiatrist they moved to Haifa in 1949.

Figure 13: Norman with his sister Irene and her husband Hanus, 1942/43.

In 1950, my mother died, and my father took a flat in London, and only lived in Chartridge at weekends. I married in 1953, and my father sold the house to Stewarts and Lloyds, and moved permanently to London. He married again in 1954, and died in 1961.

Our family donated a Reading Room, land – *Franklin Playing Field* and cottage to the village of Chartridge.

STEFAN MÜLLER (LATER STEVEN MULLER)[101]

Steven Muller, and his brother Norbert, lived in Chesham between 1939 and 1940 The brothers, Steve and Nobby, were uprooted from their home in Hamburg and transplanted to Chesham in the space of three weeks.

In Hamburg, Steve and Nobby were raised in the Jewish faith of their father, and from the early 1930s, it was clear that Jews were no longer valued or welcomed in Germany. Steve recalled, 'three of my former friends in the park, dressed in Hitler Youth uniforms, waylaid me and beat me up. I was not badly hurt, but I do still have a scar under one eyebrow from being kicked in the head.'

The brothers attended Talmud Torah Schule and sheltered there on Kristallnacht, November 9, 1938, while the synagogue next door was destroyed by fire. Their father was arrested and sent to Oranienburg Concentration Camp, but managed to obtain a visa to England. The danger escalated for the boys, who were labelled as 'Mischling', half-breeds. Steve recollected, 'my mother, reared as a Roman Catholic, received a letter from the Hamburg government, which stated that, due to the departure of her Jewish husband, she was entitled to normal Aryan status and her two sons could be granted Aryan status, become Hitler Youths, and attend the public schools, provided only that both sons would be castrated so that they could not contaminate any woman with or perpetuate the Jewish blood with which they were afflicted.'

The children, and their mother, managed to leave for England, but the boys become part of the mass evacuation out of London. The village green near Chesham train station, where the evacuated boys arrived, is no longer there, but the school he attended continues. Steve and Nobby were 11 and 10, respectively, when they left Hamburg, did not speak English and were suddenly transplanted, by train, to a small Buckinghamshire town, without contact with a Jewish community. They were unwanted foreigners to prospective host families, so 'were assigned to the German teacher of the Chesham school.'

While living apart from their parents in a foreign country was not the situation they had anticipated, Steve generally regarded the seven months that they lived with their Chesham foster parents, George and Trixie Scull, as a positive experience.

The Sculls had no children of their own, and they made Steve and Nobby feel as much at home as possible. The other boys with whom they were evacuated were English and could see their parents on occasion. The restrictions on enemy aliens in the United Kingdom, however, made it impossible for their parents, Werner and Marianne Muller, to travel so, the Sculls tried hard to give Steve and Nobby a normal English home life. Trixie taught them to knit, and they made hats and scarves for British soldiers. When it was the holiday season, the Sculls had a Christmas tree and Steve and Nobby learned about English Christmas traditions, including decorating the tree and singing carols.

In April of 1940, the visa for which the Muller family had applied in the mid-1930s was granted by the United States. Steve's English accent led to acting in seven Hollywood films and radio broadcasts. Also an academic he was tenth president of Johns Hopkins University and served as President of the hospital. Norbert also had a distinguished career, with thirty-nine years as Professor of Physical Chemistry at Purdue University.

The time that they spent in Chesham was meaningful to them. Whenever Steve spoke of that period in his life, it was with gratitude. Under adverse circumstances, he learned to speak flawless English, gained confidence and independence at an early age, and appreciated the great kindness that the Sculls and the Chesham community extended to him and his brother.

CHESHAM CONGREGATION – EISEMANN FAMILY

(Information from Rabbi Joey Grunfeld)

The highly respected Eisemann family left Nazi Germany, Frankfurt am Main, and found their way to Buckinghamshire. They lived in a beautiful house, on a hill, overlooking Chesham. The road was called Manor Way. Other Jewish residents, on the same road, included the Ullmans, next door at number ten, and Julius and Marianna Jung at number 26.

Julius Jung wrote for the *Jewish Chronicle* and several wartime articles in the *Bucks Examiner*. These were very important in developing relations with the wider community. Through this medium he was able to explain in detail about Nazi persecution. He also invited people to events in the Amersham shul, which included a talk by the famous cook Florence Greenberg. Julius Jung had a major role in building relationships with the non-Jewish locals. He also spent much time securing a kosher canteen for local Jewish families. The Jungs were friends with the Eisemann family.

Heinrich Eisemann was married to Alice and they had six children. One daughter worked on Cowcroft Farm. The farmer and his wife were Mr and Mrs Askew. They were very friendly good people, and taught one of the Eisemann daughters to milk the cows. She even helped bring a new life into the world, when a horse was in labour, recalling how once the foal was out, 'he walked backwards'. She also remembered big trout swimming in the clear stream. Her sister, Miriam became an artist, and like many other Jewish Cheshamites attended Heatherton House School. Another sister was the only bride to marry in the Isle of Man Enemy Alien Internment Camp. Heinrich Eisemann was a great scholar and ensured his children were thoroughly educated in Torah as well as having a wider education. He worked as an independent antiquarian. They were very loving and kind parents.

Rabbi Moshe M. Eisemann

The Jungs lived on Manor Way and so did we (11 Manor Way). Rabbi Aryeh (Leon) Carmel (formerly Weinkoff), the foremost student of R. Dessler who put out R. Dessler's Michtav MeiEliyahu, also lived on that street. He used to shlep us boys into his house and teach us the so called Inyanim (Hebrew: affairs, issues) of Rav Dessler. There were a couple of other Jewish families on Manor Way including the Schwartzschild (our next door neighbors) and the Ullmans.

I had no idea that there was a Jewish community in Amersham. I did go to the Amersham Grammar school for a couple of years. The principal (I think his name was Dr. Harrow) was a high officer in the air force and in fact the entire teaching staff consisted of elderly people who had been called out of retirement because the younger staff were all in the army. But I rode the bus from Chesham in the morning and back after school in time to get to the Hebrew Classes in the Cricket Pavilion. I have no idea at all of Amersham outside the school.

Chesham to Gateshead

Some members of the Chesham community were devoted to studying Torah above all else. They felt that this was the most important course to take in life regardless of any external circumstances such as war. Who would have thought that the little countryside town of Chesham could become the crucial stepping stone for the bringing together of great rabbinical minds. [102]

And so it came to pass, in Autumn 1941, a Torah scholar decided to bring the most observant and knowledgeable rabbis together. It was September, around the Jewish New Year, Rosh Hashanah, a time of reflection and forward thinking. This was a fitting month for Reb Dovid Dryan to make letters of enquiry to twenty, carefully chosen, members of the Rabbinate. [Reb is a Yiddish honourific title usually given to rabbis (teachers, or rebbes in Yiddish) but also to others out of respect. Rav and rab are Hebrew honourifics but specifically for a rabbi.]

His idea was to establish a Kolel in Gateshead, but he needed to persuade people to join him in shaping a community devoted to the education and study of Torah. Reb Dovid Dryan set up the Gateshead Talmudical College in 1929, also known as Gateshead Yeshiva. He was a controversial figure for encouraging men into a protective environment of study, isolated from engagement with war.

Of the twenty letters sent to the Rabbis, Gateshead Kolel recorded, Dryan had nineteen rejections. The only person to respond favourably was Rabbi Dessler.

Dessler is known as a great philosopher but his work was only published, after his death, by some of his pupils. Dessler worked hard to teach young people the ways of the Torah and Talmud. He taught many families which included children, who became leaders themselves, Cyril Domb (professor), Samuel Stamler (barrister) and Moshe M. Eisemann (rabbi). They were also taught by Rabbi Y Ehrentreu (cousin to the Amersham wartime assistant minister/reverend, Sonnie Bloch). Eliyahu

Dessler lived a life of spirituality, learning and improving young minds. Dessler's rabbinical appointment had been at the Montague Road in North London. War meant his congregants relocated to safer areas so Rav Dessler evacuated himself to Chesham.

In 1941, the same year that the idea of a kolel was proposed to Dessler, the place where he grew up was destroyed. On the third day of June 1941 the Nazis reached Kelm. Shortly after, everyone in that Yeshiva, pupils and tutors were murdered, by Lithuanians, and buried in mass graves.

As Gateshead Kolel reported on their website, Rabbi Dessler was so taken with the dream of a Kolel that he wrote back to Dryan, with obvious excitement, and keenness to pause 'not for a moment and all the more not for hours or days' and so new beginnings were shaped when Dessler went to his first meeting in Gateshead in October 1941.

The very first formal gathering for the Kolel was not held in Gateshead but in Chesham. Moreover, the now thriving Gateshead Kolel is able to provide the following information of the attending Rabbonim and even the address:

> It was at the first meeting that the Kolel ideal was nurtured and developed, it was the formal assembly of Rabbonim held at 46 Townsend Road, Chesham, Buckinghamshire, the wartime home of Rabbi Dessler, that the Kolel was actually born. The list of those present make fascinating reading, and represented the leading Torah luminaries in England at the time. They were; Rabbi S J Rainbow (Chairman), Rabbi Elyah Lopian and Rabbi L Gurwicz of London, Rabbi Chaim Shmuel Lopian, and Reb Dovid Dryan of Gateshead, Rabbi Dessler, Rabbi S Moscowitch (Shotzer Rebbe) of London, Rabbi I Margulies (Premislaner Rebbe) and Rabbi Yisroel Ehrentreu of Chesham, Rabbi Yehuda Segal, Rabbi H Goldstein and Rabbi Kopul Rosen of Manchester, Rabbi Benjaminson (Zhlobiner Rav) of Letchworth, Rabbi M Cohen of Northampton, Rabbi Josselowitch, Rabbi G Schneider, Mr A Goldman of London, Mr A Weinkoff (father of Rabbi Aryeh Carmell) of Chesham and Mr H E Bloch of Gateshead. At this assembly the Constitution was drawn up and the aims of the Kolel were clearly enunciated.

Incidentally, there is a connection between Alice Shalvi, and Rabbi Margulies. Alice Shalvi (Israeli resident, educator, social activist and wartime evacuee to Buckinghamshire) explained, 'He was known as the Przemyślaner Rebbe after the Galician town of Przemyśl where he originally had his court. In 1920, on his way from Galicia to England, he passed through the German city of Mannheim, where my father's family lived. While there he actually performed the wedding of my parents, Benzion and Perl Margulies (her maiden name was identical to that of my father, since they were first cousins). When my family arrived in London, Rabbi Margulies and his very large family were living in the East End where he had a "shtiebel" [a little room used for communal prayer and socialising] which we occasionally visited. One of his sons, Salomon, later became a very successful and wealthy businessman in London. I recall that Rabbi Margulies visited us in Waddesdon at least once during the war. Happy to see him, I eagerly stretched out my hand to him. He shook it but I was later severely reprimanded by my mother for taking such a liberty.'

Rabbi Eliyahu Dessler personally helped to finance the Kolel. He journeyed back and forth from Chesham to oversee it. Many eminent scholars emerged from the Gateshead Kolel. It was clear the Jewish people were being murdered and with it knowledge of Torah. By establishing the Kolel, Dessler hoped to save the knowledge of Torah from extermination.

HaRav Zushe Waltner[103]

By Moshe Musman (abridged).

HaRav [Hebrew for 'the rabbi'] Waltner was born in 1918 in Hungary. At the age of thirteen, his parents sent him to Cracow to learn in the yeshiva of HaRav Nechemiah Kornitzer *zt'l*.

In Cracow the scholar shone as a gifted *talmid chochom* [Hebrew: wise student] even before coming to England. Growing anti-Semitism manifested itself in Poland in the years before the War, and Rav Waltner experienced it firsthand when he suffered a severe beating at the hands of a local gentile in Cracow. He was advised by HaRav Kornitzer to leave the country.

He went to Switzerland as a private tutor in 1936. Rav Waltner had been in Switzerland for a year when, while out walking one day with his *talmid* near Lake Lucerne, he encountered Professor Bichler of Jews College. This meeting demonstrated to the professor that Rav Waltner possessed unusual pedagogic talents and he promised to further his cause upon his return to England. He was as good as his word and wrote informing the authorities that the young man he had met was a genius, and would be a great asset to Anglo Jewry.

The letter was effective. Rav Waltner suddenly received a call from the Consul in Switzerland and was given an English visa. He arrived in England in 1937.

Within months of the outbreak of World War Two, German bombers were subjecting the cities of England to savage attacks and many families were evacuated to small towns and villages in the countryside.

While with evacuees in Chesham, Rav Waltner first made the acquaintance of the man who had the greatest impact on his life, HaRav Eliyahu Dessler *zt'l*. He would accompany Rav Dessler on his travels and they became very close…Many aspects of his own future life and work mirrored those of his great teacher.

Rav Waltner married in 1943. His *rebbetzin* [rabbi's wife, (Amalie)] (of the Haberman-Streicher family) had arrived in England several years earlier. She came on her own as part of an agreement to take in young German Jewish girls to serve as domestic servants. This was not an occupation she relished, so she subsequently qualified as a children's teacher and was teaching Jewish school children in Chesham. Rav Dessler was their *shadchan* [matchmaker] and was also the closest that either of them had to family at their wedding.

Afterwards, the Waltners made their home in Gateshead but only Reb Zushe joined the newly opened kolel… He later came to be in Prague. Rav Waltner described that Yom Kippur, which he spent in the famous *Altneu shul*, as his most memorable one ever. The *shul* was packed with brokenhearted refugees, who had survived the war physically but as lost and rootless souls. At the sight of his British passport, Rav Waltner was inundated by entreaties to "Save us – – take us out." … He said that the people didn't *daven* on [pray] that Yom Kippur, they just cried. [Rav Waltner arranged for children to come to the United Kingdom, securing guarantors for their upkeep, and money for flights.]

While the girls took up lodgings with Jewish families, Rav Waltner took the boys and founded what developed into Yeshivas Netzach Yisroel in Sunderland, a town near Gateshead. Among them were children who had been through the camps and were severely traumatized. These were hard cases.

Sometimes when he gave them food, they hid it instead of eating it. They would have nightmares and wake up screaming. He had to sleep with them every night. Some were not *frum* at all. Some thought they were still in the camps and attempted to run away in the night. Eventually, some of the boys found relatives in the United States and went to them.

THE BLOCH FAMILY

'Our Bloch family lived in Chesham and were members of the more orthodox community. Sonnie was a reverend and would sometimes officiate at services in Amersham.'

Dr Maurice Bloch

Maurice's brother Sidney Bloch wrote a moving family memoir, *No Time for Tears: Childhood in a Rabbi's Family,* (William Kimber, London, 1980), summarised here with kind permission from the Bloch family. It portrays a pious and humble family from London and Essex. The children were Esther, Sonnie, Romie, Sidney, Maurice, Judith and Leonard. Their mother was Leah 'Lolla' (née Jung). Their father George Getzel Bloch, a rabbi from a long ancestral line of rabbis, died tragically young, but not before he had witnessed the death of one of his children, Romie. George had been the immediate inspiration for the males in the family to lead religious services. They are also cousins to the wartime Chesham rabbinical Ehrentreu family. Despite poverty the family would leave their door open to people more desperate than themselves. They would provide food, setting out the best cutlery for the homeless to use, and listen to the strangers with respect and understanding, and even took in four refugee children.

The Bloch children served Britain. Sonnie, after being reverend for the Amersham Hebrew Congregation in Buckinghamshire, became a chaplain in Burma and the Far East. Sidney was a Despatch Rider for the firefighters. Maurice was a nineteen-year-old medical student in 1945, his call up was deferred whilst studying. Years later Maurice became a Major in the Royal Army Medical Corps. Whilst they helped to defend humanity their maternal uncle, Julius Jung, son of a rabbi, and husband to Marianna, took a different kind of action in order to save Jewish children from the Nazis. He went from door to door, and community groups, making speeches and begging people to sponsor and house children. The positive results meant

Julius saved many lives. He also wrote articles which were printed in the *Jewish Chronicle* and *Bucks Examiner* to give voice to the desperate plight of European Jewry. Not only did he defend humanity in Britain but he risked his life by going to Nazi Germany to orchestrate a rescue mission.

The Bloch and Jung (was Junger) family evacuated to Chesham but by this time Rabbi George Bloch had died. Maurice (head boy and Cadet Corps leader) and Leonard went to Challoner's School in Amersham. Their eldest sister, Esther got married during the war years and lived elsewhere. Sidney took on work in Amersham, record-keeping for a burial society, but the work was dull. Perhaps the lack of excitement, in part, drew him to take huge risks. Against his mother's knowledge, aged sixteen, he rode on his motorbike, from Chesham, into the London Blitz to undertake part-time, dispatch rider, fire-fighting duties.

Sidney Bloch was taken deeper into the world of literature by German Jewish refugee, Heinrich Eisemann, father of Rabbi Moshe Eisemann, who also lived in Chesham.

After Friday night and Saturday synagogue services the Blochs would receive friends and family in their Chesham home. This included a German refugee, Arthur Stilitz, who it was believed, parachuted back into Berlin 'to save Jews from the gas chambers', and the Stamler brothers from Challoner's. Sam became a QC and David, head of Carmel College. Perhaps their brilliant young minds were nurtured in the homes of the Jewish community where much wisdom was shared. Other guests were local non-Jewish residents from law, medicine and the clergy. Professor Sam Atlas, lecturer in Comparative Religion debated with Professor David Diringer, a Cambridge lecturer. Weekends were filled with intellectual debate and games of chess. Tea 'consisted of large quantities of tomato or jam sandwiches and plates of chocolate yeast cake which was Mother's speciality.'

Later Sidney obtained a job in London, and despite an early commute on the six-thirty train, he still found evening time for Jewish studies with Rabbi Dessler.

During Christmas the Bloch family visited the Cottage Hospital, a two mile walk away, which was 'decorated with ribbons and balloons, and those who were sufficiently well sang carols and hymns with the nursing staff.'

The Blochs would ramble from Chesham to Chorleywood but

spend much of their weekends giving free Hebrew classes to the student barmitzvah sons of soldiers. Meanwhile, to bring in an extra income, the family took in an evacuee lodger, Mr Moller, and after him a German Jewish lady.

Sidney wrote he bought an old bicycle 'for 10/ – and developed an expertise in freewheeling down the steep gradients of Buckinghamshire with my shoes resting on the handlebars.' Sidney's circus antics made it into the local newspaper!

As soon as Sidney was old enough, in 1942, he enlisted with the British army and with him he took his Hebrew bible given by his mother.

MICHAEL BARNET

I am a teacher at a very orthodox Jewish school. I lived with my mother at the far end of Chesham. I walked three miles over the hill, across the fields to shul in Chesham, every Shabbos. There was a big chedar in Chesham. Many people who lived in that area were German Jewish refugees. The shul closed down mid-war.

Many of the Jewish children attended Dr Challoner's School. [Two pupils, Sidney and Sonnie were related, by marriage, to Mrs Dora Bloch.] Mrs Bloch was hijacked, on a flight, by Palestinian terrorists to Entebbe airport, Uganda. Seventy-five-year-old Dora Bloch disappeared. [She was murdered.]

The mohel [someone who performs circumcision] in Chesham, during the war, was from the Bloch family.

I also remember David Stammler, the Shaiman family, Alan Cohen (chartered accountant), Audrey Marx and Mr Goldberg, who had a 'schmutter' (rag trade) business and Sam Stammler who went on to be a member of Wembley Synagogue.

MAX SULZBACHER[104]

I don't remember the Blitz 'with some nostalgia' … but with horror and sadness. My father's entire family were killed by a direct hit on our house during the Blitz.

At the beginning of the war our family had all been brought over from Germany through the energy of my father, Martin Sulzbacher. Then he was interned, first on the way to Canada on the ill-fated Arandora Star, which was torpedoed. He survived but was then sent to Australia. My mother and we four children were sent to the Isle of Man.

However, my grandparents were too old, my uncle and aunt had already been naturalised as they had been in England five years, and my other aunt was classified C, [no security risk as an Enemy Alien, unlike B, which applied to people who were under suspicion and A, those deemed to be a high risk, arrested and interned] so they all remained in London. But the Blitz was so dangerous that my uncle had driven to Chesham outside London and booked rooms there. As it was getting dark, he didn't want to drive back in the Blackout so he returned to London by train hoping to bring the family there the next day. That night the whole family were killed and were buried in Enfield cemetery four in one row, and my aunt in the next row as her body was not found in the rubble until later.

My dear father did not hear of the disaster until Erev Yom Kippur [evening before the Day of Attonment] in far-away Australia. Forty-one years later he himself passed away peacefully on Erev Yom Kippur, so that my brothers and I say Kaddish [mourner's prayer] on that anniversary in memory of my father and of that tragedy in the Blitz so many years ago.

SHEILA SHEAR (NEE RIPPS)

I moved to Chesham with my mother and sister, Myrtle, from the East End of London. I went to South Hampstead High School which was evacuated to Berkhamsted and had enough Jewish pupils to warrant separate Jewish Prayers. If I remember correctly there was a girl from Amersham, whom I was at school with, called Elise Israel?

Also in Chesham was a family Cohen whose father was a watch repairer. He used to sit in the window of his shop and one could see him at work.

I recall a family whose surname was Gee who also lived in Blucher Street, a few doors away from where we lived. They were an orthodox family of four or five children. As they couldn't get kosher milk for Pesach they used to, each day, take a jug to the dairy and have the cow milked straight into it. You couldn't make it up!

My father used to attend Yom-tov services at the temporary synagogue in the cricket pavilion and I, for a very short time, went to cheder class there.

Sheila Shear was interviewed in *When the Children Came Home*[105], whose author, Julie Summers recorded:

> They took a train to Chesham and the four of them traipsed around the town with a little overnight bag and their silver Sabbath candlesticks, which were precious to her mother. They knocked on several doors and as it got dark a woman took pity on them and let them stay the night. For the next few weeks the four of them lived in a tiny room with no windows, their father travelling up and down to London on the early train. If he were ever late on the train they would all worry that something had happened to him in London. It was no way to conduct family life, even during a war. So they moved back to London for the second time.

However, the bombing was so heavy that they were forced to return to Chesham. Sheila continued:

'Hello Mrs Ripps,' said the billeting officer, when we turned up in January, 'I knew we'd see you again. We've got the perfect place for you. 26 Blucher Street. Go and knock on the door.'

Julie Summers recorded the details of:

...a small terraced house with a parlour, a kitchen and a scullery on the ground floor and two bedrooms upstairs and a tiny attic bedroom, which Sheila had to herself. There was no hot water, no electricity, and the loo was outside in the garden. Cooking was done in the scullery on a gas cooker and there was a butler's sink that had cold water. The house was owned by a bachelor called Harry Mayo who was an upholsterer by profession and worked for a company called Brandon's in the same street.

Both parties were strangers to the others religion and customs yet they developed a life-long friendship. Sheila recalled:

...Uncle Harry was the kindest person you could ever imagine. He took us into his house and without a moment's hesitation shared everything with us. He had the kitchen, we had the parlour. He had one bedroom upstairs and my mother, Myrtle and my father had the other. I had my lovely little attic room with a view over the garden. In the spring of that first year my mother explained to Uncle Harry that we were coming up to Passover and that there were certain customs that we had to observe. Uncle Harry was fantastic. He didn't flinch. He merely said to my mother: 'Well, well, well I never. Who'd have thought it? I always thought Jewish people must be good but now I know for sure.' And with that my mother could relax and share all the Jewish festivals. She always invited Uncle Harry to join us and he always took part. It worked the other way around too. We were invited to his sister, Nell's, on Christmas evening and we used to go along for supper and to sing and play games. There we ate plum pudding for the first time, we pulled Christmas crackers, and saw the lovely decorated Christmas tree. It was all great fun and seemed such a long way from the constant air raids, bombings, and shelter life we had left behind less than a year earlier.

Sheila continued:

> At Passover Uncle Harry ate matzos, the unleavened bread which Jewish
> people eat for this week-long festival, on Sabbath he enjoyed 'kneidlach'
> a delicious matzo meal dumpling in chicken soup, which he insisted on
> eating with a knife and fork and not with a spoon as we had always done.
> He even fasted with us for twenty-five hours on Yom Kippur because he
> thought it would be unfair for him to eat when we were not permitted.
> The fast is difficult enough, but alas on one occasion he began his with
> bacon and so suffered an unbearable thirst all day, but stubbornly refused
> to give in and waited to break his fast with us on some more conventional
> Jewish cooking.

Julie Summers noted their 'Uncle Harry' encouraged them in piano
playing, art and reading. Sheila said, 'He introduced me to the joy of
looking at paintings and my family has several of his pictures which we
treasure.' Sheila also remembered:

> His shaving routine, which took place in his downstairs room, was a daily
> ritual. He used an open 'cut-throat' razor and sharpened it on a leather
> strop, lathered his face and then carefully scraped off his beard. Myrtle
> and I watched with awe, afraid to speak or move in case we distracted or
> jogged him and were very relieved when the razor was washed and placed
> in its little plush velvet box until the next day. In fact, Myrtle, who was
> four and a half years younger than I was, saw more of Uncle Harry than
> she did of our own father because Dad only ever used to have Sundays
> off as a full day in Chesham whereas Uncle Harry was with us the whole
> time. Mother used sometimes to leave us with him if she had to go back
> into London or go out somewhere and she knew that we were completely
> safe in his company.

Harry even opened his home to Sheila's grandparents. Sheila reported:

> Neither grandparent spoke English and Uncle Harry of course had no
> Yiddish but he showed no surprise when Grandmother would bring her
> pots, pans, plates and cutlery and take over a corner of his kitchen to do

her kosher cooking. Although Grandmother didn't speak any English she was a great communicator and she managed to convey her delight with Uncle Harry by stroking him and saying: 'Ah, Mr Mayo, Mr Mayo!' He didn't seem to mind at all and would join in on evening meals whenever he was invited.

Julie Summers recorded that on:

8 May 1945 there was an enormous celebration and street party in the Broadway in Chesham to celebrate VE Day. There was singing and cheering, people danced around the war memorial and talked excitedly about the future. The bells rang out from the church for the first time in six years. Uncle Harry was nowhere to be seen. Eventually Sheila's mother found him in the garden. He was standing with his back to the house and he refused to come inside and join in the celebrations: 'Everyone in the world is happy today,' he said. 'Everyone is happy except for me, because you are leaving.' Sheila remembers her mother's immediate reaction: 'We'll stay until the new school year begins.' She told him on the spot. That way he would have three months at least to get used to the idea of their returning to London.

When the time came for them finally to leave Chesham and move back to London in September 1945 they insisted that he should remain closely involved with the family 'which you will always be a part of', they told him.

Harry Mayo and Sheila's family remained committed friends, never losing touch until Harry died aged ninety-four. Sheila reflected:

Uncle Harry had always said that he did not believe in the Church. He was not even sure that he believed in God but he was without a doubt the truest Christian I have ever met.

HILDA BAXT (NEE SAMSONOVITCH)[106]

I reside in the United States, New York. I was born in London, England. My maiden name was Samsonovitch. It was shortened to Samson. In 1939 I was eleven and evacuated, with my brother and older sister, to Chesham, Bucks.

My parents were up all night before we left, sewing coats, jackets, skirts, and blouses. My father was a master tailor and my mother was a seamstress.

My younger brother David and my older sister, by two years, were at the train station with my mother. Our clothes were in pillowcases. The station was crowded and I was not happy. The train stopped in Chesham, filled with children from all over London. We filed down the hill to a church. Inside were a lot of children and we were given tea and biscuits. I must have fallen asleep because I awoke to an empty hall apart from my brother.

My younger brother and I were separated from my older sister. Two men put us in a black car and rode down the street to a shoe shop. He let us out of the car and told us to wait inside the door of the shop. He went to the back of the shop. The woman said she didn't want us. The man asked if she would keep us overnight till he could find us a place the next day and she said no. He told her she had signed up to take children and she replied she had changed her mind. Then he put us back in the car and drove down the street again. This time they left us in the car and went inside the house. Now I was afraid. It was dark, no lights on in the street. My brother and I sat close together but we didn't say anything. I felt so terrible I couldn't say a word. My brother didn't talk. He was seven years old. It was such a horrible, horrible, feeling everything was blacked down... Suddenly the car door opened and the men told us to get out of the car and took us inside the house.

They told us that we would be staying with this family, Mrs Collins and her daughter Phyllis. Phyllis took us up to the bedroom. My sister was already billeted with another family. There was a bathroom which was very unusual as in London we didn't have bathrooms. We went to the 'out', outside. Once I got into bed that time – I was eleven years old – the tears – I couldn't stop the tears. Once I started crying my brother started crying. Phyllis came into the room and she said, 'Please, stop crying. If you want to go back home tomorrow I will take you back myself but please don't cry. We want to take care of you. We want to be here for you.' When the next morning came she took us to the drug store. She bought us hot water bottles and toothbrushes.

My mother came to visit us. Mrs Collins put my mother, and baby sister, up for the night. The next day my mother went to visit my older sister, and took her home with them. I wrote my mother and told her if she didn't come take me home I was going to throw myself out the window.

One day I said to my brother, 'We're going to walk home.' He started walking, must have been walking for about two hours. I didn't know which way was home and it was getting dark. My brother was going, 'I'm tired. I'm tired.' I said, 'All right tomorrow, we'll start out.'

I attended Germain Street School, and at no time were we informed of a Jewish community, although there were quite a few of us Jewish children. I do not remember being friendly with any of the children that went to Germain St School. I learnt about making cakes and doing laundry.

The Chesham family I was billeted to were extremely good to us. We never asked for anything and we were treated with respect. They had a daughter of nineteen who was a nurse in London. She would come in on a Wednesday and take us to the pictures and then to Woolworths to buy us movie magazines. I remember seeing the movie with Claudette Colbert and Henry Fonda in *Drums along the Mohawk*. The cinema was on the road to Germain St School.

When my brother and I came home from school we would get chocolate biscuits. Mrs Collins had a playroom upstairs and my brother played with the trains. I played Gracie Fields records.

The family did not know of Jewish people so I told them I don't eat meat unless it is Kosher. Mrs Collins would go to the fish and chip shop and buy fish for me.

In 1942 we returned to London because the bombing had not yet started, so a lot of children were leaving Chesham.

At the age of fourteen and a half, I visited with the Collins family for a week's holiday. Once Phyllis took me to the model village and that was great. Phyllis took me to Amersham and it was a wonderful day. We went to see Ginger Rogers in the picture *Roxy Hart*, and then she took me to a place that looked like a castle, with windows opened on the ceiling, and they served tea in pewter ware. It was like being in a movie. That was a wonderful experience for me. It was such a huge place – all brick with a skylight roof with the light streaming in.

QUAINTON – AMELIA ROSSELLI PINCHERLE

(Jewish, feminist, anti-Fascist, Italian poet and writer.)[107]

In her research Professor Marina Calloni (2000) stated Amelia was 'the first Italian female writer for the theatre even though present encyclopaedias show history does not mention her.' She was part of 'three liberal secular Jewish families (Pincherle, Rosselli and Nathan), whose women played a basic political and cultural role both in Great Britain and Italy.' Furthermore, she was a poet and mother. Amelia lived through what no parent should ever experience, the death of not one but 'three distinguished sons, all killed for the "love of the country", the ideal of freedom, the perspective of social justice and the fight against tyranny.' The first son, Aldo, was killed in action in WW1. For the political activities of this family, Amelia's Italian house was ransacked, her possessions destroyed. Her sons, Carlo and Nello, fled to France but the fascists pursued them. They were murdered. Amelia Rosselli Pincherle came, with her remaining family, to the Aylesbury Vale area of Buckinghamshire from 1939 – 1940.

It was a dangerous time to be socialist and Jewish. Marina Calloni stated, 'after the national unification in 1871 they were considered Italian citizens until 1938, when the racial laws and the persecution started. Amelia wrote in her memoirs "Jewish? Of course, but *first of all* Italians".

After the funeral of her sons, in France, Amelia did not go back to Italy. Calloni stated 'Carlo's and Nello's wives (Marion and Maria) took the same decision…' They left for Switzerland but the children were not granted residency,'so that they decided to go to the UK.' The trauma did not end there. The UK labelled and interned the three women as enemy aliens although 'Carlo's wife, Marion Cave, was a British citizen'. Friends successfully petitioned for their release.

Calloni recorded that Amelia wrote on 18th September 1939 from Quainton: "We spend anxiously our days, waiting news. But all what is private, personal, disappears and loses importance facing the grandiosity of events..." Amelia believed "the time for justice will come one day" (4th February 1941).

Paola and Silvia Rosselli

(Sisters reflecting together on their shared memories)

We were in England not as Jewish refugees, but as political refugees, having left Italy after our uncle and our father, Carlo and Nello Rosselli, had been murdered by the fascists in France on June 9, 1937, because of their anti-fascist activities. This is the reason our family (our paternal grandmother, Amelia Pincherle Rosselli, our mother, Maria Todesco Rosselli, and we four children: Sylvia, nine years old, Paola seven years old, Aldo two-and-a-half and Alberto only a few months old) left Italy in 1937, before the racial laws in 1938. We are Jewish, but we are not "practicing" Jews and so we do not remember ever having taken part in any Jewish religious activities during our stay in Quainton, or if there was a synagogue there or nearby.

On leaving Italy, we first went to live in Switzerland (in Villars-sur-Ollon, Valais), but in 1939 the Swiss government did not renew our permit, and we decided to leave for England. We arrived in Eastbourne in August 1939, but in September, war was declared; and for fear of a possible invasion of the Germans, it became dangerous to live on the coast. So we decided to move to a safer place, and the choice fell on the little village of Quainton, in Buckinghamshire, where a young couple, Manuel Benaim and his wife Sara, with their small son Ruby, friends of our family, already lived. A house was found, owned by Mr. Black. It was quite near the village, with a large garden and an apple orchard around it.

What do we two sisters, ten and eleven years old at the time, remember about our stay in England?

Arriving in Eastbourne, we lived in a boarding house, and the two of us were sent off to a nearby school where we began learning English. After the war broke out, we remember rolls of barbed wire on the beaches, and the street signs indicating the direction for other cities, such as London, changed around to mystify eventual German invaders or parachutists. We also remember the first air raid alarm in Eastbourne; as we had not yet had our gas masks, we were quite frightened, although we had been told that if worst came to the worst, we could hold handkerchiefs dipped in vinegar in front of our mouth and nose. When our family moved to Quainton, my sister and I were sent off to boarding school; the school was Queen's College of London, which had been evacuated to Brackley, Northamptonshire, for the duration. The school was in an old manor house, no central heating, and windows open in the dormitories all night, even during the winter (ah, the spartan habits of the English people!) We remember how cold it was in the morning getting up, with a thin layer of ice on the water we used to wash with! But it was a good school, and we were quite happy there, and particularly remember the nature walks we took in the fields and woods surrounding the school, and the lessons about nature and water painting.

We were only in Quainton during school holidays. We do remember the village, the few small shops which had not much of anything to sell, due to the war shortage; going to fetch drinking water at the fountain near the village green; our mother buying yards and yards of heavy dark blue wool material with which to make curtains for the black-out; and air raid alarms. But after a year, our mother and our grandmother decided that

Figure 14: In front of the Quainton house,
left to right: Silvia, Paola, Aldo and Alberto Rosselli.

England was no longer safe especially for us children (of Italian, Jewish and antifascist family) and so, with much difficulty, we managed to obtain visas for the USA and tickets for the last ships leaving for Canada, taking English children there for the duration. The ship that sailed before ours (City of Benares) was tragically sunk by German U-boats.

We left Quainton in August 1940, spent one night in a hotel in London on our way to Liverpool, also in order to say goodbye to the many friends and relatives living there. There was a bad bombing that night, and we remember the whole family (in the meantime we had been joined by Carlo's widow, Marion Cave, and their three children, John, Amelia [distinguished poet] and Andrea, who were leaving for the States with us) going down to the air raid shelter.

The sea was quite rough during the first day of our crossing. For the first few hours we were "escorted" by a plane of the British Air Force, and for the first days by two warships, perhaps two destroyers, but then they turned back and we were on our own. But after eight days of navigation, we arrived in Montreal safe and sound. We lived in the States until the end of the war and our return to Italy was in the summer of 1946.

That one year in England was important for us, for the shelter and the protection it gave us in those difficult times. It also meant the possibility of learning to read, write and speak English, and of getting to know a different country. We remember our stay in England with gratitude for the hospitality and friendship we found there, and with great admiration for the courage of the English people during and after the war.

THE STEINHARDT FAMILY AND THE CEDAR BOYS – WADDESDON MANOR[108]

Jeremy Godden's mother was Lore, his aunt, Helga and their parents were Hugo and Lilly Steinhardt. They fled 'Germany and came to live in the English village of Waddesdon' with thirty-one school boys from the school in which Hugo was a teacher.

Hugo's grandson, Jeremy Godden stated:

Many Jews of Germany had wanted to be part of the enlightenment or 'Haskalah' [Hebrew word] since the 1770's. Most of all they had wanted to be considered good Germans. They learnt German rather than a Jewish dialect, adopted German first names, wore the same clothes, adopted the same styles as the rest of the population and believed fervently that their commitment to all aspects of German life would finally lead to their full acceptance.

Then the Nazis came and people were divided 'into 'Aryan' and 'non-Aryan' and the Jews, as 'non-Aryans', were barred from state service. On 26th June 1933 Hugo…was dismissed.'

In 1937 Hugo became head of a Jewish boy's home, the 'Flersheim Sichel Stiftung' in Frankfurt am Main. Godden reported:

The appointment included an additional teaching post at the Jewish School, the Philanthropin, which was a very prestigious establishment. He was to teach English. The job included a situation for Lilly to use her office training and Bertha [Hugo's sister] was engaged as cook. Lore entered the grammar school section of the school with the boys and Helga also joined her there at the age of ten.

238

Germany was a terrifying place, the 'home had continuous visits from the SS at six o'clock in the morning.' Resident, Bernd Katz, was a day away from his eleventh birthday. It was the 9ᵗʰ November 1938. Godden noted, 'The atmosphere had been tense and full of rumours all day. Fathers of the children had been arriving from the villages to escape Nazi attacks. (They were mainly after males at the time)'

Godden recorded Bernd's recollections:

As night fell…we heard a rushing noise like a huge wave coming ashore during a severe storm. The noise kept getting louder and louder. Then we heard the chanting, "Kill the Jews, kill the Jews," and rocks started to fly through the windows. The children were sent to the back bedrooms and climbed under the beds.

Hatred toward Jews escalated, twenty-seven 'male teachers, Hugo and his brothers, were imprisoned in Buchenwald concentration camp.' They beat Hugo. Helga thought it was because 'Hugo was too gentle in his speech and manner. Some of the teachers returned but two died and others never regained their health. Fifteen teachers managed to emigrate at this point.'

Godden continued:

During Hugo's imprisonment in late 1938, Helga and Lore wrote letters abroad pleading for help. Helga addressed a letter to President Roosevelt and received a reply but no offer of help from the American consulate. In July 1938 Roosevelt had convened the 'Evian' conference in France where 32 countries met to discuss the fate of the Jews. But no doors were opened and no hope was offered after much debate and discussion. The Nazis gleefully noted the refusal of America, Britain and the other countries to offer safety to the Jews. Hitler said, "They complain in these democracies about the unfathomable cruelty that Germany …uses in trying to get rid of their Jews…they affirm with complete coolness that over there, evidently there is no room!"

One of the girls had a breakthrough, when they wrote to a stranger in England. The envelope was simply addressed to "Lord Rothschild, London". It was duly received by Lord Rothschild. The letter was given 'to his cousin James de Rothschild who promised to help to rescue them from the ever worsening situation.'

Jeremy Godden noted:

> The home was now searched several times a week. Nazis would come and deliberately storm around about 5am, claiming to be searching for weapons. Helga remembers being very scared. Helga recalls that another Jewish home nearby had burned down at the same time as the local synagogue while Lore, Helga and the Boys were at school. They ran about 3 miles home to make sure it wasn't theirs.

No permission to leave was given for the Jewish governess and a cousin. Another cousin, Helmut Rothschild (the son of Hugo's sister Bertha and husband Theo Rothschild), [not related to the famous Rothschild banking family] escaped to 'The Cedars', a mock-tudor home, made available to the refugees, on the Rothschild Waddesdon Manor estate in Buckinghamshire. Lilly's sister Bertha continued as their cook. Godden added that, 'eight more boys arrived, mostly in their teens but also one six year old. Some parents arrived late that summer, seizing the last opportunity to leave before the war broke out.' The children became known as 'The Cedar Boys'.

Jeremy Godden related:

> Lore had been very fond of Werner Florsheim (now Bernard Florsham). He accompanied her after school and he came out with the Kindertransport. He arrived in Coventry but stayed in Waddesdon during the bombing of Coventry. His parents took over the Frankfurt Boys' Home after the Steinhardts left. Another 40 boys were admitted in the late 1930's. Plans to evacuate them (from Germany) to Ecuador failed and the Florsheims, their younger son and all the new boys were deported and perished in Litzmannstadt (Lodz) in Poland. Miss Casparius, the governess, had suffered a similar fate. I remember Lore telling me of the agonising decisions by some of the boys' parents about whether to let them go to England on their own. Most of those who chose to stay with their loved ones in Germany perished.

Those who made it to *The Cedars* 'were provided with furniture and basic necessities by the Rothschilds.' Lore had mentioned 'that they had to go to the manor to ask for extra money to cover extras, such as clothes, visits, presents etc. as they had left Germany with nothing of value and just a few belongings.'

Godden re-counted Bernd Katz stating 'There was a club in town where they put on shows and boxing matches'. Godden continued, 'Heinz Meyer Bender (who changed his name to Henry Black) was the boys representative in the boxing and was very successful. He won the North London Junior Boxing title in 1940. Henry became an estate manager in Norfolk.' Furthermore, 'Uri Seller (originally Ulrich Stobiecka), eventually, worked for the Israeli Embassy. Hans Bodeinheimer worked in a Golf Course near the coast in Israel. He was active in three major Israeli wars as well as having a role in the raid on Entebbe.' Godden added, after 'the war others were reunited in the USA with relatives who had survived. Two who had no surviving relatives settled on a kibbutz in Israel.' Godden stated:

In 1939 the first of the boys left for Israel. In 1940 four more went to the USA, including Bernd Katz. Some were reunited with relatives. Those over 18 were keen to enlist to fight against the Nazis. At first they had to join the Pioneer Corps but eventually joined the regular British armed services. German sounding surnames were changed in preparation for the invasion of Europe thus protecting any Jewish soldiers who were captured.

The following are extracts from Lore's diary:

July 13th 1942

...next thing is the forces – what if they don't accept me?... Daddie is of the opinion we have to help the war activity or England will turn against us afterwards...

Monday July 29th

I have not been writing in this book for a considerable length of time, perhaps I feel happy in spite of having to join the ATS [Auxiliary Territorial Service] and having to work hard all day in the gardens, dumb and dull work mostly the same, from planting lettuce, picking up potatoes, picking fruit, pulling out carrots, cauliflower stumps, weeding all by myself in a potato field, clearing out stables.. get the same everyday, quite nice company, if it's the girls, less pleasant is working with

*the men, accept for Mr Wise and the dullest is being by myself. At the end of the week
I am expecting .. with the recruiting officer-I am hoping to get a job in PT [Physical
Training] but I doubt it.*

*After 4 monotonous weeks in the gardens I am hoping to go camping with the
Habonim* [Zionist youth organisation] *for a week. There is a boy from…(?)
who comes every week to talk on Zionism. He made an impression on me first time
I saw him carrying water cans in the garden. He made me think that he is probably
very enthusiastic and energetic and that everybody can be like that to make life worth
living…It seems very queer and silly to me that I can ever have doubted it, feeling as
normal and ordinary now I must have been going bonkers.. Now I am independent,
earning my own money, it sounds great but I get about £2.80s a week, 15 shillings
of which I have to pay home – but army pay is less.. We had an excellent discussion
on the night ..(?) about the Jewish problem. I hope he has not influenced me too
much with his talk, although it is only to the good. I am too easily influenced by
other people. I am looking forward to next time, because it is so dumb and dull in
the evenings.. weeding all day makes you think and when I think I want to write it
down..*

Now for the day in London…ATS…

*First of all I left a pair of gloves on the bus before the interview – coming up
I addressed somebody else by the name of the person I had an appointment with.
I stammered and staggered and he knew nothing about it, but it was only for a
minute until the secretary rescued me but the Commander Glen, quite friendly but
she disappointed me to tears I am afraid to say. I feel an awful fool afterwards, a friend
of Mrs Rothschilds and seeing me cry, but still there was no PT, nothing but a place
of a cook or jobs like charwoman open for me and knowing that I had to say yes did
not make it too easy. 'Had I tried the WAAF?' 'No, I did not know that they would
take non-friendly aliens, such as I am cursed to be.'*

Jeremy Godden resumed:

In February 1943 Lore took up a training course with the Ministry of
Supply and started work in Cambridge as a lab technician. It was here that
she met Ken Godden whom she married in 1946.

Lore and Helga attended a prep school in Aylesbury. Lore was about
to take her School Certificate in May 1940 when she was interned as

an enemy alien... Hugo was granted exemption, presumably on health grounds. Lore was sent to the Port Erin internment camp on the Isle of Man where Helga says, she "enjoyed the company of others in her age group". She went swimming daily and took part in activities organised by the refugees. Whilst on the Isle of Man, Helga believes that Lore met a young man who wanted her to emigrate to Palestine with him but her parents were not keen to lose her. She was released from the Isle of Man after six weeks, and had to change to a better school so she could retake her exams.

During her spare time in 1940 – 41 Lore entertained the villagers and evacuees with her performances as a skilled acrobat and gymnast. She also took part in dancing displays and drama. In the holidays she worked in the Manor nurseries and assisted the WVS. [Womens Voluntary Service] She applied to join the WAAFs [The Women's Auxiliary Air Force] but was rejected, Helga thinks possibly because of her nationality.

Lilly had to carry on as well as she could on her own, with two daughters and the boys to look after. Bernd Katz remarks about the Steinhardts, in his account: 'We did not appreciate their efforts at the time. In retrospect...it could not have been easy to raise thirty boys, most of them in their teens, in a new and strange country.' Some of the boys were really happy in Waddesdon. However, not all the boys were happy. The Rothschilds helped with George who had a breakdown... Most of the boys were successful...Otto Decker who eventually went to Puerto Rico where he owned an engineering company; [said] "I think our experience made us more determined and more ambitious to succeed in life, to justify why we survived when so many died."

Helga and Lore both worked as teachers. Lore worked in Secondary and Primary schools and with excluded children. Helga...teaching at a training centre for children with cerebral palsy. Lilly moved to a smaller house in Waddesdon when the boys and her daughters had all left. She continued to find great satisfaction in offering hospitality to her family and her "boys", who were now spread all over the world.

The wording [of a 1993 memorial] reads "This plaque is dedicated to the revered memory of Mr and Mrs de Rothschild by the Cedar Boys and Girls in gratitude for sanctuary at a time of conflict, 1939".

CEDARS 1944: G. HEUMAN, P. GORTA, U. SELLA, W. KUGELMAN, O. DECKER, H. ROTHSCHILD, MRS. STEINHARDT, H. BODENHEIMER, R. DECKER, G. GRUENEBAUM, D.FIELDS

Figure 15: Cedar Boys (Top) and below Henry Black. British armed forces 1940s.

Helga Brown (nee Steinhardt)

James and Dorothy de Rothschild did not seek publicity. James de Rothschild was very helpful and visited 'The Cedars' regularly – enquired about our welfare and could not have been more helpful with obtaining medical treatment for my father Hugo Steinhardt who passed away in 1942.

Dorothy de Rothschild had many interests during wartime such as WVS. She was a magistrate and active in village activities.

Waddesdon was a small village, without a Jewish population, when we arrived there.

The Cedar Boys:

Alfred Bieler
Ludwig Bieler
Manfred Bacharach
Hans Bodenheimer
Georg Bodenheimer
Rolf Decker
Otto Decker
Irwin Freilich
Theo Freudenthal
Werner Gonsenhauser
Peter Gortatowski
Gunter Gruenebaum
Hans Hellmann
Gert Heumann
Bernd Katz
Walter Kugelmann
Fritz Lebrecht
Heinz Maier Bender
Hans Spier
Ulrich Stobiccka
Bodo Wurzburger
Rudi Hirsch
Helmuth Rothschild
Kurt Marx
Arthur Marxsohn
Heinz Lowenstein
Siegfried Pappenheimer
Gert Simon
Herbert Tint
Ralf Katz
Hugo Steinhardt
Lilly Steinhardt
Lore Godden née Steinhardt
Helga Brown née Steinhardt

My father prepared the boys for their barmitzvahs and the older ones had learnt Hebrew at their Jewish school in Germany. As time went by Jewish evacuees moved into the village and assisted with services conducted in the Dining Room at 'The Cedars'. Especially active was a factory owner, Benno Margulies, who set up his firm in Aylesbury with his brother who moved there from Hatton Gardens.

There was no synagogue in Waddesdon or Aylesbury. Some Jews had a room there in a prayer hall. The Harrow synagogue lent us a Torah and other items.

In Frankfurt we had attended the West End Synagogue, where services were conducted by Dr G Salzberger. He was a friend of Hugo Steinhardt and after his arrival in London he travelled to Waddesdon, at the beginning of the war, to preside over barmitzvahs and services in our Dining Room. His grandson Jonathan Wittenberg has written about his journey to Frankfurt from Finchley.

Werner Gonsenhauser and Ludwig Bieler had their barmitzvah on 19th August 1939. Dr Salzberger read the sermon assisted by H Tints, Hans Hellmann and evacuee, Mr Doll.

On the 9th December 1939 was the barmitzvah of Heinz Lowenstein. His aunt attended having travelled up from London.

We celebrated all of the Holy Days and took time off school, much to the envy of non-Jewish pupils.

We had Chanukah celebrations and the presents were donated by the father of the Bieler boys, Mr de Rothschild, Mr Margulies and Mr Wolf.

In May 1940 Lore Steinhardt, Herbert Tint, Kurt Marx and Gerd Simon were interned as enemy aliens.

On the 15th February 1941 the barmitzvah of Hans Spier and Walter Kugelmann took place. The 5th October 1941 was the barmitzvah of Gunther Gruenebaum. The Bieler barmitzvah was combined with Chanukah festivities on the 20th December 1941. Rolf Decker had his barmitzvah on the 11th April 1942. On the 22nd August that same year Dr Schreiber came from London, and officiated over the barmitzvah of Gert Heumann. In October Hugo Steinhardt, my father, passed away. In December Fritz Lebrecht had his barmitzvah. His mother, aunt and friends came from London to be there. In May 1943 Peter Gorta and Ulrich Stobiccka had their barmitzvah.

We never went hungry because we were self-sufficient. We dug up the beautiful lawns to grow vegetables. We were given an orchard nearby, full of seasonal fruit. We also kept chickens, looked after them, ate them and the eggs. We made jams. In addition, because some of the boys worked on farms, their received double rations of cheese and other items. We missed sweets, bananas etc. We still made fruit flans.

There were frequent air raid warnings. As far as I know only one bomb fell in Waddesdon. At the sound of the sirens, often in the middle of the night, we trooped down to the cellar with our gas masks but we gave that up eventually. We didn't have a shelter.

We walked and took part in village activities, once we had mastered the language. The village hall was a hive of activity and my sister was a talented gymnast and acrobat who displayed her talents. We played table-tennis. The British Council gave us games and books. We acquired second-hand bikes and cycled miles. If we wished to go to a cinema we had to walk five miles or cycle. The agent in charge of the Rothschild Estate was Philip Woolf, who was the brother of Leonard and brother-in-law of Virginia. He very kindly treated us to cinema visits but not transport. The boys were expected to collect salvage from the village households.

The boys had all attended a Jewish Grammar School in Germany and some were disappointed at the prospect of going to village schools and leaving at the age of fourteen. A few insisted on finding an alternative. There were no places on offer at the Aylesbury Grammar School, but only one boy passed the 11 plus, after only one year, and several others were able to take a 13 plus exam. Those who left at fourteen were asked to work on the Estate. A few emigrated to join relatives in the US between 1940 and 1942.

I was sent to a private school in Aylesbury. There were pupils at the council school and the Church school. There is now a C of E Secondary School and the 'boys' and I contributed to the 'Cedars Fund Prize' which is still awarded annually.

There was a Jewish nursery nurse who worked with the children at the Manor. My aunt worked as a cook at 'The Cedars'. Her name was Bertha Butzbach.

A contingent of Jewish people evacuated from the East End. Many only spoke Yiddish and couldn't write in English. They slept in the village hall and came to our services on a Saturday, but all returned to London in spite of the Blitz.

The following boys lost their relatives in Nazi concentration camps:

Hans and Georg Bodenheimer – parents
Irwin Freilich – mother
Theo Freudenthal – Mother. Father died 1943.
Gunther Gruenebaum – mother
Walter Kugelmann – parents and two siblings
Fritz Lebrecht – sister
Heinz Lowenstein – mother
Heinz Maier Bender – father and brother
Kurt Marx – parents and brother
Hans Spier – parents
Herbert Tint – parents
Helmuth Rothschild – parent and brother
Ulrich Stobiccka – parents

All the boys who took the place of those in the Children's Home in Frankfurt, who managed to escape i.e. 'The Cedars Boys', were murdered together with the wardens, their son and the Governess. My father, Hugo Steinhardt, was tortured during his stay in Buchenwald Concentration Camp and died as a result three years after.

Waddesdon Village – Professor Alice Shalvi (nee Margulies)[109] in Interview.

My parents, Benzion and Perl Margulies, and my brother William initially came to Waddesdon at the end of 1939, having been preceded by my uncle, Alexander Margulies and his wife Stella. They had bought a fairly large house (complete with tennis court) named Warmstone, at the end of a lane that turned left off the main road from Aylesbury, about a quarter of a mile outside the village. The neighbour, Mr Evans, owned a herd of cows and a dairy. Meanwhile, I was with my school in Northampton.

When the Blitz broke out, we all moved to Waddesdon. My father bought 20, High Street. The house had a large back garden, in which we grew vegetables that kept us plentifully supplied, both fresh and when bottled. We also grew strawberries and enjoyed the fruit of a large plum tree that stood in the back yard of the house. This was separated from the vegetable garden and a large field that lay beyond by a stable-like structure that was divided into coal-shed, laundry (with a large cauldron in which bed linen and other whites were boiled) and a general storage space. We also kept chickens, an occasional turkey, and sometimes other animals. We continued to live there until the end of WW2.

At the outbreak of war a fairly large number of Londoners arrived in the village, many of them Jews from the East End. Most of them did not remain long in the village. Among those that did were friends of my father: Gudel Lazar (a refugee from Nazi Germany) and his London-born wife Beate (née Mendelson) and their little son, Martin. Another newly-wed couple was Barry and Trudy Mindel. He was an employee of the Mizrachi Zionist Congregation, of which my father was for some time treasurer.

Also among these was another family of refugees from Germany, the Goldmans. Mrs Goldman was the sister of my aunt by marriage. Their daughter Edith was about my age. Together with the Steinhardt girls, we organized Chanuka parties at the Cedars. At one of these we performed a very pro-Zionist sketch we'd written that drew praise from Mrs de Rothschild, who expressed warm support of our ideology!

Another classmate was Doris Lewis, who lived in Aylesbury with her widowed mother and sister, Lily – she married Bertie Black.

Probably the most important impact that my sojourn in Buckinghamshire made on me was through my becoming closely acquainted with the English countryside, with nature in general, in a way that is impossible in urban settings. I learned to love the countryside and, with it, the poetry it inspired, especially among the 19th century Romantics. That, in turn, led me to study English Literature at Cambridge and, in consequence, also led to my career in teaching English Literature at the Hebrew University.

One of the Cedar Boys, younger than myself, was the only one who was allowed to study at AGS. Then called Gerd Heumann, he is now Geoffrey Hartman, emeritus Professor of English Literature at Yale University, with a worldwide reputation. He once told me that all he remembers from those days is that he was always hungry, because the bigger boys took his food. One other, older, boy, Herbert Tint, went to grammar school in Bletchley (I think), returning to Waddesdon for the weekends. Many years ago, I chanced to meet him in a Jerusalem restaurant and learned that he, too, had become a professor. Not a bad record for Waddesdon's Jewish population.

My uncle established a factory in Aylesbury, at which my father and brother were also engaged, apart from the time (1940-1943) my brother was at LSE (evacuated to Cambridge.) The factory produced bullet-counters for use in fighter planes.

On the corner of the lane that led to Warmstone was a large Pioneer Corps army camp where a fairly numerous group of refugees from Germany served. My father took responsibility for finding Seder night hospitality for all of them.

The evacuees in Chesham included the Stammler family. The older son, Sam, was at King's College, Cambridge a year ahead of me.

From Professor Shalvi's unpublished memoirs:

During the war, when we lived in the village of Waddesdon, grew our own fruit and vegetables and raised poultry, we had two "regulars," who every week came either for Friday night dinner or for Shabbat lunch, or both. One was Mr. Kurenitz, a short, plump, dapper Russian-born Hebrew teacher whom my father had hired to instruct not only my brother and myself but also the residents of The Cedars, a large house in the village where James de Rothschild, the local squire, had installed an entire orphanage of Jewish boys rescued from Germany. Leaning back in his chair with a sigh of contented repletion, Mr. Kurenitz would end every meal with the same remark, for which Willy and I waited as being the sign that he was about to depart: "Mrs. Margulies, you deserve the DCM." Every week my mother duly responded, as if it were a part in a play which she had dutifully learned by heart, "What is that, Mr. Kurenitz?," to which the answer was "The Distinguished Cooking Medal", followed by a hearty laugh, in which the rest of us were clearly expected to join.

The other guest, who sat through the meals without saying a word, was Mrs. Pulver, a plump, sad-faced widow who was, like us, an evacuee from London. Occasionally, other evacuees would be invited to join us. Among them was Beate Mendelson, the daughter of my father's former landlady, who had coached me in English. She had been my favourite candidate for marriage to Uncle Alex, but he had in fact married another refugee, Gudel Lazar, whom my family had known before they left Germany.

The most remarkable and memorable instance of hospitality came at Passover in 1943. My father had taken upon himself the task of finding homes that would host the numerous Jewish soldiers stationed in and around Waddesdon for the traditional Seder meal with which the festival begins. After considerable effort, he succeeded in accounting for only some of them. For the remainder, about twenty-five in number, he could find no more hosts. So he came home to my mother and asked her whether we could accommodate them all. It was inconceivable that a Jewish soldier should be without a Passover Seder. It was equally inconceivable that my mother would refuse. And so, at the shortest of notices, there began an extraordinary flurry of preparation. Turkeys and chickens were sacrificed to the slaughterer who came especially from London. Vast pots of soup steamed on the stove. Dozens of kneidlach, the dumplings that traditionally accompany the chicken soup at Passover, were prepared and dozens of eggs hard-boiled. My own particular specialty was sponge cake, because my arms were strong and I could spend hours beating the egg whites to a stiff froth with a metal fork or mixing the butter and sugar until they attained the desired creamy consistency. The cakes rose like a dream and emerged from the oven one by one, lemon-scented and fragrant.

Providing and preparing the necessary amount of food was one thing. Because we had become land-owners, poultry farmers with a vegetable garden and fruit trees, my mother had all the necessary ingredients even at this time of strict rationing. Space was more of a problem. Unlike the large farm house my uncle had bought on the outskirts of the village, ours, on the High Street, was comparatively small. The parlour-cum-dining room in which we spent most of our time proved barely adequate for the extraordinary assortment of men who filled it that night. My father had borrowed some benches from the village hall, our dining table, extended to the full, was augmented with the table from the kitchen and we were all jammed in so tightly that I had to slip under the table in order to help my mother bring in the food once the preliminary part of the Haggadah had been completed. But the initial astonishment and subsequent manifest delight of our guests, the relish with which they partook of my mother's delicious food, their compliments on my baking skills, the gusto with which they joined in the songs that end the Telling, all these were ample reward for the effort my parents had invested. Of all the memorable Seder nights I have experienced, that in Waddesdon at the height of the Second World War remains most vivid in my memory. For me, it was yet another example of my parents' unquestioning, warmhearted kindness and their ingenuity at collaborating in overcoming material obstacles that would have daunted everybody else I have known.

WARTIME

We listened to every news bulletin and grew more and more concerned and depressed as country after country fell to the Germans. Holland, Belgium, France, Norway, Denmark … The threat seemed to be coming ever nearer.

My parents and my brother had left London to join my uncle and aunt in Waddesdon, near Aylesbury, about forty miles from London. Perhaps because she once again felt herself a not entirely welcome guest in someone else's household, my mother was profoundly unhappy and soon became ill, suffering from severe abdominal pains and vomiting after almost every meal. Without my being informed, she was hospitalized in London and diagnosed as suffering from gall-stones.

At the end of the school year, emboldened by the London calm and reluctant to have me continue to live away from them in a non-Jewish home, however hospitable, my parents decided to bring me back to London.

Although the East End of London, the dock areas and the City suffered severe bomb attacks, the north-west districts where we lived remained relatively undamaged. But one night the sounds of explosion came perilously near and suddenly the ground heaved below us as if hit by an earthquake. At once came an urgent banging on the shelter door. It was my brother, badly shaken, wanting to be admitted. A bomb had fallen some hundred yards away, on the other side of the main road that ran through our neighbourhood.

A few days later, before we settled down outside, my brother, who had gone upstairs to the toilet, called us to join him in my bedroom at the front of the house. In the distance we could see the night sky glowing bright red. The City of London was burning. A few days later, my parents once again moved to Waddesdon. This time they purchased a house of their own in the centre of the village and this time I went with them.

★★★

Waddesdon, with a population of about one thousand, was one of a constellation of villages that surrounded the market-town of Aylesbury, renowned for its ducks, which served as their commercial centre. Not only was there a weekly cattle and market-gardening market in the town square on Saturdays, but the local branch of Boots, the chemists, had a lending library from which one could order even the latest publications; there were two cinemas, both of which changed their programmes on Thursdays, thus offering a weekly total of eight films in their combined programmes, and there was also, most important, so far as I was concerned, a grammar school where I would be able to continue my war-interrupted education.

Aylesbury was a mere five miles, a short bus-ride, from Waddesdon and rural buses ran frequently then, as they unfortunately no longer do. However, my father's attempt to register me at the school at first met with a negative response. Aylesbury Grammar School, like the Northampton School for Girls, had been compelled to host an entire London establishment, in this case the Ealing Boys' School, and although not all the Ealing pupils had chosen to be evacuated, the premises were grossly overcrowded.

At the time, there was a general assumption that the war would soon be over and the Londoners able to return whence they had come, so that there was no great readiness to come to their assistance. Londoners were considered outsiders; "foreigners" was the local term applied to them. The tightly-knit rural communities, unlike large towns such as Northampton, disliked and resented the intrusion upon their placid lives. The poorer families perceived us as in some way depriving them of space and income, while the snobbish "county" families, whose children went to private schools with smart uniforms, wanted nothing to do with the middle-class city parvenus. Somehow, we fell into a strange hybrid, all grouped together as "evacuees," although families like my own had little in common with the bombed-out East Enders who were all accommodated in the totally inadequate space of Waddesdon's village hall, where camp beds were set up for them, and the few toilets soon became smelly and squalid, thus contributing to a further deterioration in the evacuees' reputation.

After a few weeks spent restlessly in the little house on High Street which my father had purchased for £1,000, I decided to write to the headmaster, describing my frustration at not being allowed to continue my studies and begging him to admit me to the school as soon as possible. Whether my letter moved him or whether he or the local education authorities now realised that, given the continued bombardment of London, our stay in Buckinghamshire was likely to be longer than initially anticipated, I do not know, but almost at once I was invited for an interview and allowed into the school and so found myself, for the first time since leaving Wykeham in the summer of 1938, at an entirely co-educational establishment.

The difference was that I was now an adolescent, very conscious of what I considered my plain face and heavy body, scared of how boys would react to me, profoundly aware that academic distinction could never compete with the pert sexual attractiveness of some of my classmates. I recall the amused look the school secretary, herself an "old girl" of Aylesbury Grammar School, gave me, when I anxiously enquired, while I was waiting to be escorted to my classroom, whether I would have to be studying together with boys. She was able to allay my fears by assuring me that my particular class was comprised entirely of girls, since in the interest of economy both of space and teaching staff, all the female evacuees had been herded together, irrespective of age, while the boys were, for the most part, assigned to the Ealing school.

Now, as the possessor of a bicycle which my father bought me for my fourteenth birthday soon after we arrived in Waddesdon, I rode around the beechy Buckingham countryside, enchanted by the vast fields of corn, the haystacks, the grazing cows, the herds of sheep whose wool got caught in tufts on the barbs of wire fences that divided one field from another.

Waddesdon Manor, the home of James and Dorothy de Rothschild, around the grounds of which the village lay, has a large park which was open to the public. The house itself was partly occupied by convalescing soldiers, while many rooms were temporarily shuttered. In the park, a row of statues had been bound in canvas to prevent bomb damage. To me, they looked like prisoners awaiting execution and every time I cycled, with accelerated speed, along the path between them, I expected one of them to come to life and pounce on me. I was forever coming upon new vistas in the park and one spring day, turning a bend, I suddenly found myself confronting a vast bank of golden daffodils. I had never before seen such an abundance of what appeared like wild flowers thronging an open space. When, a little later, I read Wordsworth's poetry for the first time, I instantly recognised the similarity between his response and my own.

In addition to Boots' Lending Library, from which we were able to obtain even more recent publications, Aylesbury had another source from which we could acquire reading material. Weatherby's, located in a back street, was owned by a true book lover, who delighted in bibliophile customers who appreciated both his excellent stock and his readiness to order anything not in stock. At the end of my first term at AGS, I was pleasantly surprised to receive the sum of fifteen shillings as a refund for my bus fares. Delighted, I stopped at Weatherby's en route home and for the first time purchased a book with my "own" money – the Complete Works of Lewis Carroll in the fine Nonsuch edition. On the bus ride home I discovered how much he had written apart from the two "Alice" books I already knew so well. Thus began a lifetime of almost obsessive book purchases, with which I built up a very impressive and eclectic library.

Bicycling in the villages around Waddesdon I saw the imagery of Keats's "Ode to Autumn" visibly embodied in the mellow fruitfulness of cottage gardens. In September, I picked pounds of blackberries from the fertile hedges around the village. Even at home, we were harvesting the apples from the tree behind our house and the plum tree outside the kitchen window supplied us with an abundance of fruit, which my mother learned to bottle once she had made as much jam as our meager sugar rations allowed.

Indeed, we had become farmers. My father, ever ready to experiment with new interests and occupations, and impelled by a desire to supplement what could be purchased either at the village grocery or, on market days, in Aylesbury, decided to go further than growing a variety of vegetables. We had over an acre of land behind the house, a large part of which remained vacant even after we had planted potatoes, cabbages, marrows, beans and peas, celery and cucumbers and even a strawberry patch. We kept some thirty chickens, which provided us with a steady supply of unrationed eggs, as well as the joy (accompanied by the considerable care required to ensure that the brooding hens did not trample either on the eggs or on the newly hatched chicks once these appeared) of seeing the little fluffy yellow balls break out of the shells and watching them grow.

Encouraged by our success with chickens, my father decided to purchase some turkeys, but these proved to be far more temperamental than the placid hens. No sooner had the hen turkey laid a couple of eggs, than she flew up on to the roof of the coop my father had bought to house her and her mate. It was much higher than the chicken coop and its roof could not easily be reached. Unable to lure the bird down with either food or water, my father set up a ladder, hoping to catch her by the legs and bring her down by force. Hardly had he reached the roof, than the bird hopped to the far end of the coop; up went my father on the other side, and away went the bird. Thus the battle continued, my father reluctant to admit defeat, the bird determined to remain aloof, insouciant regarding the fate of its young. The eggs were never hatched, the turkey hen died of starvation – but my father remained obstinate. New turkeys were brought in, this time proving less temperamental, and finally we were the proud breeders of our own turkey chicks.

My father then decided to branch out further. He bought a calf, but it proved so ferocious that my mother and I refused to enter the field in order to feed the chickens and my father was forced to sell it, unfortunately at a loss. He then went on to sheep, not realising that they have to be frequently moved from one field to another if they are not to develop foot disease. Smirking, our more expert country neighbours observed these ventures, none of them ever deigning to advise my father before he made a purchase, but never failing, after the event, to explain why he had been mistaken.

This happened again when my father decided to dig a pool in order to keep some ducks. No neighbour bothered to warn him that the ground was unsuitable and that, within a matter of days, the water would be absorbed into the porous local soil. My father, the initiator of all these investments in livestock, was not, however, their major caretaker. That task was left to my mother, who found it far from congenial, though she competently utilised the varied fruits of our farming to provide delicious meals that were produced with unfailing regularity and fascinating variety.

One stormy day I returned home from school to find her, a winter coat draped over head and shoulders, running out of the front gate to the stationer's shop a few houses down our street. In consternation, I enquired where she was going in such extraordinary garb and at this strange time of day, when she would usually be preparing dinner. "I'm going for the ducks," she explained bitterly. These creatures had scrambled out of the pond and through the hedge into the stationer's back garden, where they were devouring his greens. Joining my mother, I helped her chase the birds, which obstinately refused to return via the hedge through which they had come. We had no alternative but to pursue them around the garden, pick them up, grasp them as firmly as possible under our arms and return them, one by one, to our own premises. No sooner had we successfully brought in one pair and set out for another, than we found the first pair busily scrabbling through the hedge to reach the inviting greens. This pursuit continued for about an hour, until my mother and I, drenched to the skin, angry and exhausted, decided to abandon the chase and await my father's return from town.

The ducks bedded down for the night and the next morning, assisted by our handyman-gardener, my father somehow drove them back home, fixed up a wire fence between us and the sadly depleted greens, telephoned the slaughterer and, albeit reluctantly, abandoned duck-rearing. His decision came none too soon, for a few days later there was no water in the pond and we were left with only an ugly, swampy patch of ground to remind us of this particular venture.

It was not until later, that I learned of the Holocaust and the extinction of the Jewish communities of Europe. I was unaware that among those murdered soon after the German occupation of Poland were my Uncle Mendel, his wife and my three pretty cousins. Since I learned that fact, I have felt considerable guilt at my own carefree existence at that same time.

Although my father was better informed, he kept the knowledge away from us – for what reason, I do not, and shall never, know. Paradoxically, the war years were among the happiest I spent in England. We were far away from the blitz, though on one occasion a German bomber returning to base released some incendiary bombs over the village, one of which landed in our front garden. We had spent the evening at Warmstone, my uncle's home about half a mile away, and had been followed, annoyingly, by Rip, his terrier, whom we tried in vain to shoo back to his own home. Soon after we had gone to bed, leaving Rip outside in the hope that he would go away, he began a frantic barking. My father went back downstairs in order to quiet him. On opening the door, he found our front hedge in flames, Rip still barking and neighbours appearing at their windows to see the cause of the unwonted commotion. The fire was soon extinguished and Rip gratefully admitted to the kitchen to spend the night in comfort, as a reward for so cleverly alerting us to peril.

Until 1944, when for several days convoys of army lorries passed through the village in an unceasing flow, announcing without a word the impending invasion of Europe, the village remained totally immune to what was happening elsewhere. Most of the evacuees, finding no suitable accommodation or employment in the village, returned to London or went elsewhere within months of arrival. Some, like my own family, set up businesses in Aylesbury, or, like my father, from time to time commuted to London to keep up whatever business they had run there.

I made new friends at school, growing particularly close to my fellow pupils once we were in the Sixth Form, which was comparatively small because most of our classmates had left at the age of sixteen, once they had, or had not, passed the Lower School Certificate. By this time, the girls and boys, both locals and Londoners, had been gathered in one class, though for most of the hours we spent at school we were divided according to our electives, the science pupils sharing virtually no lessons with those of us who had chosen the humanities.

In my memory, most of the time seems to have been summer, and those summers appear to have been spent playing tennis (at which I became sufficiently proficient to play for the school in competition against visiting schools from the surrounding towns) and watching cricket, which I learnt to appreciate under the tutelage of our art teacher, Mr. Harrison, who, himself an addict of the game, would take us out to sketch from the pavilion, interspersing his instruction with comments on the progress of the game.

I read a great deal, particularly in the winter months, when the entire family sat in our parlour, snug and warm with an anthracite stove, listening to the radio, which continued to provide BBC staples such as the wonderfully comic ITMA, acronym for It's That Man Again, in reference to its star, Tommy Handley, who appeared together with a singular cast of characters, each of whom had defining speech-characteristics and catchphrases that helped distinguish one from another. One such was Mrs. Mopp, the charwoman, whose opening query was always "Can I do you now, sir?" This, as well as other catchphrases, rapidly entered British idiom.

In addition, my brother and I became addicts of the AFN (American Forces Network), where we first encountered American comedy shows, such as those featuring Jack Benny, Fred Allen, George Burns and Gracie

Allen, and also the great band leaders of swing – Harry James, Jimmy and Tommy Dorsey, Duke Ellington, Louis Armstrong and Glenn Miller.

Among the closest of my friends were two Londoners, one of them Jewish. Her name was Doris Lewis, and she lived in Aylesbury itself, with her widowed mother and older sister, Lily. Doris, too, studied English and History and was a clever, diligent pupil, whose only hope of going to university lay in her winning a state scholarship which would cover the fees her mother could never afford to pay. This she duly did. Indeed, we Londoners proved to be the brightest stars in the school's firmament.

With another classmate I maintained contact for much longer, because he was accepted to Cambridge. M.P. (Martin Peter) Frankel had the distinction of being the son of a Member of Parliament and himself hoped to add the same initials to his surname as already preceded it. He had a freckled face, an undisguisably "Jewish" hooked nose, and, unlike the other boys, who invariably wore sports jackets and slacks, occasionally appeared at school in an elegant dark blue or grey suit. His father, Dan Frankel, a tailor by profession and a member of the Labour Party, represented the overwhelmingly Jewish working class constituency of Mile End, where his main rival was another Jew, Harry Politt, a member of the small, radical, Communist Party. Martin was staunchly left-wing, as were most of the Jews in Britain at the time, and he had no intention of concealing his political opinions. These were not, however, the predominant views of the conservative provincial society in which we now lived. Once, following the German invasion of the Soviet Union which transformed the Russians into Britain's allies, we pupils were enthusiastically singing the Internationale at a school assembly, as part of the repertoire of allied national anthems which we had duly memorized in English translation. One of the teachers, who had sat through the Marseillaise and "Poland's might is not departed," abruptly got up and demonstratively left the hall, obviously finding this rallying call of the downtrodden workers too much to swallow, allies or no allies.

Martin Frankel was a year older than I, but in the Sixth Form, in which we spent our final two years of school, pupils of both years studied together and age became less of a barrier than it was in the lower classes. Martin Frankel turned me into a public speaker. I had on occasion spoken briefly and far from memorably from the floor, but one day I found myself chosen to second Frankel in proposing a distinctly political topic related to war crimes. At home, I composed a carefully argued presentation and, on the morning of the debate, showed it to him, ardently hoping it would meet with his approval. It did not. "This isn't a speech, it's an essay," he snarled at me contemptuously and took my speech away to rewrite its arguments in a rhetorical style better calculated to arouse passionate feeling rather than appeal to the rational mind. Cowed, I read the speech that had been written for me, investing it with all the ardour that its style required. We won the vote with an overwhelming majority and I found myself surrounded by admiring fellow pupils and even staff members, who for days complimented me on my eloquence.

We were studying Rostand's *Cyrano de Bergerac* at the time and I experienced some guilt at being like the handsome Christian benefitting from his ugly friend's poetic skills to win the hand of Roxanne. But Frankel never revealed that he, not I, had authored the fiery speech and I continued to benefit from this initial experience, gradually developing a no less successful debating style of my own, which however, like his, relied on dramatic emphases, repetitions, rhetorical questions and scornful satirical dismissals of my opponents' specious arguments.

★★★

How was it that, in a region where no Jews had ever lived until the outbreak of the war, there should nonetheless be virulent anti-Semitism? (The Rothschilds were not identified as Jewish by their tenants, most of whom in any case never came into close contact with their landlord.) This question began to exercise my mind almost immediately after my arrival in Waddesdon, for I soon encountered preconceptions and prejudices founded on deep-rooted mythological stereotypes which stunned me with their primitivity. In all seriousness, one of my neighbours, a girl slightly younger than myself, who waited with me every morning for the bus that took us to Aylesbury, asked me to show her where we Jews kept our horns. From her I also learned that the entire village was convinced that we had built a munitions factory under the field behind our house. When I hotly denied this allegation, she smiled slyly and said, "Well, of course, you can't *talk* about it, can you? I mean, it's a war secret." At school, frequent allegations were leveled at Jews as being black-marketeers.

I felt helpless, unable to combat this suspicion and hostility. Anything I said was perceived as the deception natural to the tribe that killed Christ (another allegation frequently flung at me). I did not want to trouble my parents with my own perplexities and tribulations, but soon the insults and allegations became too much for me to bear. One day, in the school grounds, as I was about to enter the building after the lunch break, two boys hissed "Dirty Jew!" as I passed them. At a loss as to how to respond, I continued on my way trying to look as though I had not heard, but when I reached the classroom and found Martin Frankel there, I tearfully told him of the incident. To my surprise, he marched out of the room without a word, returning only after the next lesson had just begun. A few minutes later, the school secretary arrived and called me to the headmaster's study. Appalled, I wondered what I had done to warrant such a summons, which usually involved punishment or rebuke. In the study, I found myself face to face with my two tormentors, who glared at me angrily. Mr. Furneaux turned to them and uttered just two words, "Now, apologise!" The culprits muttered a few indistinguishable words and suddenly I felt as though I were the guilty party. Confused, I began to dismiss the apology. "It's not that *I'm* offended," I lied. "It's my *people* you've insulted." I could find no words to convey to them how hurt I was. I knew they now hated me more than ever and that this conversation would serve only to exacerbate their loathing, since my "tale-telling" (they were unaware that it was Frankel who had reported the incident) had got them into trouble.

Sure enough, the harassment continued. The next morning, when I came into the library, which served as the sixth form classroom, all my books had been swept off the shelf assigned to me, pages had been torn out of my neatly-kept loose-leaf files and everything lay scattered on the floor. I did not dare to complain, fearing that further punishment would only arouse fiercer responses. I was most afraid of physical attack. I had seen Chaplin's *The Great Dictator* and feared being beaten up, having my head bashed against the school's stone wall, being waylaid on my way to the bus terminal, perhaps even being pushed under a passing vehicle.

But above all, I was troubled by the awareness that this attack on me was in fact based on a distorted perception of our entire race. Naively thinking that increased knowledge would bring about a change of heart, I asked my father to bring me a supply of pamphlets published by the Board of Deputies of British Jews, which detailed the Jewish contribution to civilization at large and to European culture in particular. These I left in conspicuous places around the library.

But what were monotheism and the observance of a weekly day of rest from physical labour, Einstein and Freud, to these country louts? I doubt whether they even looked inside the pamphlets, the covers of which were soon defaced, the pages torn out and the entire stock eventually consigned contemptuously to the wastepaper basket.

Defeated in my attempt at enlightenment, I shrank into a shell of self-protection, trying to efface myself, never to refer to my Jewishness, my religious beliefs and customs. Far from expressing pride in my identity, I tried as best as I could to obliterate the differences between myself and my English classmates. When in their company I as it were detached my Jewish self, which I could express and gratify in the privacy of my home. I even began attending morning prayers, from which I could have been excused. Only with Doris [friend] could I be open and frank, and alone together we would often mock the boorishness and ignorance which characterized the majority of pupils in the lower classes, most of whom could hardly wait for the moment when they would legally be able to give up attending school.

This response to torment was one way of coping with the persecution resulting from being "other," "different." As I discovered later, when I met Martin Frankel again at Cambridge, he was to choose a very different route.

I also had a boyfriend in the village, where I struck up a relationship with one of the inmates at The Cedars. Early in 1939, the Rothschilds had put this imposing residence, the largest house in the village, which derived its name from two large trees in its front garden, at the disposal of a Jewish boys' orphanage from Frankfurt, which was headed by the Germanic formal Dr. Steinhardt. Several Jewish parents had seized the opportunity of saving their sons by sending them off together with the genuine orphans, who were comparatively few in number. The boys ranged in age from thirteen to seventeen. Only those who were below the official school-leaving age of fourteen were permitted to continue their education, either at the village school or, in the case of one of them, at Aylesbury Grammar. One other exception was a seventeen-year-old named Herbert Tint, who went to school in Bletchley rather than, like myself, in the nearest town. I never learned why he was thus singled out, unless it was because he appeared more talented than his fellows. Possibly his parents had been able to send him off with some money, which enabled him to cover the school fees.

In any case, he soon asked me to go for walks with him on those weekends on which he returned to Waddesdon, about once every three weeks, and we discovered many common interests in reading, music and films. I think he felt a certain superiority to the boys at The Cedars and that I somehow satisfied his need to demonstrate that superiority vis-à-vis the others by showing them that he had a relationship with a member of one of the "superior" families in the village.

I became acquainted with The Cedars primarily because the Steinhardts had two daughters, one of whom was my age, the other a year or so older. There were two more young girls among the evacuees, both of them also refugees from Germany. One of them was a distant relative; her mother, who had died some years earlier, was the sister of my aunt by marriage, Esther, the wife of one of my father's brothers, who had, like us, lived in Essen. It was natural that the five of us would form a kind of clique and equally natural that we would most frequently meet at The Cedars, rather than at my home or in the small cottage rooms occupied by the other two families, who had not even found (or had not been able to afford) houses to rent.

But in addition to these meetings, my father's connection with The Cedars also brought me into contact with the residents there. Having both organised and led the prayers for the High Holy Days that occurred soon after our arrival in Waddesdon, he had rapidly discerned that Dr. Steinhardt, a typically semi-assimilated German Jew, lacked not only the knowledge required to give his charges an adequate Jewish education but even the desire to provide it. With his usual sense of personal responsibility, my father therefore offered to procure an appropriate teacher and also (presumably in order to overcome any possible opposition) to pay his salary.

At first, my brother and I also participated in these classes, but it rapidly became clear that our knowledge far outstripped that of even the most talented of the Cedars boys and so Mr. Kurenitz came to us every Sunday, to instruct us in what was his specialty, Hebrew grammar. My brother, having attended a Jewish secondary school, was proficient even in this and thus able to progress to more interesting material such as Bible and even the classical poetry of the Middle Ages. Throughout the four years that preceded my departure for Cambridge, I was stuck with the repetitious conjugating and parsing which I loathed, with only very occasionally the relief of reading a few verses of Bible.

I tried as often as possible to cancel my lessons, pleading a headache or excess of homework to be done by Monday morning, but my father was too intent on my having a proper command of the language to let me off entirely and if a lesson was cancelled on Sunday, I found it rescheduled for the middle of the week, when I usually *did* have a considerable amount of homework and, in addition, wanted to be free to listen to the radio or to read.

Thus the time passed. I was, on the whole, extremely happy. I had become close to my brother, with whom I shared not only a fondness for the same books and radio programmes, but also a bedroom, where we chatted and exchanged jokes before falling asleep. We went for walks together and he helped me with my homework, when necessary. The range and depth of his knowledge never ceased to amaze me.

A year after our move to Waddesdon, he left to study at the London School of Economics, which had, like a number of other London colleges, been evacuated to Cambridge. From there, early in 1943, he sent me the requisite forms for application to both the Cambridge women's colleges and so it was really he whom I have to thank for the fact that, in October 1944, I found myself a first-year student at Newnham.

Upon visiting Aylesbury Grammar to say goodbye before my family's post-war return to London, I discovered that none of the evacuees who had distinguished themselves by winning State Scholarships, exhibitions or comparable university awards, had been listed on the school's Honour Board. We were, to the last, "foreigners," outsiders, even though, by failing to note our achievements, the school was depriving itself of the distinction of having enabled us to achieve our success. It was a true case of provincial xenophobia and of shortsightedly cutting off one's nose to spite one's face.

BRIAN TESLER –
BUCKS AND ME

Adapted by the author from his family memoir, *Before I Forget*, published by Mind Advertising Ltd, 2006.[110] Brian Tesler CBE had a long career in television as a producer and a director chairman of London Weekend Television amongst many other illustrious roles.

Before the Second World War, my family – David, Stella, my seven-year old sister Rosalind and eleven-year old me – lived in Markmanor Avenue in Walthamstow and my Uncle Mick Chason, Auntie Eve and their little son Derek lived in Clapton, both in East London.

In the spring months and early summer of 1939, war between Britain and Germany seemed inevitable, and Londoners didn't need the gloomy prophecies of the newspapers to believe that, if it came, London would be the immediate and principal target of Nazi air-raids, bombs and poison gas. The Government decided on the mass evacuation of London's most vulnerable inhabitants – children, pregnant women, mothers with babies and pre-school children – taking them out of densely populated areas like the East End and the docks and into the presumed safety of the countryside, moving no fewer than three-quarters of a million people in a mass military-style exercise.

Markmanor Avenue and Clapton were not in the East End and the Teslers and Chasons were not among those scheduled for evacuation, but we still felt vulnerable enough to want to get out of London, so we decided on an evacuation of our own. Uncle Mick was a salesman, and on his travels he had found a little house to rent on the Micklefield Estate, a new building development on the outskirts of High Wycombe. On Friday, September 1, 1939, the two families piled into Uncle Mick's white van and made their way into the countryside. Micklefield Estate was then a vast area of new, characterless houses in a grid of rigidly straight streets, but happily for us the house Uncle Mick had rented was at the end of the Estate and beyond us were the glorious woods and fields of Buckinghamshire.

By the Sunday morning of that first weekend, the families having sorted out the accommodation and finished the unpacking, my mother and Auntie Eve prepared lunch while Rosalind and I and little cousin Derek went exploring. We wandered for hours, collecting baskets of delicious cob nuts, this being the season for them, and made our way back to our new home in the glorious autumn sunshine. We were greeted with gloomy faces. This was Sunday, the third of September, 1939; Prime Minister Chamberlain had made a statement on the radio while we were out. England was at war with Germany.

And nothing happened.

No air-raids, no bombs, no poison gas.

The newspapers began to call this The Phoney War, and by Christmas half the evacuees had drifted back to London, including the Chasons. The Teslers stayed on for a few weeks longer. It was impractical to maintain a house just for the four of us, so we knocked on doors and found a family on the edge of the estate that would rent us a room in their little bungalow.

Our accommodation was cramped; the bungalow was in the middle of a plot of totally uncultivated land – no, not land: *earth*. The family kept chickens – scores and scores of chickens; the weather was atrocious; and the earth surrounding the bungalow quickly turned to mud. All I remember of that awful period is mud, rain and the all-pervading smell and sight of chicken-pooh. I couldn't wait to get home, which we did before the end of the year.

That was my first experience of living in Buckinghamshire. The second was very different.

The Phoney War became very real four months later. German armies invaded first Denmark and Norway, then Belgium and Holland; and then France. Outnumbered and out-manoeuvred, the Allied forces on the continent were on the run. They began to be evacuated from Dunkirk and other ports along the French coast and Hitler prepared to invade England. When he failed to win mastery of the air in the Battle of Britain he tried to undermine the nation's will to resist invasion by razing our major cities to the ground, starting with the capital itself, and the nine horrendous months of The Blitz began in September 1940.

Incredibly, Walthamstow was unscathed during its early weeks. As far as we knew, not a bomb fell on it. Every evening, when the air-raid sirens wailed, the Tesler family made its way down to my maternal grandmother's house at No. 13 and into her Anderson shelter. In the morning, as the sirens sounded the blissful All Clear, we'd make our way home again to wash and brush up and have a little breakfast. My father would go off to his millinery factory in the City and I would go off to school.

And then, one night early in the November of 1940, the noise of aircraft and guns and exploding bombs seemed louder and nearer to No.13 than usual. When the All Clear sounded and we walked back up the Avenue to our own house we could see neighbours gathered in the street and a rescue team at work in front of some heavily damaged houses a few doors further up. Markmanor Avenue had suffered a direct hit.

No-one had been hurt and No.44 had suffered no damage, but my parents thought it was time for another evacuation, and quick. They talked to friends of theirs, Mr and Mrs Lewin, who were similarly concerned, and within days the Lewins had closed up their flat in the Finchley Road and collected us in their large saloon car and we were on our way to High Wycombe once more. I could not know, and would not have believed, that we would never live in Markmanor Avenue, or Walthamstow again.

The Lewins had heard from friends that Holmer Green, a little village between High Wycombe and Amersham in Buckinghamshire, was a pleasant place in which to live, and since this time we had no Uncle Mick to pre-plan and pre-arrange our accommodation, the four adults decided that we would simply drive there and knock on doors, as we ourselves had done the previous year at the end of our stay on the
Micklefield Estate.

Mr and Mrs Lewin fairly quickly found a cottage in Holmer Green itself that could take in the two of them, but it wasn't so easy for a family of four. This was a small village with small dwelling-places and we had exhausted its possibilities in only an hour or so of fruitless knocking on its doors; so we decided to look beyond it. The Lewins drove us around until we discovered a pleasant little lane just outside the village, off the road to High Wycombe, with a white-washed house at its end which seemed large enough to accommodate another four people. We knocked on the door and, weary and despondent by now, explained our problem.

The very pleasant lady of the house, Mrs Salethorn, invited us in for a cup of tea and having given us the once-over said she thought that, since her husband was away in the Army, her daughter Jean could sleep in her bedroom, so if the four of us were prepared to share the other bedroom we might all be able to make a go of it. The Teslers could more or less take over the sitting room although Jean, who was about a year older than me, would have to come into it to practise her piano-playing; and we could share the scullery and the kitchen, which was furnished with a large table and enough chairs for us all to have our meals around it.

"And the bathroom?" my mother asked.

"Bless you, there's no bathroom: you won't find a bathroom anywhere in the village, my dears; we bring the tin bath into the scullery from the garden shed whenever we need a bath and fill it with water we've boiled up on the kitchen range– but there's a basin in the bedroom and a jug that you can fill from the scullery tap so you can wash yourselves any time you like."

"A jug and basin?"

"Yes dear."

"And" – my mother said, rather quaveringly – "the toilet?"

"Oh that's outside of course."

"Yes. Of course."

And so it was; a little wooden hut, with a little wooden seat, and torn-up newspapers on a hook for lavatory paper, and no chain to pull because there was no running water: the bucket had to be emptied regularly into a covered cess-pit in a neighbouring field, which council workers cleared every week or so. Ah well, we felt, if that's how you live in the country, that's how the Teslers will live.

And that's exactly how we did live for the next two years. Once we had sorted ourselves out and fallen into a practical routine, they were good and happy years. The bed in our bedroom was just about big enough to accommodate my parents, and my father in any case was going to have to spend his weekdays in London, coming out by train and bus to join us at the weekend. They bought camp-beds for Rosalind and me; and any family belongings that wouldn't fit into the chest of drawers and wardrobe in our bedroom were installed in the sitting room below.

We got on well with the Salethorns and happily ate our meals together during the week, joined by Corporal Salethorn on the rare occasions that he was on leave. At the weekends, when my father was with us, the Salethorns would let the Teslers catch up on their respective weekday news and had their own meals separately at different times. The village was a pretty and friendly one, well served by buses that ran between High Wycombe and Amersham. High Wycombe itself was an agreeable market town with good shops and three cinemas; the countryside surrounding us was beautiful and welcoming; the air was fresh and clean. And it was so quiet: there were no air-raids, no anti-aircraft guns to disturb our sleep...But shouldn't I be going to school?

In Walthamstow, in September 1939, I had left Sybourn Street Elementary School, a little mixed school where boys and girls of different religions – Jewish, Protestant, Catholic – happily and unquestioningly mingled. Sir George Monoux Secondary Grammar, to which I had managed to achieve entry, was a very different proposition. It was clearly more upmarket than Sybourn Street and it wasn't at all welcoming. It was an all-boys school, and I appeared to be its only Jewish boy.

In the school playground, during the mid-morning break a few days into the beginning of the autumn term, I had found myself in the middle of a ring of threatening, grim-faced eleven-year olds who were calling me "Jew boy!" and accusing me of having killed Jesus Christ: I mean, literally, they were crying out "You killed Jesus! You killed Jesus!" Me? Me, personally? I didn't know what on earth they were talking about.

I went home for lunch that day very unhappy indeed, and it didn't take my mother long to realise that something was wrong. It took her even less to persuade me to tell her what had happened; whereupon she said "Right! Get your cap!", put on her coat, marched me back to school, demanded to see the head and gave him a large and forceful piece of her mind. He apologised for the behaviour of what he was certain was only a small and untypical group of pupils and said he would see that it didn't happen again. I had to tell him the names of those responsible and he obviously had a word with them, and it didn't happen again; but now I had the reputation of being a sneak, and a baby for having to have my mother fight my battles for me, and the school became even less congenial than before.

What was it John Betjeman said in his mock denunciation of wartime Slough– "Come, friendly bombs, and fall on Slough"? The bomb that dropped on Markmanor Avenue was friendly for me, as well as timely.

It rescued me from a school in which I had never felt comfortable and which was never likely to help me realise whatever potential I might have possessed. But was I going to be any more fortunate with a Buckinghamshire alternative?

There were secondary grammar schools in both Amersham and High Wycombe, but High Wycombe was nearer and the Royal Grammar School in High Wycombe sounded grander, so when my mother thought I'd had more than enough time away from study it was to the Royal Grammar School that she took me for an interview with its Head.

The interview was pleasant enough, but at the end of it the Head informed us that, alas, his school was completely full and there was no room for me in it. However, the reason why the Royal Grammar School was short of space was that a London Grammar School had been evacuated to it and was currently occupying a third of its classrooms. This school, the Chiswick County School for Boys, might possibly have a place for me. So, a phone call from one Head to another, a walk along the corridor to another part of the building, an interview with another Headmaster, the formidable Dr Carran, and I was in. The former pupil of a snooty, anti-Semitic East London school was now the pupil of a totally unfamiliar West London school billeted on another school in the middle of the Buckinghamshire countryside. Had I gone from the frying-pan to the fire?

In one wonderful, liberating, energising word: No!

In the months that followed, I found to my delight that Chiswick County was a marvellous school: friendly, receptive, with enlightened teachers, a decent but not exacting standard of sport and physical training and a reputation for first-class school plays which instinctively intrigued me. On that first interview day, Dr Carran showed my mother and me round the school, and in the assembly hall we saw the boys rehearsing a production of Julius Caesar with impressive scenery and full stage lighting. Now *this* was a school! As for anti-Semitism: I discovered in due course that nearly half the boys in the class I was to join were Jewish; I never experienced anti-Semitism in school again.

The next two years were pretty idyllic. I enjoyed school, and got on well with both teachers and fellow-pupils. Once we had accustomed ourselves to the rural way of life in Holmer Green the family found it pleasant and relaxing. Rosalind was happy in the village school; we got used to having our weekly baths in the tin tub dragged into the kitchen; we even got used to the outside loo, though we cursed it in the winter months. There was always a good movie on in one or other of High Wycombe's three cinemas. And the BBC had launched a morale-boosting new radio service – The Forces Programme – introducing us for the first time to legendary American radio series like The Bob Hope Show, The Jack Benny Show and The Fred Allen Show as well as its own new wartime light entertainment productions like Garrison Theatre, Happidrome, ITMA and Much Binding in the Marsh.

My father spent every weekend with us, and every now and again he would take us all to the movies in High Wycombe, sometimes including the Salethorns. I remember the joint excursion to the Rex – including Jean's father, who was on leave that weekend – to see Charlie Chaplin's The Great Dictator early in 1941. Dad was particularly pleased with this film, not just because he thought Chaplin was funny and its satirical treatment of Hitler and Mussolini inspiring but because he was proud that this genius Chaplin was Jewish. Jewish people like to think that their heroes, especially the artistic ones, are also Jewish, and that's particularly easy to believe of film stars, so: "Did you know that Tony Curtis is Jewish? And Lauren Bacall? And Leslie Howard? and Kirk Douglas? and Hedy Lamarr?" In actual fact, all these others are or were Jewish. Chaplin wasn't.

The idyll wasn't to last.

Chiswick County School for Boys had evacuated itself to the safety of the countryside at the beginning of the war, as so many schools had done. Not all its pupils had chosen to go with it, however, and by the Christmas of 1939, when the war still appeared phoney, some of those who had fled to the country drifted back to London with their families, which is why there had been room in its High Wycombe contingent for me. Those who had stayed in Chiswick and those who had gone back to join them needed to continue their education, but they couldn't use the School's premises in Burlington Lane because the Office of Works had requisitioned them.

They had found an alternative home in the old Victorian building vacated by Isleworth County School when its own new School was completed. But now, early in 1942, the Chiswick School's own buildings were being relinquished by the Government, so at the end of the Spring term it was able to announce that at the beginning of the Autumn term both its sections would be going back to Chiswick, to be united once again on the school's old site.

My parents found themselves in a serious dilemma. I was very happy at Chiswick County and working well in it. What were they to do? Remain in Holmer Green and get me into the Royal Grammar School, to start all over again with new teachers and new schoolmates? Go back to Walthamstow to pick up where I had left off in a school with unhappy memories of both teachers and pupils?

What they did, and what I will always be profoundly grateful for, was remarkable. They decided that the family would go back to Chiswick with the County School. David and Stella would tear up their East End roots and move to the other side of London – the other side of the moon as far as they were concerned – to a West London suburb of which they knew nothing and where they knew nobody, simply to ensure that I could continue my education with a school I was happy in. I would owe everything in my future education and professional career to that decision and I would never forget it.

But I would never forget Bucks either. It had not only given me two idyllic years in the healthiest and most beautiful of settings. It had also, by pure chance, in one of life's little ironies, given me the school and the education that would shape my career. So thank you, Bucks!

MAIDS MORETON HOSTEL

My name is Susan Hatton (née Jones). I can remember about what we called *The Jews Hostel* – politically incorrect now but that is what it was called in the early 1940s.

I grew up in the village of Maids Moreton. The Hostel was situated on the left hand side of the main road into Buckingham. As far as I can remember it was two long prefabricated buildings. I assume one for women and one for men. [Plans discovered by a local resident, and shared with Susan Hatton, revealed separate male and female blocks.]

We would see the people who lived in the Hostel going for long walks, around Foxcote and into Buckingham. They didn't buy from village shops but had their own food delivered. As children, going into Buckingham, we would be intrigued by their festivals, especially weddings which took place under a canopy.

As far as I can remember, the men wore skull caps and the women were plainly dressed. But then we all were in those days of rationing. They smiled at us children as they passed us but had little conversation. I do not know if they spoke English. Certainly we were brought up to respect each other's way of life but they kept very much to themselves.

In early 2005 my brother asked the question "What became of the people who lived in the Hostel?" This was a good question and I was determined to look into it so I wrote to the Jewish Board of Great Britain who looked into it for me. They heard back from someone living in New York. I was able to fit another piece of the jigsaw together and wrote an article, *A Wartime Hostel*,[111] in which a German Jewish refugee stated:

In December 1948, my sister, Erna (Chava) Bernet (who was not a member of the 'kibbutz') was married there to a member, Herbert (Michael) Kahn. Shortly after that, the majority of the members emigrated to Israel, where they founded a kibbutz, Lavi, in the Galilee near the Horns of Hittim, about half way between Nazareth and Tiberias. Lavi today is today a flourishing kibbutz with agriculture, industry, restaurant and guest house.

Furthermore, local resident to the area, Geoff Kirk, uncovered a tragic incident. Refugee of only twenty-one years of age, Julius Plaat was killed in a road accident on his way to work, opposite Wootton's bakery.[112]

Geoff also found an article in the *Buckingham Advertiser*, following the inquest, which stated Platt was 'due at 7.30 a.m. that morning at Mr Fisher's farm, Chetwode.' The doctor at the scene described, 'definite wheel marks on the abdomen' caused by the lorry. Julias Platt, who had fled Nazism for the freedom of England, died two hours after the accident.

Geoff Kirk also discovered a conflict between a landlady, Mrs Lines and Mr Bryant.[113] Both were members of the council. The latter expressed disgust, to the council, at the state of houses being rented at exorbitant fees to evacuees. He commented of the rat-infested house, 'Any night the ceiling may drop down in both bed-rooms. You can push them up in places with your hands...' Then came the defence for the tenant, who it seems was attacked by the landlady for her religion. Mr Bryant continued, 'I will never allow a respectable woman, Jewess or not, to be abused in this Council Chamber: especially one who has no home and whose husband and six brothers are fighting for us. I call it disgraceful. This Jewess is proud of her religion.' The council were unable to help the tenant, who had moved there after being 'bombed out', as she refused to complain.

Geoff Kurt also found an article, about an *alien* summoned for not registering a change of address, when she moved to Padbury for employment.[114] German Jewish Paula Theresa Goldmann was the first to be facing prosecution at Aylesbury despite the Metropolitan police, from where she was first living, not taking up the case. It highlighted a problem of not having instructions given directly at police stations. Instead, rules were printed in the media, and individuals expected to know them. The charges were dropped, for a fine, as it was concluded there was "a certain amount of wrong and a certain amount of right."

It is to be hoped living conditions were better in Maids Moreton Hostel, which was actually part of a kibbutz.

The Vow: Rebuilding the Fachler Tribe after the Holocaust

Summarised from Yanky Fachler's book.

Based on the journals of Eva and Eli Fachler[115].

Yanky Fachler's parents, Eli and Eva (Hebrew name Chava) both came on the Kindertransport train to Britain. They didn't know each other then, but before long they would meet and marry in Buckinghamshire.

In their wisdom, the British proceeded to intern many of the 'lucky' few thousand German Jewish refugees who had managed to enter Britain as enemy aliens. They were sent to internment camps on the Isle of Man, Canada and in Australia (where the British have a habit of sending their unwanted). The order specifically covered 16 to 60 year-olds in the north and east of Scotland, and the coastal areas of the east and south of England. Fortunately for Eli, the General Internment Order distinguished between enemy aliens (people with German, Austrian or stateless passports) and friendly aliens. Eli's Polish passport meant that he belonged to the latter category. The police came to examine Alien Registration Certificates at his school for Jewish refugees in Whittingehame, Scotland. The school was meant to be a safe haven, a place to learn agricultural skills for a future in some other country. At aged eighteen they would no longer be allowed to remain in Britain. The police took away 36 pupils over the age of 16 who were designated enemy aliens, as well as half the madrichim [teachers]. Many of Eli's friends were included in the round up.

Accompanied by British soldiers, they were taken south to Lingfield Racecourse, which had been turned into a POW camp for 500 German sailors caught in British ports at the outbreak of war. The Germans had established an efficient Nazi organisation in the camp, and the arrival of Jewish youngsters was a recipe for trouble. Before the Germans were shipped off to Canada, there were frequent altercations between the two groups. The Whittingehame group did however befriend the Italians and a small group of anti-Nazi Germans. Most of Eli's friends were then sent to the Isle of Man.

By mid-August, the Home Secretary Herbert Morrison realised the idiocy of interning Jews. Most Jewish internees were released, including the Whittingehame contingent. But for the rest of the war, the released (and now friendly) aliens had to report to the police whenever they wanted to travel anywhere in the country. Eva was unaffected as a British subject.

Another internee who was sent to Canada was a young scholar named Joel Litke, who later married Eli's sister Miriam. Yoel was originally to have sailed to an internment camp in Canada aboard the Andora Star. Luckily, he was not on the vessel when it was torpedoed by U-boats, and over half the 2,000 internees and crew perished in the Atlantic. When he did eventually set sail for Canada, Joel was treated by the Canadian soldiers as if he were a Nazi.

Another internee was a young German rabbi called Asher Feuchtwanger, one of hundreds of internees who sailed to Australia in 1940 aboard the Dunera. A book has been written describing the horrific conditions of the trip and the even more horrific attitude of the British crew. Rabbi Feuchtwanger was later to become the communal rabbi of the Letchworth Jewish Congregation.

Eli Fachler was earmarked for Hachshara, the kibbutz-style communal farms under the auspices of the Ministry of Agriculture. This was via the Bachad, (a pre-war orthodox Zionist group of Germany, who trained in agriculture intending to live and work in Palestine, now Israel. Fleeing the Nazis they came to England for sanctuary and continued to learn how to tend the land). Eli was assigned to join the tiny Hachshara Kibbutz at Hardmead, near Newport Pagnell in Buckinghamshire in July 1941.

Land work was an important activity. The needs of the British Government and the goals of the Zionist movement converged to achieve an unusual symmetry and synergy during the war years. There were about half a dozen Hachshara kibbutzim in England, Wales and Scotland. There were also large contingents of Bachad youth in Grwych Castle (North Wales), Whittingehame Farm School, Manchester and Bedford.

Eli had been a member of his miniscule Bachad kibbutz in Hardmead for just a day or two when Eva found herself organising a summer camp on the same kibbutz. A couple of weeks after the summer camp, Eva's call-up papers arrived. What more natural, she thought, than to become a Land Girl together with a lovely bunch of youngsters working on the land in Buckinghamshire. The rest, as they say, is history.

Eli joined Hardmead on July 9th. On the 10th of July, his Aliens Registration Document was endorsed once more: "Permission is given for holder to commence work for Bucks War Agricultural Committee at Lodge Farm, Hardmead, Bucks."

Eli Fachler described the kibbutz:

Conditions at Hardmead were primitive in the extreme. You had to walk for over a mile along a path through the fields to reach the bus stop on the nearest main road connecting Bedford and Newport Pagnell. Water came from a spring in the field. The kibbutz numbered about 12 males and 6 females, including one married couple. We were housed in a cottage. I shared a room with a boy from Vienna. He was very frum, [Yiddish for devout] an academic type, and his name was Erich Roper.

Because Hardmead was so isolated in the middle of fields, we worked on surrounding farms as near to the kibbutz as possible. We got around either by walking or by bicycle. Our employers were the local War Agricultural Committee, a branch of the Ministry of Agriculture.

Our kibbutz may have been small, but we just about had a minyan, [prayer group of ten men] including boys from Frankfurt's Breuer yeshiva [Hebrew for place of study of Jewish text]. The girls included the daughter of Rabbi Joseph Carlebach from Altona, whose lectures had so inspired me... We had regular shiurim [Hebrew for lessons on Torah] in Hardmead on all manner of Jewish subjects.

Eva recalled:

I started corresponding with Hardmead about our Summer Camp, and found out that we could hire tents, and eat our meals in the kibbutz. I ordered beds, blankets and supplies...

We found a small house in the middle of fields, no gas, no running water – they had to use a pump. All very primitive, but very friendly. One of the group, Betty Einhorn, was a friend of ours from Frankfurt. She showed us the kitchen which was of course strictly kosher. Betty had told us that most of the group had gone to a nearby Hechalutz kibbutz to hear a lecture. By the time we were about to leave, they all returned, amongst them a tall, very good-looking fellow called Eli Fachler from Berlin.

I asked Betty about him and she told me that he had arrived only a day or so before, that he was much younger than he looked, and that he had come from Whittingehame Farm School. Fritta and I were very favourably impressed with Hardmead... Eli, and another chaver [Hebrew for friend], Heini Mehrgut, from Hamburg, were most attentive to me and we had a great time.

The Summer Camp was a great success. We had three young rabbinical students from Jews College as our spiritual leaders: Lippa Baum, Stanley Woolf and Immanuel Jakobowitz. Other participants included Israel Cohen and his sister Gita, Manny Lehman and his sister Hanna from Letchworth, my good friends Lola and Thea Eisemann, Jenny Wechsler and many more young people. The weather was good, the food excellent, and the atmosphere was terrific. There was another camp, from Bnei Akiva, [Jewish youth group] on a nearby field and we had long discussions, debates, shiurim and wonderful sing-songs on Shabbat. We left the camp with great reluctance but promised to correspond with our new friends.

Eli reflected on the first same meeting with Eva (Chava):

On that Sunday, we were visited by two young ladies from London who were members of the Ben Zackai Youth Group of the Adass in Stoke Newington, whose spiritual head was Rabbi Dr. Solomon Schonfeld (who himself had extricated almost 1,000 children from Europe before the war). Our visitors were Chava (Eva) Becker, aged 19, and Fritta Diller, aged 20. Their mission was to suss out the location, particularly the kashrut facilities, for a summer camp they were planning under canvass.

Three weeks later... Chava and her Ben Zackai camp descended on us, together with a camp from B'nei Akiva. We became friendly with all the chaverim from both camps, including Immanuel Jakobowitz, whose brother Georg had been my classmate in Berlin. One of our chaverim in Hardmead was Heini Mehrgut. I made a bet with him, over a small bar of Cadbury's chocolate that I would succeed in getting friendly with Chava. I won.

Chava and I went on bicycle rides to the local pub for cider (was I in contravention of the licensing laws?), conversing most of the time in French. If we had been overheard speaking German, we may have created the wrong impression.

After this Eva received her call-up papers and became a Land Girl with the Hachshara Kibbutz Movement. Eva even became the face of the Bachad recruitment posters. She moved to Hardmead, in September, 1941. Eli recalled 'certain boys belonged to certain girls: Leo and Zilly, Jack and Betty, Yoine and Eva. As a newcomer, she had better 'keep off'. That certainly restricted Chava's field of conquest.' Eli continued:

One Friday night around September, my roommate Erich Roper left the Shabbat candles on our table under my coat, absent minded as he was. Of course it caught fire, as we discovered to our horror during the Shabbat meal. Yoine and some others promptly grabbed some buckets of water and put the fire out – much against the objections of Erich who maintained that we should leave the house and let it burn down, as one is not allowed to be Mechallel Shabbat (break the Sabbath) for material things. Poor old Erich, he just could not think beyond that. He had no concept of Chillul Hashem [desecration of God's name and expectations] or Pikuach Nefesh, [all Sabbath laws can be discarded in order to save a life] he did not realise how delicate and precarious was our status as aliens in a country at war. Did he not know how many of our orthodox brethren did Fire Watch and Fire Fighting on a Friday night during London's Blitz?

Eli lost his clothes and photographs in the fire but there was already a move planned as Hardmead merged with Hachshara Kibbutz, Sealand. The joint kibbutz, with Manchester and London members, would be known as Buckingham. Many of them, as in Hardmead, had been to school in Grych Castle in Wales, the contemporary farm school established at the same time as Whittingehame, except that it consisted entirely of Bachad members.'

Eli's Aliens Registration Document stated: "Will move to The War Agricultural Hostel, Maids Morton Road, Buckingham, 23rd November 1941."

Eli described the new kibbutz:

After the primitive conditions of Hardmead, Buckingham represented a great leap in our standard of living. Accommodation was in purpose built Nissen Huts. One hut was the boys dormitory, (at 18, I was one of the youngest), one hut was the kitchen and dining room, one hut was for the girls, and one was the boiler room, washing facilities and toilets. There was also accommodation for our manager, Akiva Kornbluth and his wife Ray, and for the cook, Mrs. Epstein.

We were now over 50 people, over three times as many as our Hardmead group. The place had been built specially for us by the Ministry of Agriculture, who also organised our work schedules. The works organiser, Mr. Cranwell, who lived down the road, sent us out to work on various farms within a radius of about 20 miles. We mostly cycled to work. Larger groups were taken by vans or lorries.

Chava and I continued our relationship where we had left off, and got quite friendly. We attended lectures together at the neighbouring Hashomer kibbutz. Once we heard Manya Shochet, already then a legendary figure, a founder of the early kibbutzim... Chava and I went on shopping expeditions to Marks & Spencer in Bedford, and of course we continued our cycle rides to the Chester Arms for cider. I was just eighteen, and Chava nineteen and a half.

The work in Buckingham was much more varied than just digging ditches, which is what we had spent most our time doing in Hardmead. Chava did milking in Tring, thatching roofs near Buckingham, raising plants at nurseries in Bletchley (now Milton Keynes), and work in the kitchen and sewing room. I was sent out with gangs on harvesting and threshing work, and sometimes I went by myself to help with general farm work. In the winter, we burned bushes.

We were paid by the Ministry according to a National Agricultural Wages Scale. That scale paid according to age, length of service, and how skilled you were in a particular branch. As one of the youngest, I could not possibly have lived on the money I earned. But because we were a kibbutz, all our earnings went into a common kitty. We received our basics in clothing, food, and shelter, plus some pocket money to be spent as we liked.

The Vaad (Organising Committee) were Kulli Landau, Johnny Mantel and Henny Haskell. The works organiser was Eric Schneider who was responsible to two officers of the War Agricultural Committee.

Eva (Chava) explained procedures:

In true kibbutz fashion, we pooled our wages, had a well-equipped kitchen, washing machines and pantries. We had our office in the boys' hut. A large dining room which also served as our Synagogue was in the girls' hut. The girls took it in turn to work on "outside work", kitchen duties, washing and ironing and mending duties. We had sewing machines and some of the girls were sewing dresses etc. We were fully equipped by the WAC with bed linen, kitchen utensils...

As farm workers, we received double rations of cheese and meat. We baked our own challot [Sabbath plaited breads] and cakes, and the girls did a splendid job in the kitchen under the supervision of first Mrs. Epstein, and later Mr. Akiva Kornbluth. Obviously, quite a few firm friendships developed and of course we also had the usual heartbreaks, but many of these friendships ended in marriage. We had a lot of visitors over the weekend, such as Bnei Akiva Camps. We also had our tragedies. One of our Hardmead boys, Yoine, died when the bike he was riding on his way to work collided with a lorry, and we heard of a girl who was murdered while hitchhiking between two other kibbutzim.

Eli reflected:

Almost from the word go, as soon as Buckingham opened, there was a stream of visitors from London. We were the closest showpiece to London of what the Bachad movement stood for, a practical example of religious Zionism in a kibbutz environment. Our visitors included the machers (movers and shakers) of the Mizrachi movement, young rabbis and their families, and of course hordes of young Bachad and B'nei Akiva members (in the 18 to 25 age group) from their numerous groups in North West London, the (then still very Jewish) East End, and from Stamford Hill.

We really did create for ourselves a very cohesive religious community. Shiurim (Hebrew lectures), English Literature groups with outside teachers, psychology lecturers from Oxford, the mandatory ideological talks by members of the Hanhala (the movement's London head office), as well as visits from Aguda [orthodox religious and political group] orientated young hopefuls like Shammai Zahn. Shammai became Rosh Yeshiva in Sunderland, [succeeding Rabbi Waltner in what was the Sunderland kollel which moved to Gateshead. He also knew Rav Dessler in Chesham] and after the war he rescued many children from Casablanca in Morocco to be taught in his yeshiva. Of course, it was inevitable that in a group like ours there were also frictions between individuals, and when people took sides, there was friction between groups. Yet the overall feeling was one of harmony and belonging...To the outside visitor, it must have made a powerful impact for positive, joyful Jewish living.

The kibbutz experience left me with the conviction that spending at least a year in such surroundings should be mandatory for every youngster after school, and before entering places of higher education. The discipline of having to consider the wants of others, the necessity of sharing and making do with very little, the acceptance of responsibilities for certain tasks on which the whole group may depend – all these are character forming in a most positive way. Certainly society as a whole would greatly benefit from such an idea.

So it was that members of various London-based religious youth groups came to visit, sometimes with friends, sometimes alone. Some of the boys I knew from school in Berlin, or from the Hardmead camps. The girls were obviously looking for potential mates among the orthodox committed undemanding manhood of our kibbutz. I was not aware of it at the time. Nor was I thinking of marriage before the age of 21.

Our kibbutz had an elected vaad (executive) of about 5 members, including the gizbar (treasurer). Our cook was also a refugee. My appetite then being huge (was I always like that, I wonder?) the cook would say to me: "Sie essen ja nur um mich zu argern" (you're only eating to annoy me). This became a catchphrase for all kibbutz members whenever someone asked for more food. Akiva and Ray Kornbluth, our wardens / managers /

housekeepers were British born. They also were paid by the Agricultural Committee. Their domain was buying provisions, supervising the smooth running of the hostel, as it was called, and representing us vis-à-vis the authorities.

The Assefa Clalit (general meeting) was the forum for all aspects of our activities, as well as financial policies. At one of those meetings, I proposed the idea of using our accumulated funds to acquire a threshing machine. A gang of our boys and girls could then go round the farms and do the threshing and bundling of straw for set fees. This would generate far larger income for the kibbutz than the wages we received at present. If this idea proved successful, we could buy more than one machine.

Eli's proposal was supported, but not by enough people, and control was lost to the head office. It was decided their current earnings, without further investment, must go to those in greater need. A kibbutz in St. Asaph, Wales, couldn't even afford to repair their own shoes. Eli realized it would soon be time for him to leave Buckingham.

D Day arrived and Eva remembered she was milking cows when the farmer's wife called her over to hear a radio broadcast about the invasion by British troops into France. Following this, Eva and Eli decided to marry.

It was Chanukah, the festival of lights when Eva (Chava) and Eli had first a civil wedding and then on the Buckingham kibbutz, what Eli described as the 'real' wedding. Eli recalled his mother mother-in-law, Melanie Becker, managed to get a pickled tongue from Moishe Chaim Grunbaum, who was now the kosher butcher in Letchworth. Eli wore his army uniform (having joined the Royal Fusiliers in March 1944) for Shabbat Chanukah, December 15th and 16th 1944. He explained, 'that Rabbi Broch from Letchworth performed the Chuppah, which was held outside. It was cold but dry. My good friend from Berlin and Whittingehame, Emil Lowenstein, had made drawings as table cards, and Chava's wedding dress was inherited from Emil's wife Mia.'

Eva continued:

In the kitchen, Kuli Landau and his brother Manfred, whose parents had a baker shop in Berlin, were busy baking cakes and challot for two nights running, and the kitchen staff worked overtime too. The pickled tongue that Mama obtained (with the greatest difficulty) from Stern and Grunbaum was THE dish of the wedding feast.

On a very cold and windy day, Sunday 17th December 1944, the last day of Chanuka, with Nazi Doodlebugs flying overhead, we got married beneath a large Tallit (prayer shawl) in the garden of our kibbutz. The Buckingham choir under the capable leadership of Israel Alexander sang wonderful melodies (he would later lead a choir in Carmel College... poetry was recited by Richard Feist, and other festivities were in the programme. We had a wonderful feast...

As Eli and I stood under the chuppah, we were both mindful of the possibility that he may never see his family again. [Indeed, they perished] We made a vow that we would re-establish the Fachler tribe.

Tyler's Green – Rev Bernd Koschland

I was born in Fuerth, nr Nuremberg, in 1931 into an orthodox family. I lived through the growing severity of Nazi persecution of the Jews. It climaxed for me on the infamous Kristallnacht, when my father was taken to Dachau Concentration Camp. On his release a while later, my parents decided to send me to England on the Kindertransport and in March 1939 I sailed for the UK. My older sister followed a couple of months later. How my parents must have felt in sending us away, not knowing whether we would see each other again. We did not, as they perished in 1942. How I felt at the time I cannot recall.

I, like the majority of Kinder, knew no English. I was taken to a Jewish hostel in Margate, learned English and went to school. In 1940 evacuation set in and this took me to a non-Jewish family in Staffordshire, who were extremely kind and supportive. In 1941 I moved again to another hostel in Tylers Green, Bucks, run by the Munk's Shul of Golders Green. Passing my 11+ exam allowed me to go to the Royal Grammar School, High Wycombe, which I had to leave when the hostel moved to London in 1945.

Eventually I entered Jews' College, graduated and worked as a Minister for 12 years. After that I went into teaching at JFS (Jewish Free School) and lastly City of London School for Girls from which I retired.

I married in 1957 – my wife died in 1996 – I have two children and six grandchildren, two of whom are married.

In retirement I have involved myself in a variety of activities, working with the local Authority (Barnet), Inter-faith work, Hospital and Police, Jews' Temporary Shelter, etc.

TYLERS GREEN – A JEWISH 'VICARAGE'

The 'community' of Tylers Green was the hostel, which was founded in 1940 by the Golders Green Beth Hamidrash (Munks) at the instigation of the late Rabbi Eli Munk, assisted by members of his community. The hostel held about 25 boys of Kindertransport or of refugee origins – in the latter case children whose parents, family came as refugees to the UK. In the village itself there was, as far as I remember, just one Jewish family, Zwirn (well-known furriers of the time). [Another resident was Sidney Bratt. He stayed during 1940-41. Sid explained, 'I went to school there and was in an orthodox hostel. The hostel was run by Mr. and Mrs. Max Baer from Frankfurt on Maine, Germany. I stayed there until shortly after my bar mitzvah and then left for Edinburgh, Scotland.']

The Committee, who were frequent visitors, engaged the Wardens, cooks, helpers and a teacher. Everything was conducted on strictly orthodox lines. The warden's wife was the matron. As the teacher was on the staff, there was no need of a cheder as we had lessons in Jewish studies every day. Religious guidance was ensured by the Warden and his wife. Rabbi Munk would visit regularly.

Being a 'self-contained' community, services were held daily, taken by the boys, even straight after bar mitzvah. There were a few internal bar mitzvahs, and even one from a family in Beaconsfield. Thus as a local 'Shul', we attracted occasional persons from round about, including a serviceman now and then.

There was some contact with the community in High Wycombe, e.g. when we went there for Chanukah parties and other odd occasions. I cannot recall contact with Amersham or Chesham, though one of the committee lived in Chesham for part of the war.

Kashrut was strictly observed; meat was sent from Frohweins in London by train or sometimes picked up by older boys directly from the shop. Pesach goods were ordered through Selfridges. The garden provided fruit and vegetables.

Air raids were few and far between. Looking back I do not think we had an air-raid shelter. The nearest incident was a V1 which fell a short distance from the local Royal Grammar School which several of us attended. Two of us even joined the school's army cadets. Anti-Semitism was non-existent in the village. The only 'Jewish problem' was that the Grammar school had formal lessons Saturday morning. Rabbi Munk obtained permission from the Head for us to be excused, though other Jewish pupils attended. We were also able to leave early on Friday in the winter.

All in all, life, as I found it, was pleasant under the circumstances. We received visits from family and friends. There were also occasional visitors who stayed for a few days. (One frequent visitor eventually married my sister a few years after the war!) Despite school, Hebrew lessons or visitors, we had time for ourselves to enjoy the large grounds. The committee and others provided games, even bicycles, magazines and books for us to enjoy. Speaking for myself, I also made friends with local boys through school. When permitted we could also go away to visit families, e.g. for a Shabbat or chag [festivals]. Summertime, we were enabled to join youth camps.

Whilst life was the best it could be under the circumstances, Kinder who came on Kindertransport had a cloud on the horizon. Where were our parents? What happened to them? Why no communication? Answers to these questions had to wait – if there were answers.

The archives (given into my possession) show a well-run hostel, with active and loving committee members and staff. I would call it a show-place in the midst of a village which probably had never seen Jews. We were accepted by the locals, not as intruders, but as a peaceful oasis with well-behaved youngsters (most of the time! Boys will be boys!)

The idyllic village life ended when we had to vacate the building after the end of the war in Europe. We dispersed temporarily to various places in London but came together again in new premises in North London, October 1945, where we became part of the larger Jewish community.

Recently I was back in Tylers Green, filming as part of a BBC film on the Kindertransport. The house no longer stood; the grounds and adjoining field had become a housing estate. Where was the gate for the short-cut to the hostel? Taking it was a punishable offence in hostel terms, as I found out on a birthday of mine. I was caught because I had dropped my yarmulke in the churchyard! [St Mary's Church was designed by a Jewish man, David Brandon. It seems a fitting place to lose the Jewish skull-cap – known in Hebrew as a yarmulke or kippah].

Filming done, we repaired to a local hostelry and sat in the sun supping local brew. On leaving a lady called out Shalom to me; I was wearing my kippah. I turned and she asked if there is a local rabbi and synagogue. I replied that the last 'synagogue' closed in July 1945 at what was the 'Old Vicarage,' the site of our hostel.

The Royal Grammar School (RGS) in Wartime – High Wycombe. Bernd continued...

I was an "alien" refugee as I had come to England from Germany in 1939 and only arrived in Tylers Green in 1941 at a hostel located there.

In my last year at Tylers Green primary school, then headed by Mr Filby, I took and passed my 11+ examination which allowed me to go to the RGS. However Buckinghamshire County Council had laid down certain criteria for youngsters of my age. As an "alien", fees of 5 guineas (£5.25p in modern currency) had to be met. I had to have the right level of English for my age so as not to hinder progress, and finally no English boy could be excluded at the expense of an "alien". All conditions were met, so I started at the RGS in September 1942.

It was somewhat daunting to enter the portals of a school, founded by charter in 1562, with its large open space in front of the building. I had passed by on the bus. The then Head, Mr. Tucker, welcomed us in to start our secondary education. In those days, Latin was compulsory in the first year (Year 7). Miss Pollard – she liked to be addressed as "Sir" – ensured we all slaved away at Kennedy's Latin (commonly known as "Eating") Primer. Her punishments were severe if declensions and conjugations were not known fluently, including exceptions. Latin was in addition to French and the usual subjects. Maths consisted of three separate lessons, Arithmetic, Algebra and Geometry; Trigonometry came later. Logarithm tables became our vade mecum for maths; no slide rules were allowed; calculators did not exist.

As in other schools, there were Prefects, all from the Sixth Form, with various forms of punishment for misdeeds; this included the cane, administered by the Head Prefect. For a particular "crime", I was summoned for trial by a Prefects' meeting, found guilty and given a stroke of the cane. Thank you, Head Prefect, Wicks!

Further major crimes that were to be punished severely was the breach of the school rule that to go to High Wycombe every pupil had to walk into town – no bus down the hill. From High Wycombe one could take the bus, because of the steep hill. Also school uniform, including caps, had to be worn outside school.

For a short time, facilities of the school were shared with Chiswick County School, part of which was temporarily evacuated to RGS. This meant readjusting timetables to allow sharing of facilities. In turn this had the effect on some boys of the orthodox Jewish faith as we would have to leave early on winter Fridays because of the Sabbath. Likewise formal lessons on a Saturday morning caused a problem for some Jewish boys. Mr. Tucker and the Governors agreed to allow early leaving on Fridays and missing Saturday morning. None of this had adverse effects on our ultimate scholastic achievements.

Saturday afternoon was given over to sport, especially as the facilities of the vast playing field were excellent, for rugby, soccer and cricket. Sport was also part of the normal weekly curriculum. The playing fields also had another use: punishment. To run round the perimeter was most unpleasant. The Fives Courts were an additional facility, but usually the more senior pupils claimed them as their preserve.

THE BRONZE TENNIS HERO – JOE WOHLFARTH

(By Bernd Koschland)

We were both in the same hostel in Tylers Green, near High Wycombe. Joe was always interested in football and good at it. So it was no surprise when at the age of 18 he was spotted early by a coach of the Maccabiah [Jewish Olympics] Committee and selected for the English Football Team for the Maccabiah in 1950 and again for the 1958 Games. He continued playing for a local team in England for some years.

Joe took up tennis only in his mid-fifties. Now in his "younger" years over 75, Joe played tennis for Israel for the over 75's in the Games… as a result of the urgings of his youngest son, Adrian. The outcome? He won a Bronze Medal. Joe, congratulations, and well done!

His story as a Kind [German for child. Joe came to Britain on the kindertransport] was told by Israel's Prime Minister at the opening of the 18th Maccabiah. PM Netanyahu said,"…And to Joe, the tennis player, I say: your story is a source of inspiration for every Jewish child, for every Jew, for every athlete and is a living example of the revival of our people and of the spirit raging within us."

In an interview with the Jerusalem Post, he is quoted as joking about competing in the next Maccabiah at the age of 80. Typical of the Joe I know from many years ago, he commented, according to the Post, "When my friend and I walk off the court, we say to each other, 'Baruch Hashem, [God Willing] we are able to do this. But what will we do when we get old?"

What I say to you, Joe, is Yishar Kochacha, [may your strength grow] with the koach (strength) to play at 80. Perhaps 'bis 120?' [Jewish blessing, may you live for 120 years, like Moses, who died with no pain but with the kiss of God taking his soul].

Joe trained and practised as an architect. Eventually he and his wife Dinah went on aliyah [Hebrew for emigration to Israel] where they joined their children, Caron, Michael and Adrian. Dinah and Joe are now proud grand – and also great grand-parents.

High Wycombe – Dr Geoff Freed[116]

I was born on the 7th November 1938 into the Jewish Faith, and this was later to save my life.

Many families were evacuated to the countryside to escape the bombing. For a short while we were in Tebay in West Moreland, a small farming community. Our stay there was not pleasant, I fell out of a window, my mother was sick, my Dad was agitated, and my brother had trouble with the local ladies. I do not know what made us move back. I suspect my family wanted to be among Jewish people, and so we were moved to High Wycombe Buckinghamshire, where there was a small synagogue and Jewish Community. My Hebrew name is Yosef ben Moshe Mordecai, Joseph the son of Moses Mordecai.

My family rented a big house shared with my parents, brother, uncle, aunt and grandmother. My parents were Rose and Maurice Glickenfried. My aunt was Millie and uncle, Ben Lenz. My grandmother was Jane Bilangroski who was Russian. We were all evacuated to High Wycombe. I went to two schools, Miss Hathaway's private school and the public Green Street School.

One day, when I was four, my dearest beautiful late Mother took me for a pram walk, in one of those old prams. It was in winter and apparently bitter cold.

There was the recreational Ground with the river at top and Fryers Lane to the right leading down from the house. The address, of our home was 200 West Wycombe Road, High Wycombe, Bucks. Anyway, as we came near to the waterfall I leaned to the left. The strap broke. I fell out into the freezing cold water and floated out to the middle. I somehow doggy paddled to the bank where a passer-by and my mother pulled me out. A few yards more and I would have drowned going down the waterfall.

It took nearly 45 minutes to get home and I was shivering cold. This

Figure 16: Geoff Freed aged five and a half.

went on to be a severe cold and eventually congestion of the lungs, pleurisy, and then pneumonia. I was put on some awful tablets named M and B. [Geoff became critically ill].

On a Friday night, November 20 1942, I was clinically pronounced dead by Doctors Thomson and Young. They wanted a post mortem done but my mother said it was the Jewish Sabbath and it would have to wait until Sunday the 22nd.

I was then taken to the morgue at High Wycombe General Hospital. I was in the morgue from 19.30 Friday 20 November 1942 till awakening at 10.00 am Sunday 22nd November 1942. A person was saying prayers in Hebrew and when I awoke, he was startled to say the least. The man praying over me nearly fainted right into my face. He called the doctors and I was saved from a post mortem and burial by half an hour. The doctors had thought I must have been in a coma.

[Geoff described this as a Near-Death Experience (NDE) of going into space]

I perceived lights like stars and shapes like planets all in an inky, jet black…there was a massive Bright light and I knew if I went into this there is no coming back… [Geoff described an approaching figure, indicating an alternative direction into a coloured ball.]

... The ball was turning slowly and I remember counter clockwise, reluctantly I began to go towards it, slowly at first then really speeding, it got larger and larger, and gigantic. I impacted with it and awoke in a cold dark place, banged, and was let out of the box which was in the morgue. ... I had seen the Earth from deep space...in 1942, I kept doing drawings and was told it was a dream and I had been very ill.

I was telepathic until the age of 9. I used to say 'Why is it that grown-ups think one thing and say another'. I could and still 'see' auras. I used to sit in trees and watch wildlife. The other kids thought me weird. I was a sickly and not a healthy child and for a while after the NDE I was a thin as a rake.

The next part involved an American Airman named Joe. The Americans came to Booker Aerodrome near our house, and as they had not built billets for them the villagers were asked to temporarily house them. Joe's dad had been in the USA merchant navy and studied Ju Jitsu at Dojo (exercise hall) which was run by Zen Buddhists Monks. On seeing me so pale and skinny he started to teach me Ju Jitsu and This experience of the NDE has shaped my life and is the clearest memory etched into my brain as it were. I gave up all religions having tried everyone in some form or other. I am regarded by some as a kosher Buddhist and by others as non-religious Jew and a deserter. It is the inspiration to keep on going on and to welcome the return to that 'space' when the call comes to travel back home.

I stayed in High Wycombe until the age of six or seven. My family kept kosher and the holy days but were not Orthodox or Federation or anything like that.

The synagogue was above a shop in a big room between the guildhall and the cinema. I only vaguely remember the synagogue run by a Rev. Freed (not a relative) in a street just off of the High Street. Instead of going to synagogue on Saturday mornings I went to the cinema next door!

The first film I ever saw was in High Wycombe. Alice Faye was in a romance which my mother took me to and I didn't like it. After that I went to the Saturday morning pictures and watched the incredible Flash Gordon, Tom Mix and Roy Rogers cowboy films.

There was some anti-Semitism. A group of school boys chased me. I got behind a not – well-constructed gate that opened both ways and had a bolt. I held the gate with both hands. I was so determined not to let them through.

There was a lane called Mile End Lane with, I think, a technical school down there and a caravan that sold sausage rolls. I used to sneak there. My mother never knew, and with a farthing or ha'penny I would buy bread in dripping.

Behind our house was the mainline London to Oxford railway. I'd do something very dangerous and put a ha'penny on the track, so that it was flattened by the passing steam train, and then I'd pass it off as a penny.

Once, I kicked a ball over the vicarage wall but was caught by Mr Roberts, the policeman, who wore an old cape. The policeman swiped me with his gloves. We had to address him as 'Sir'. He took me to my father and made me apologise to the vicar.

I recall one Jewish man who did brilliant impressions of Danny Kaye.

I remember one bomb fell nearby but I was too young to recall the details.

Uncle Ben took me to Marlow to Jones' Tea House near the Thames in Marlow. My uncle was six foot tall, had a shock of white-gray hair and a red nose. He liked his tipple! His wife was timid. Down the lanes he would sing, on the top of his voice, rude Jewish songs in Yiddish 'Yuck im un and yuck der un.' This is of course a rough attempt at the words that meant 'S*** them all'. Residents would come out and say, 'Do you mind being quiet. It's Sunday.' My Uncle would look at me and say, 'Well, there you are then.'

My brother, Woolf was a drummer and a boxer for Wycombe Technical School. He was a ladies' man.

I saw Glen Miller with my parents. They were playing 'In the Mood.' I think Glen Miller wore glasses. The band played under the Guildhall. It was from High Wycombe that Glenn Miller took a flight out and disappeared forever.

TRAUTE MORGENSTERN

A refugee from the Nazis at Wycombe High School 1941-1947

As far as I am aware – in my years at WHS there were two Jewish teachers, namely Mrs Davidson, one of the Jewish mistresses, who lived just at the top of Marlow Hill (and would have found the present location very convenient) with whom I exchanged very few words. The other one was Peggy Franklin, our Latin teacher, quite a remarkable lady, so much so that we requested, and were granted to have her for the second year running as Form Mistress. (Miss Downs, the headmistress, never gave her the satisfaction of telling her of our request!) Peggy never admitted her Jewish background, not until our relationship pupil/teacher turned into friendship. She often came to Milan and I visited her in Bristol right till the end. She was a very bright person: she even tried and partly succeeded in picking up not only Italian (easy for a Latin teacher) but also my partner's northern Italian dialect!

As far as I know there was only one other refugee pupil, Ursula Grossman, still living in High Wycombe, but she was not Jewish. Her parents came out purely for political reasons – very praise-worthy. There were a few other Jewish girls but I cannot tell you anything about them.

My brother lived in High Wycombe between 1940 and '41. He came into contact with a group of Jewish, orthodox boys, who brought him back into the Jewish world. At first he did not practice but later on the Jewish faith became an important factor in his life. Our wonderful guardians were non-practicing Jews.

Article Extracts from 'High Flyer' The Wycombe High School Magazine:[117]

With the words "So you are the new Welsh girl", a stout, rather imposing lady, but of gentle manner and voice, welcomed me to WHS at the start of the 1941 autumn term, well aware – as I was to find out later – that Wales did not come into the picture at all. Obviously, the lady – as I was soon to learn – was no other than Miss Dessin, the Headmistress of the school, who just wanted me to feel at ease. She wished to give the impression that I was Welsh from my surname which, according to the identity card we all had to carry during the war, was Morgan. Yet that very same document, besides giving my first name as Truda, also added that Truda Morgan was an alternative to Traute Morgenstern.

The explanation for this is very simple – I was a Jewish refugee, born in Vienna in 1929. Thanks to the foresight and spirit of sacrifice of my parents and, even more so, thanks to the law passed by the British parliament immediately after the dramatic events of Kristallnacht in November 1938, my little brother Peter, aged 8, and I, nearly 10, were put on the first train leaving Vienna for England in early December 1938. This was one of the so-called KinderTransport, whereby 10,000 Jewish children were allowed to flee from the Nazis (mainly from Germany, Austria and Czechslovakia), providing certain conditions were met, the most important being that there would be guardians available to care and provide for us.

As luck would have it, the guardians for Peter and me were the families of the then famous catering concern J. Lyons and Co. I say "luck" not from a financial point of view, which must have been a factor, but because of the extraordinary, never-failing kindness, attention and generosity with which they cared not only for us but for some 20 Jewish refugee children for whom they provided a home in Kentish Town in London, appropriately called "The Haven". Our names were anglicised and we were sent to schools according to our ages. For the second time we were evacuated with these schools after the outbreak of war, with labels round our necks and also gas masks and emergency kits. Peter followed his primary school whereas I, with Parliament Hill School (which still exists today) was assigned to a family in St Albans who either would not or could not care for me, whereupon, Peter and I were reunited on the Isle of Wight until the first bombs fell there. Then we were split up once more, but after a year in Cornwall, I was kindly taken in by a family in Marlow so as to be nearer to Peter who was then in High Wycombe. It was this new family who contacted Miss Dessin and, though my entrance exam must have been a complete disaster, she agreed to give me a place at Wycombe High school, purely on humanitarian grounds.

Miss Dessin, whom I hope I have not let down, is one of the many people to whom I shall remain grateful for all of my life. She was an exceptional figure for most of us. She knew us all by name and she would often stop us in the corridor to enquire about our well-being and progress. She set very high standards and the school enjoyed an exceptionally good reputation, which I believe is still true today. The daily routine ran very smoothly, despite what must have been many additional problems owing to the war – sharing premises with Ealing High School which had been evacuated from London and consequently having to organise lessons in the school (then at Benjamin Road) and in the Baptist Church Hall.

Certainly for me, there was a special atmosphere, taking into account attitudes of those times. Firstly there was no religious discrimination and at a later date we very few Jewish girls were allowed to hold our own services in a separate classroom. However, I, not practising, soon returned to the assemblies in Main Hall. Secondly, the short piano recital by one of our Music teachers offered a very enjoyable and relaxing start to our day. Thirdly, what might appear to be unimportant, proved to be of considerable value to me –at the start, when we brought sandwiches, my family was asked not to make them too lavish, to avoid embarrassment to others!

And so, still a very quiet, shy (though that changed within the next few years) twelve and a half year old who had only attended primary schools until then, I was put into the 2nd form (Year 8 now). As was the strict principle of those times, I had to catch up with what I had missed from the first year i.e. Physics, Chemistry and French, not to mention English, and I had to do so on my own. I was put into the "A" stream which, though not perhaps a democratic system, was a blessing as well as a challenge for me, as I was with a particularly lively, bright group of more than 30 girls from very different backgrounds including some evacuees. I am still in touch with many of these, even after more than 60 years, whether having left WHS at the end of the 5th form (Year 11) in 1945 or the 6th form in 1947.

This strong bond can perhaps be explained partly by English team spirit, partly by war memories and partly by growing up and studying together and I think, by a certain atmosphere fostered at WHS, thanks also, to dedication to one's House (Beck, Gray, Hampden, Milton, Penn) with much encouraged but friendly competition between them. However, compared with today, it may sound surprising that, with the exception of two families only, none of my classmates or their families ever invited me home. No doubt all had their own serious problems because of the war, transport was difficult, but neither they nor even the staff were aware of my great need for affection. However good or kind my guardians were, they were living in London and I saw them on special occasions only. However considerate the family in Marlow was, no one ever put their arms around me in all my nine and a half years in England, not even during my two 6th form years living with the family of an old WHS girl. I kept in touch with her right until the end and also with her sister, Barbara Taylor, another old girl, who passed away.

...In those days, generally speaking, no allowances were made for particular, even if justified psychological problems or needs or any out of the ordinary demands. I recall months of a knee cartilage problem. It was no joke walking up and down the hill (Priory Road) to and from WHS or waiting for a bus, though the "get-on-with-it" spirit proved to be a blessing later on, because it prepared us for worse blows that then had to be faced and overcome.

Being the only (apparently promising) Maths student in the 6th form, I was granted three teachers all to myself. I fear I did not repay this extraordinary privilege when I re-joined my parents in Milan after the war. They had managed to survive in Italy but by then they had become complete strangers with whom it was difficult to communicate since I had completely forgotten German.

At WHS we had our Parliament (involving staff and students); we had been taught to read a newspaper; we had been sent to hear Anthony Eden speak at the Albert Hall, London. I had been made a Prefect and Head of House, which meant taking on responsibilities and learning to deal with others. The qualities acquired in these roles are essential as basic background for life in general. Culture can be learned at a later stage while behaviour is developed right from the start.

I consider myself very privileged to have reaped so much in my six years at WHS, becoming a well-integrated evacuated refugee.

The London Jewish Chronicle and the Holocaust – Professor David Cesarani[118]

At the outbreak of war, the *Jewish Chronicle* management put into effect a plan for evacuating the paper from London. The editorial, composing and circulation departments were removed to High Wycombe, a small town in Buckinghamshire. Here the staff and office equipment were crammed into the premises of the *Bucks Free Press*, which were shared with the *Catholic Herald*, the Church of England *Guardian* and the Christadelphian *Mutual Magazine*. Working conditions were far from comfortable or convenient.

The dangers to the paper and the staff were brought home by the destruction of the main office at 47-49 Moor Lane, in the City, during an air raid on the night of 29 December 1940. Irreplaceable files containing correspondence, press cuttings, obituaries, and photographs were burned. The temporary office established in Queen Victoria Street was also hit in an air raid on 11 May 1941. These blows, comparable to stunning and amnesia in a sentient being, had an incalculable effect on the paper's ability to sort and assess incoming information.

Wartime rationing affected the paper drastically. From September 1939 to July 1940, the amount of newsprint allotted to the press in Britain was reduced by 60 per cent. As the German U-boat blockade tightened, the Paper Control Office limited the number of pages in periodicals. The amount of newsprint allotted to the *Jewish Chronicle* was cut in March 1941 and again in early 1942.

Many features had to be dropped, including Simon Gilbert's incisive comment column. Henceforth, his distinctive and often critical voice was sublimated into the editorials. In order to squeeze more into less space, the

301

size of type was reduced with each cut in the paper ration. By 1943, the *Jewish Chronicle* was appearing on brittle, discolored paper and taxed even readers with perfect eyesight.

The paper's trading position suffered badly from the effects of war. The evacuation or voluntary relocation of Jewish people from the main centers of Jewish settlement disrupted sales and circulation. Casual sales fell since continuous nights of bombing in 1940 – 41 left people with little time or energy for perusing the press.

The circulation of newspapers was eventually fixed by the government in March 1941 and each paper was allowed only enough newsprint to supply subscribers. In November 1941 new regulations compelled the *Jewish Chronicle* to suspend casual sales altogether. In 1942 a further tightening of paper rationing meant that no more fresh subscriptions could be accepted. The paper advised readers to pass on finished copies to friends and to send them to servicemen.

Advertising revenue slumped since non-war related production declined and consumption was strictly controlled. The daily press was buoyed up by the Government's public information campaigns, but not the religious or class papers.

The combined effect of pegged circulation, rising production costs and diminishing advertising pushed the paper into the red. Michel Oppenheimer was forced to dip into personal capital to stave off financial ruin, while the employees actually took a pay cut to help it survive.

Hostilities damaged the staff situation in other ways. By the end of the war, thirteen staff members were in uniform. Fewer personnel were doing more work in worse conditions.

The *Jewish Chronicle's* correspondents on the continent were eliminated in step with the advances of the German army. Its own correspondents in Germany and Vienna had been forced out years earlier. Now, its reporters in eastern and Western Europe had to flee. Several unfortunates were caught by the Nazis and shared the fate of the Jewish population in general.

News gathering was significantly affected by the severance of the editorial department from the offices of the paper and the environs of Fleet Street. The editorial staff was cut off from channels of information in the capital: the governments-in-exile, the embassies of neutral states, visiting diplomats, and the members of foreign armed services were all a long, hazardous train ride away. It was left to the diminished, overstrained band of operators in London to cover these sources and to phone in reports (when lines were available). Otherwise, the editors were limited to picking up news off the wire services, including the Jewish Telegraphic Agency (JTA), or from other newspapers.

Formal and informal censorship further limited what news the *Jewish Chronicle* could obtain or publish. In 1939 the Ministry of Information issued guidelines stating that it was inadvisable to invoke the suffering of the Jews in propaganda directed at the Middle East. Anything that fostered sympathy for Jewish refugees attempting to reach Palestine was undesirable as it would embarrass British policy and irritate the Arabs. In 1941, the Ministry issued a memorandum stating that "horror stuff ... must be used very sparingly and must always deal with the treatment of indisputably innocent people. Not with violent opponents. And not with Jews."

Until late 1942, the Political Warfare Executive, which had a powerful role in setting the propaganda agenda, insisted on stringent proof of stories about the fate of the Jews. British officials and military personnel were keenly aware of the extent of anti-Jewish feeling in Britain and Europe, and were apprehensive that any sign of favor towards the Jews would play into the hands of Nazi propaganda. It was also felt that "atrocity stories" had become counter-productive because their fabrication for propaganda during the First World War had later been exposed and the genre was discredited.

Official displeasure towards the publication of potentially dangerous "tittle-tattle" compounded the ingrained professional scepticism of the *Jewish Chronicle* editorial staff. The confusing, ambiguous nature of the information concerning the Jews which emerged from the occupied countries all contributed to the demotion of the place it was assigned in the paper and the toning down of the editorial comment.

PEACE AT LAST

VE day allowed evacuees to return to the cities, and refugees to find a permanent home. This reduced membership of Buckinghamshire synagogues. However, people loved the Chilterns and some stayed. High Wycombe continues to have a congregation. Amersham and Chesham merged some years after the war but took the decision to close in October 1966 as there were less than ten members. The land was sold in 1968. Gerrards Cross, Beaconsfield, Bletchley and Haversham all closed after the war. Slough used to be part of the County of Buckinghamshire. Slough formed a synagogue, with Windsor, post war, which remained open until 1970. An off-shoot from Northwood and Pinner Liberal Synagogue re-established a community, called South Bucks Jewish Community (SBJC), formally launched in 1990. Prior to this the small number of Jewish people reflected the early wartime community and held services in people's homes, halls, and then in the Quaker Meeting House, Whielden Street, Old Amersham. This is where Katie Krone, the person who sparked the mystery of the rabbi in the green jacket, used to meet with other German Jewish refugees during WW2.

THE MOTORBIKE REV

There were no rabbis but there were three excellent leaders that officiated in the corrugated synagogue on Woodside Road, Amersham. A few people recalled the green jacket but no one could tell who wore it! So now you think you've just read so much to find the answer to this question, and what do you get – nothing – oy! Well, stop your hand, before you hit your head. The question as to who the rabbi, actually reverend, in the green jacket was, has finally been answered. Amongst others, Ivor Delman remembered the motorbike. Devorah Wolkenfeld, whose husband the chazan conducted services, confirmed, 'the motorbike belonged to dear Sonnie Bloch'. Sister Katie Krone linked the motorbike to the jacket. The Reverend Sonnie Bloch, adored by many, was 'The Rabbi in the Green Jacket'.

Figure 17: 'Sonnie' Sebastian Morton Bloch in canonicals.

Bucks Examiner Newspaper

Jewish Related Extracts – 1939–1945

28.3.41
PASSOVER

Letter below, signed by Mr. Julius Jung, Chairman of the Chesham Kosher Canteen, 26 Manor Way, Chesham:

"Ever since the committee of the Chesham Cricket Pavilion kindly let their pavilion to be used as a house of worship for the Jewish citizens temporarily residing here, it has been our endeavour to use the hall also, on a non-profit basis, as a canteen where children and adults can receive a hearty luncheon prepared in accordance with Jewish dietary law. The canteen will be opened on Friday, April 11th, which is the Eve of Passover. As invitations have already been extended to all Jews young and old whose addresses have been known to us to inform us how many of their family would be anxious to have their meals at the canteen during Passover. There must be many others whose addresses we do not know, but to whom an equally hearty invitation is being extended. There is just one condition. It would be a crime in war-time to buy more food than necessary, unless people therefore communicate during the next few days with the Rev. S. M. Bloch, Rosemont, Eskdale Avenue, Chesham, no promise can be made that they will be accommodated at the last moment. May I therefore beg all Jewish readers of your valuable paper to contact him immediately."

4.4.41

THE JEWISH COMMUNAL CANTEEN
A TIMELY EXPLANATION

To The Editor, Bucks Examiner.

In view of the discussion at last week's Food Committee, this is a timely letter of explanation from the Chairman of the Kosher Canteen:

Dear Sir,

In the last issue of your valuable paper, there appeared a report of the meeting of the Chesham Food Committee relating to the Kosher Canteen. May I be allowed to notify your readers that every possible step will be taken in conjunction with the Food Executive Officer to prevent anybody getting double rations?

The number of persons who will take advantage of our canteen during Passover will be about 75 schoolchildren and 40 adults.

I have offered the Food Executive Officer to let him have the ham and bacon coupons of all observant Jews in the Town as they are never using them.

Yours faithfully

JULIUS JUNG, Chairman

11.7.41

THE CHILDREN AND ORANGES
WHAT ARE WE FIGHTING FOR?

Sir,

In your issue of June 27th, which I have just seen, appears a report of a discussion of a meeting of the Chesham Food Committee, requesting a kosher canteen. I am not so much concerned with the discussion itself as with the remark made by a lady member of the committee. It is to be noted that this lady's name is not given.

It would appear that she had a serious grievance in which she found Jewish children eating oranges, apparently brought by their parents from Town. I have yet to learn that it is a crime either against morality or decency for a child to eat an orange, unless of course it may be so in case of a Jewish child, but it seems to me that the very nadir of intolerance is reached and such an argument is used, and by a woman, in any discussion at all. Everybody can get what he or she wants as long as it is legal, and as long as it is able to be obtained.

We are fighting a war for the freedom of the human spirit, but how far removed we are from reality is shown by the mental attitude of a woman who classes herself, no doubt, as a Christian, and airs a grievance that some children can get oranges. I myself have not yet seen an orange since the war. I am a family man, and would like my children also to have oranges, but if other children have them all I can say is that they are fortunate, and that is an end to it.

It is about time we woke up to the plain fact that there are quite a number of people in this country who are so afflicted with narrowing vision, with racial hatred and with bigotry, and they are quite unworthy of being described either as English or Christian, but I think one would have to go far to find so glorious an example of the depth of human nature can sink as this lady committee member, whose soul is grieved because some Jewish children actually ate oranges.

Yours faithfully, E. Davis.

5.9.41
TO MAKE THE BEST OF FOOD

For over an hour, to a closely attentive audience, Mrs. L. J. Greenberg, the Jewish Chronicle expert, talked to ladies at Chesham Town Hall on Tuesday upon food: there were animated interjections and questions, and it was evident that all thought the talk well worthwhile. In that hour Mrs. Greenberg packed advice as to food values, how to cook food, how to prepare salads and what to use. Recipes for cake making, salad making and so on. The talk was full to the brim with information, and she promised ladies that inquiries through the Jewish Chronicle would be answered if a stamped, addressed envelope were sent.

Mrs. Greenberg made the point that in spite of the fact that we were short of some foods, there were the essential foods, as the good health of the nation showed, and in fact we were better now than we were when we had so much fried foods and sweetstuffs.

She dealt with the body-building foods, the energising foods, and the protective foods, and stressed the value of wholemeal bread, which she said we should insist upon having, oatmeal, beans and lentils, nuts, potatoes, and green vegetables. Further she pointed out that amongst these could be found all the properties for body building, energising, and protection.

Salads were described, and their value given, as well as the economy of preparing, and the lecturer pointed out incidentally the good properties of watercress and mustard and cress because of the iron in them. As an aside, she said she had failed to get watercress in the Chesham shops, and immediately there was a chorus "They grow it here". Cook vegetables as slowly as you can, and utilise the liquid: fish is good food value, especially herrings: meat braized and pot roasted was meat from which you had the full value. Do not soak vegetables a long time, was one of her slogans.

Mr. W. G. Payne, Chairman of Chesham Food Committee, presided, and was warm in his praise of the lecture, and pointed out a personal experience of preserving runner beans for out-of-season times, a course recommended by Mrs. Greenberg.

There were queries raised as to substitutes now on the market, and Mrs. Greenberg, while advising proceeding with caution, pointed out that many of the preparations were carefully analysed by experts, and had stood the test.

The difficulty of securing herrings locally was spoken of, and Mrs. Greenberg said she was aware that in some areas there was a difficulty, but in others there was plenty, and she promised to put the matter before the Ministry of Food, with a view to getting better distribution if possible.

5.6.42
AMERSHAM

A JEWISH SYNAGOGUE is now under construction in WOODSIDE ROAD (near Sycamore Corner). Good progress is being made with the building and it is expected to have it completed by the autumn.

12.6.42
A JEWISH COMMUNAL HALL

The building now is in the course of erection in Woodside-road, which is being built by the United Synagogue Membership Group of Amersham and District (of which the Rev. I. Rapaport Ph.D., is secretary) is not only to be a synagogue, as was the general impression. In an interview with our representative, The Rev. I. Rapaport explained that it is to be a Communal Hall for the Jewish community at present residing in the district. Its main use is to be for the religious education of the Jewish children, of whom there are now about 100 in the Amersham area. For this purpose, the rearmost section of the hall is to be divided from the main portion, and the latter curtained off when required, to give accommodation for three separate classes, which will be so used on three or four days of each week. On other occasions, including each Saturday, the main body, with the curtains withdrawn, will be used as the central place of worship for all the Jewish community in the district. The hall will also be available for their social functions, and for this reason, the Rev. I. Rapaport prefers to call it a "war nursery and army hut," rather than a Synagogue. It had long been felt, he said, that some such centre was badly needed in the district by those of the Jewish faith who, 20 months ago, were evacuated to this district, and for whom, so far, no such accommodation had been found. Up to the present their worship has had to be made in a variety of halls in different parts of the district and the children's religious education conducted, somewhat scrappily, in various places. At the height of the evacuation movement there were upwards of 300 Jewish children drafted into Amersham, but there are now only 100, and these will in future receive their religious education in one body of the new Communal Hall. The Rev. I. Rapaport expressed the thanks and appreciation of all Jews at present in our midst for the many kindnesses extended them by the residents, and particularly to the clergy of those churches who had afforded them accommodation in their halls and church-rooms – the Rev. G. H. Lawrence for the use of St. Leonard's Hall, and the Rev. E. Murray Page for that of the Free Church, amongst others. He explained that the new hall under the emergency conditions upon which it had been possible to build it, cannot remain after the conclusion of the war, and in the meanwhile it remains at the disposal of the local Council, should emergency arise for its use, for any purpose by them. It may not be generally known that since the earliest days of the evacuation a canteen hut has been carried on in Bois-Lane, Chesham Bois, by a committee of Jewish ladies, under the superintendency of Mrs. Hirschfeld, where children can get a good dinner for 4d., and adults for 1/-. Originally opened to cater for Jewish children, it has more recently been used almost exclusively by non-Jewish, as so many evacuee children have returned to their London homes. It is used so regularly by a number of children from Chesham Bois School. The Rev. I Rapaport, who was appointed secretary of the Synagogue Membership Group of Amersham district nearly two years ago, and is in spiritual charge of the community in the area, hopes that much benefit will be gained by the better accommodation being provided for the children's religious education, for he holds that such education is more essential to-day than ever it was, and will become increasingly so when peace comes again.

11.9.42
WOODSIDE HALL. AMERSHAM

A special intercessionary service held by members of the Jewish faith was one of even greater solemnity than the intercession services frequently held by them. Rev. Dr. I. Rapaport conducted the service, and an address was given by the Rev. A. Scaper, B.A. The Prayer for the king and royal family, and for the Fallen, was said, during which the Rev. Rapaport held the scroll of the law, taken from the Ark. The Service closed with the blowing of the Shofar, or ram's horn.

18.12.42
A JEWISH DAY OF FAST AND PRAYER [EXTRACT]

Sunday was declared by all Jewry in Britain as a day of fast, prayer and mourning for the massacred Jews in Europe during the war.

The fiendish murder of millions of Jews in Poland fills us with horror.

Instead of January 3rd, previously mentioned, I do now, as the ecclesiastics head of British Jewry, call upon every Jewish community to make Sunday, December 13th, a day of fast, and prayer, a day of mourning and of abstention from work and amusement. May God hear our prayers and be peaceful unto His People." Such was the special message sent by the Chief Rabbi to the United Synagogue Membership Group of Amersham (through the Minister, the Rev. Dr. I. Rapaport) in common with all other Jewish Groups throughout the country. And so a special Service of Intercession was held at Woodside Hall on Sunday afternoon, upon which very solemn occasion the hall was filled to overflowing. The solemnity of the service was most impressive, and many members of the great congregation were reduced to tears...

28.1.44
APPRECIATION OF DR. I. RAPAPORT [EXTRACT]

Last week we referred to the fact that Dr. I. Rapaport, who has been minister of the Jewish community in Amersham for the past three and a half years, has left Amersham to take up an army chaplaincy...

... One of his most remarkable achievements was his complete mastery of the English language in so short a time, for as recently as 1936 he was unable to speak a word of our language, and now there is not even a trace of accent discernible in his speech. In 1940 he graduated at the Jew's College for the ministry.

There was a large gathering at Woodside Hall, over which Mr. M. E. Mosley (warden) presided, to bid the doctor farewell, and wish him good luck in his new work, and he was made the recipient of a cheque, a gold wristlet watch and a leather attaché case from the respective societies of the community, the presentations being made by Mr. M. Levy. Mrs. A. Winer also presented him with a gift on behalf of the Ladies' Knitting Circle. Mr. Levy expressed the regret all felt at Dr. Rapaport's departure, and their appreciation of the good work he had done whilst in Amersham.

11.8.44
NEW CHAPLAIN TO THE FORCES
REV. S. M. BLOCH

(BY MR JULIUS JUNG, OUR SPECIAL CORRESPONDENT)

Recently I attended a very pleasant function at Amersham Synagogue. The local community had met in full force to big good luck and God-Speed to the Rev. S. M. Bloch on his appointment as Chaplain to the RAF.

Mr. J. L. Feuchtwanger, who presided, stated that Mr. Bloch had been with them since the inception of the Synagogue some four years ago and had endeared himself to all by his devotion to duty, by his exceptional ability to win the attention and love of the children, and by the self-sacrificing manner in which he had been spending all his spare time in furthering the interest of all the sections of the local Jewish community. Amersham was very sorry to lose him but appreciated his desire to give his services to King and country by volunteering for the chaplaincy. He wished the Rev. Bloch, on behalf of the community and especially the Religion Classes, God's blessing, in his more onerous duties, and a safe return.

Chaplain Amias, who had come down for the occasion, welcomed Mr. Bloch as a new colleague and assured him that officers and men – Jewish and non-Jewish – would greatly appreciate his work.

Rabbi J. Ehrentreu, of Chesham, in paying tribute to the Rev. Bloch, recorded that he was a Cheshamite, living as he does in Eskdale-avenue, Chesham, and that he had done very successful work in Chesham, both in connection with the local billeting officer as regards billets for Jewish evacuees, and as chairman of the O.R.T. Millinery and Dressmaking Classes, which during the last blitz taught (gratis) women and girls in town these most useful trades.

The Rev. Indech, the new minister of the Amersham Jewish Community, revealed that Mr. Bloch had become a chaplain because his conscience had convinced him that he could do more for his people at the moment in that sphere than in Amersham, although he had loved every minute he had spent there. The Rev. Indech felt sure that Chaplain Bloch would earn the undying gratitude of the officers and men if he would lavish on them the same devotion and love that he had hitherto given the boys and girls of Amersham.

Mr. A. Winer, a warden, presenting Mr. Bloch with a cheque on behalf of the community, stated that on one occasion the Rev. Bloch refused part of his salary because he feared that the community could not then afford it.

Other speakers were Flt.Lt. Scott, who assured the Rev. Bloch of a right royal welcome as only the R.A.F. can give it; Mr. M. Levy, the senior warden; Mr. A. Moseley, the treasurer; and Mrs. Hirschfeld, of the Ladies' Guild, who were responsible for a nice tea for all present. There were two further speeches: Mr. B. Grossman, who presented the Chaplain with a beautiful leather bag on behalf of the local Jewish Service Club; and last but not least, a few sweet words and a beautiful pipe from pretty Ann Mays on behalf of the Jewish children of Amersham.

The Rev. Bloch suitably replied.

Chaplain Bloch's younger brother is out in the Far East. He is Cpt. Sidney Bloch, R.F.M.F. The next younger one is Sergt. Cadet Maurice Bloch; the youngest, Leonard, can but dream of his duties when he grows up.

We join the Amersham and Chesham Jewish Communities in wishing Chaplain Bloch great success in his new duties, and a happy return to his mother, with the speedy and glorious germination of the war.

10.7.45
A LETTER OF THANKS

From Mr. David J. Goldberg of 32 Chessmount-rise Chesham dated 16.7.45 to the Editor of the Bucks Examiner.

"I would be grateful if you would allow me space in your valuable journal for a word of thanks. As Chairman of the Hebrew Congregation for more than 4 years, I feel that I cannot leave Chesham without expressing our appreciation and gratitude to the people here who have helped us find refuge in their midst. Your Municipal Officers; your food office staff who made great efforts in our food problems; your Cricket Club Committee, (especially Mr. Vine), have all done their utmost to help us. To the Headmasters and Mistresses and their staffs, we owe a special word of thanks, for it is through their interest and efforts that our children have received the ideal education which will enable them to become true British citizens. I would also like to voice appreciation to your tradespeople. They have always been civil and helpful to us, although short-handed, and working under difficult conditions.

We came to Chesham at a time of great distress; but retain now only happy memories of these years between. So, "Good-bye, Chesham", and on behalf of us all, "thank you".

Glossary of (Mainly) Hebrew Terms

Barmitzvah – boys aged thirteen read from the Torah. Girls aged twelve – Batmitzvah.

Chanukah – eight day Festival of Lights to celebrate religious freedom.

Chaverim – 'friends' and also members of a kibbutz.

Cheder – a Jewish children's Sunday school.

Chuppah – a canopy under which a couple are married.

Chumash – one of the five books of the Torah.

Daven – pray aloud.

Frum – Yiddish for devout.

Haggadah – Passover (Pesach) book for the order of the service which is called a seder.

Kibbutzim – plural for kibbutz; communal group living and working in equality.

Kashrut / Kosher – Jewish dietary laws.

Minyan – ten men required for communal prayers.

Pesach – (Passover) festival celebrating freedom from Egyptian slavery, involving a **seder** – a gathering to a traditional meal, with wine, songs and prayers.

Purim – celebrates Queen Esther saving Persian Jewry from annihilation.

Rav and **Rab** are Hebrew honourifics specifically for a rabbi.

Reb – Yiddish, honourific title usually given to rabbis (teachers or rebbes in Yiddish)

Shabbat – Sabbath (Shabbos in Yiddish)

Shul – Yiddish for synagogue, Jewish place of worship.

Sifrei Torah – handwritten Hebrew scrolls containing the five books of Moses.

Sukkot – harvest festival

Topfen – Austrian for Quark, a cream cheese often used in Jewish cooking.

Yeshiva – an Orthodox Jewish college where the sacred texts are studied in depth.

Yom-tov – a day of joy designated to particular festivals.

References

Abrams, N. (2010) 'Hidden: Jewish Film in the United Kingdom, past and present', *Journal of European Popular Culture* 1: 1, pp. 53–68, doi: 10.1386/jepc.1.1.53_1)

Bedoire, F and Tanner, R (Translator), (2004) *The Jewish Contribution to Modern Architecture, 1830-1930*, KTAV Pub. House, Stockholm

Berman, R. (1997) *Dear Poppa: The World War II Berman Family Letters*, St. Paul, Minnesota Historical Society Press

Bloch, S. (1980) *No Time for Tears: Childhood in a Rabbi's Family,* London, William Kimber

Board of Deputies of British Jews and the German Jewish Aid Committee. (1933 – 1939) *While You Are In England: Helpful Information and Guidance for Every Refugee.*

Brasch, C. (1980), *Indirections: A Memoir 1909-1947*, Oxford University Press, Wellington

Buckingham Advertiser (1940 and 1943)

Buckinghamshire (Bucks) Examiner (1940-1945)

Canetti, E. (2005) *Party in the Blitz*: London: The Harvill Press

Cesarani. D. (2003) 'The London Jewish Chronicle and the Holocaust.' In: Shapiro, R. M. (ed.), *Why Didn't the Press Shout? American and International Journalism During the Holocaust.* New York: Yeshiva University Press & KTAV Publishing House, pp. 175-195

Chamberlain, N.(1939) *In Search of Peace*, p. 393; and *Parliamentary Debates, House of Commons* (London: HMSO, 1938) vol. 339, 12th vol. of session 1937-1938, pp. 361-369, 373

Chilvers, I and and Glaves-Smith, J. *Freedman Barnett, A Dictionary of Modern and Contemporary Art,* Oxford University Press Inc. Oxford Reference Online. Oxford University Press

Donnerer, J and Lembeck, F (eds), (2006) *The Chemical Languages of the Nervous System: History of Scientists and Substances*, S. Karger AG, Publishers, Basel, Switzerland, Karger

Edelman, M. (1946) *SMALL TOWN THEATRE, Picture Post*, London: Hulton Press LTD

Fachler, Y. (2003) *THE VOW*: Rebuilding the Fachler Tribe after the Holocaust based on the journals of Eva and Eli Fachler, Canada: Trafford Publishing

Fry, H. (2014) *Spymaster: The Secret Life of Kendrick,* Marranos Press, London

Green, D. (2012) *Denise Levertov: A Poet's Life,* Chicago: University of Illinois

Gulland, Diana. (2014) *Basque and Jewish refugees at Tythrop House, Kingsey,1937 to 1940. Records of Buckinghamshire,* Volume 54, pages 179-200

Harding, T (2013) *Hanns and Rudolph,* London: William Heinemann

Hollenberg, Donna Krolik. (2013) *A Poet's Revolution: The Life of Denise Levertov,* Berkeley: University of California Press

Ison, L. (2013) *From There to Here: A Family's Journey,* Oxfordshire: Words by Design Ltd.

John Jagger, M.P., '*Obituary*' *The Times,* London, 10 July 1942

Jewish Chronicle 1941

Lloyd, J. (2007) *The Undiscovered Expressionist: A Life of Marie-Louise von Motesiczky,* New Haven: Yale University Press

Masters, P. (1997) *Striking Back: A Jewish Commando's War Against the Nazis,* Novato, CA: Presidio Press

Rose, N. (2000) *The Cliveden set: portrait of an exclusive fraternity,* London: Jonathan Cape.

Samson, V. (1993) *Landsleit of Amersham and surrounding areas: A History of the Amersham Hebrew Congregation 1939-1945, Amersham, SBJC*

Schellenberg, W. (2001) *Invasion, 1940: The Nazi Invasion Plan for Britain*, with an introduction by Erickson, J. London: Little Brown & Company and the Imperial War Museum.

Sugarman, M. (2002), *More than just a few: Jewish pilots and aircrew in the Battle of Britain Jewish Historical Studies Vol:38, p183* Jewish Historical Society of England

Summers, J. (2011) *When the Children Came Home: Stories of Wartime Evacuees,* London: Simon & Schuster Ltd.

Tesler, B. (2006) *Before I Forget: A Family Memoir,* London: Mind Advertising Ltd.

The Royal Society, Dr Otto Loewi archives.

Vessey, B. (1995) *British Boys for British Farms: The Story of the YMCA's Farm Training Scheme,* London: YMCA England.

Websites:

Abrams, D. (1984) John F Hall's website. *An Interview with Mark Abrams* [Online], Available: http://surveyresearch.weebly.com/an-interview-with-mark-abrams-transcripts.html. In addition:

Wartime at the BBC [Online], Available: http://surveyresearch.weebly.com/uploads /2/9/9/8/2998485/abrams_8_-_wartime_at_the_bbc.pdf

AJR, The Association of Jewish Refugees, Werth, *Upstairs, Downstairs,* [Online], Available: http://www.ajr.org.uk/index.cfm/section.journal/issue.Jun09/article=2833

(Sulzbacher M*)* (2011) http://www.ajr.org.uk/journal/issue.Apr11/letters

(Pressburger O) (1995) http://www.ajr.org.uk/journalpdf/1995_may.pdf

Anderson, D, (for a list of modernist houses in Bucks) [Online], Available: http:// daveanderson.me.uk/houses/england/bucks.html

Bean, K. *'Afternoon Tea with Renee Asherson'* [Online], Available: http://vivandlarry. com/general-discussion/afternoon-tea-with-renee-asherson/

Bombs over Buckinghamshire, [Online], Available: http://www.buckscc.gov. uk/media/130641/WW2 bombs over bucks.pdf
http://www.buckscc.gov.uk/media/130661/WW2_schools.pdf,
https://ubp.buckscc.gov.uk/SingleResult.aspx?uid=TBC554 (King Zog)
https://ubp.buckscc.gov.uk/SingleResult.aspx?uid=TBC554 ('Allies and enemies')

Calloni M "Body, Gender, Subjectivity" – Bologna, 28-9/ 1-10-2000 Section 8: "Refusing to forget" [Online], Available: https://www.women.it/cyberarchive/ files/calloni.htm

Capristo, L, ed. (2004) *'From Hitler's Hamburg to Hollywood: Growing Up in Germany' The Mulberry Tree*; [Online], Available: http://web1.smcm.edu/mulberrytree/_ assets/PDF/summer04/growingupingermany.pdf

Czechs in Exile, [Online], Available: http://www.czechsinexile.org/places/aston abbottsabbey-en.shtml

Dei'ah veDibur, 'Torah for the Taking, Torah for the Giving: HaRav Zushe Waltner Zt'l' (Musman M) (2003) [Online], Available: http://www.chareidi.org/ archives5763/KRH63features2.html

Freed G, [Online], Available: http://www.geofffreed.com/2013/03/post-11.html

Freud Museum London, The Sigmund Freud archive catalogues, Archive [Online], Available: http://www.freud.org.uk/archive/catalogue/letters/id/ASC/18/

Gateshead Kolel, [Online], Available: http://www.gatesheadkolel.org/history. html

Harry Ransom Center, The University of Texas At Austin [Online], Available: http://www.hrc.utexas.edu/collections/books/holdings/knopf/ (Alfred A Knopf publisher)

Haversham & Little Linford Heritage, Blake S [Online], Available: http:// www.mkheritage.co.uk/hav/index.html

Haversham & Little Linford, [Online], Available: http://www.havershamvillage.co.uk/stlenshisto.html

Harvard Law School Library, Harvard University, *Frankfurter, Felix. Letters to his sister Estelle, 1933-1964* [Online], Available: http://oasis.lib.harvard.edu/oasis/deliver/~law00106

Jewish Chronicle, 'Children's favourite Roald Dahl: proudly antisemitic', Elgot, J and Sheinman A, (2011) [Online], Available: http://www.thejc.com/news/uk-news/54747/childrens-favourite-roald-dahl-proudly-antisemitic

Jewishgen, 'Jewish Civilian Deaths during World War II excluding those deaths registered in the Metropolitan Borough of Stepney', Pollins H [Online], Available: http://www.jewishgen.org/jcr-uk/static/excludingthose listedinstepneyregistry.pdf

Jewish Museum London, Jacobs, D. (interviewer) Oral History Collection Transcript (1976) Lipschitz, H (interviewee)

Jewish Virtual Library, Sugarman, M. *Jewish Pilots and Aircrews in the Battle of Britain*, [Online], Available: http://www.jewishvirtuallibrary.org/jsource/ww2/sugar4.html

Katz, D, S. Oxford Dictionary of National Biography, 'Margoliouth, Moses (1815–1881)', [Online], Available: http://dx.doi.org/10.1093/ref:odnb/18055

Lawley, M. *Edmund Fredric Warburg* (1908-1966), [Online], Available: http://rbg-web2.rbge.org.uk/bbs/Learning/Bryohistory/Bygone%20Bryologists/EDMUND%20FREDRIC%20WARBURG.pdf

Leeser, H. [Online], Available: http://www.ratsgymnasium.de/

Nobel Prize.org, [Online], Available: "Otto Loewi – Biographical". *Nobelprize.org*. Nobel Media AB 2013. Web. 6 Jun 2014. http://www.nobelprize.org/nobel_prizes/medicine/laureates/1936/loewi-bio.html

Princes Risborough Town Council, 'Memorials', [Online], Available: http://www.princesrisborough.com/memorials.html

Roll of Honour, Edwards M (Webmaster) Cannell, G & Dishman, A. (2008) [Online], Available: http://www.roll-of-honour.com/Buckinghamshire/Winslow BritishLegion.html

Slough History Online, '*Aspro History*', [Online], Available: www.sloughhistoryonline.org.uk/.../sl-sl-S000002706_aspros-d-00-000

Sugarman, M. (For a detailed account of Jewish personnel and lists many names.) [Online], Available: http://www.bletchleypark.org.uk/resources/filer.rhtm/595696/breaking+the+codes-+jewish+personnel+at+bletchley+park.pdf

The Commonwealth War Grave Commission, (CWGC), [Online], Available: http://www.cwgc.org/

The Crash of Bristol Beaufort AW288 at Roscroggan: In Memoriam, (2012) Steele M. & Ward B [Online], Available: http://213.228.233.205/aw288/

The Gazette, (*London Gazette*) [Online], Available:

Issue 36145, 24 August 1943, https://www.thegazette.co.uk/London/issue/36145/page/3811/data.pdf

Issue 1277, 18 March 1947, https://www.thegazette.co.uk/London/issue/37908/supplement/1277

Issue 2994, 5 May 1939, https://www.thegazette.co.uk/London/issue/34622/supplement/2994/data.pdf

Issue 38128, 21 November 1947, https://www.thegazette.co.uk/London/issue/38128/page/5513/data.pdf

Issue 27293, 12 March 1901. https://www.thegazette.co.uk/London/issue/27293/page/1760/data.pdf

The Guardian, Watkins, N. (2009) *Harry Weinberger obituary: A trenchant defender of traditional painting with a melancholic and haunting style* [Online], Available: http://www.theguardian.com/artanddesign/2009/sep/25/harry-weinberger-obituary

The Listening Project: Hilda Baxt, Brooklyn, by D, Rice [Online], Available: http://www.listeningprojectbrooklyn.com/participants/hilda-baxt/

The Marie-Louise von Motesiczky Charitable Trust, (2011) [Online], Available: http://www.motesiczky.org/

University of Birmingham, Cadbury Research Library: Special Collections YMCA archives [Online], Available: http://calmview.bham.ac.uk/Record.aspx?src=CalmView.Catalog&id=XYMCA

Victoria University of Wellington Library, *Indirections: A Memoir 1909-1947,* C Brasch, Chapter 14, *The Abbey,* The New Zealand Electronic Text Collection, [Online], Available: http://nzetc.victoria.ac.nz/tm/scholarly/tei-BraIndi-t1-body-d3-d2.html

Wiener Library, [Online], Available: http://www.wienerlibrary.co.uk/Search-document-collection?item=943 (see entry 35, for Lewis Erlanger at Flint Hill Farm). Also: http://www.wienerlibrary.co.uk/Search-document-collection?item=1161 (Strauss family of Radnage Farm)

Wilton Park, *'History of Wilton Park'* Archive [Online], Available: https://www.wiltonpark.org.uk/wp-content/uploads/History-of-WP.pdf

Winslow History, [Online], Available:

http://www.winslow-history.org.uk/

http://www.winslow-history.org.uk/images/plane%20crash%20report.jpg

Wycombe High School, *High Flyer,* Archive, [Online], Available: http://www.whs.bucks.sch.uk/explore/the-guild/archive

Yad Vashem, Shoah Resource Center, *Evian Conference*, [Online], Available: http://www.yadvashem.org/odot_pdf/Microsoft%20Word%20-%206305.pdf

(In addition permitted use of their timeline as historical guide): http://www.yadvashem.org/yv/en/holocaust/timeline/

BIBLIOGRAPHY AND FURTHER READING

Albright, M. (2012) Pra*gue Winter: A Personal Story of Remembrance and War, 1937-1948*, New York: HarperCollins Publishers

Amersham Museum, Samson, V & D, (2015) *Wartime Jewish Amersham*, [Online], Available: http://amershamhistory.info/research/wars/wartime-jewish-amersham/

Blaug M [Online], Available: http://markblaug.wordpress.com/about/

Epstein, T. Scarlett. (2005) *Swimming Upstream: A Jewish Refugee From Vienna, Middlesex:* Mitchell Vallentine & Company

Jewish Historical Society of England [Online], Available: http://www.jhse.org/

Jewish Women's Archive, [Online], Available:
http://jwa.org/encyclopedia/article/preston-rosalind
http://jwa.org/encyclopedia/article/shalvi-alice

Katz, V. (2008) *The Blue Salon and Other Follies: A Jewish Boyhood in 1930s' Rural Germany*, Xlibris Corporation

Kops, B. *The World is a Wedding*, Five Leaves Publications, 2007

Marks, L. (1998) *Between Silk and Cyanide: A Codemaker's Story 1941-1945,* London: HarperCollins

The United States Holocaust Memorial Museum, [Online], Available: http://www.ushmm.org/online/film/docs/about.php (film footage of Jewish refugee children on a YMCA farm in Buckinghamshire.)

Notes

1. *While You Are In England: Helpful Information and Guidance for Every Refugee*, pamphlet produced by the German Jewish Aid Committee and the Board of Deputies of British Jews, 1933 – 1939.

2. Archive of the National Council of YMCAs (Young Men's Christian Association) 1838-200.

3. Barbara. Vessey, *British Boys for British Farms: The Story of the YMCA's Farm Training Scheme*, YMCA, London, 1995, p9.

4. Wiener Library, 'Reunion of Kindertransport Documents 1987-2002', http://www.wienerlibrary.co.uk/Search-document-collection?item=943, 2002, (accessed 12 February 2014). (See entry 35).

5. Ibid, 'Kurt Strauss: Family Papers, 1938-2011', http://www.wienerlibrary.co.uk/Search-document-collection?item=1161, 2005.

6. Yanky Fachler, *The Vow: Rebuilding the Fachler Tribe after the Holocaust*, Trafford Publishing, Canada, 2003.

7. Diana Gulland, 'Basque and Jewish refugees at Tythrop House, Kingsey, 1937 to 1940'. *Records of Buckinghamshire*, Volume 54, 2014, pages 179-200.

8. Yad Vashem, Shoah Resource Center, Evian Conference, http://www.yadvashem.org/odot_pdf/Microsoft%20Word%20-%206305.pdf (accessed November 12 2013)

9. In addition permitted use of their timeline as historical guide throughout our book: The Holocaust, http://www.yadvashem.org/yv/en/holocaust/timeline/

10. Norman Rose, *The Cliveden Set: Portrait of an Exclusive Fraternity*, Jonathan Cape, London, 2000.

11. Peter Masters, *Striking Back: A Jewish Commando's War Against the Nazis*, Presidio Press, Novato, CA, 1997, p23.

12. Helen Fry, *Spymaster: The Secret Life of Kendrick*, Marranos Press, London, 2014.

13. 'History of Wilton Park', https://www.wiltonpark.org.uk/wp-content/uploads/History-of-WP.pdf, (accessed 21 October 2013).

14. Ted Enever, *Britain's Best Kept Secret*, Sutton, Stroud, 1994/1999. Cited by M. Sugarman, Jewish Virtual Library, World War II: 'Jewish Personnel at Bletchley. Park', http://www.jewishvirtuallibrary.org/jsource/ww2/bletchleyjews.html#_ftn4, (accessed 15 January 2014).

15. Martin Sugarman, Jewish Virtual Library, World War II: 'Jewish Personnel at Bletchley Park', (accessed 19 November 2014). http://www.jewishvirtuallibrary.org/jsource/ww2/bletchleyjews.html

16. Ibid.

17. Fredric Bedoire and Robert Tanner (Translator), *The Jewish Contribution to Modern Architecture, 1830-1930*, KTAV Pub. House, Stockholm, 2004, p.139.

18. Leo Marks, *Between Silk and Cyanide: A Codemaker's War 1941–1945*, HarperCollins, London, 1999.

19. Thomas Harding, *Hanns and Rudolph*, William Heinemann, London, 2013.

20. Jessica Elgot and Anna Sheinman, September 15, 2011, *Jewish Chronicle*, 'Children's favourite Roald Dahl: proudly antisemitic' http://www.thejc.com/news/uk-news/54747/childrens-favourite-roald-dahl-proudly-antisemitic (accessed 19 October 2014)

21. Sugarman, *World War II: Jewish Pilots and Aircrews in the Battle of Britain.*

22. The Commonwealth War Grave Commission, (CWGC), http://www.cwgc.org/, (accessed 5 December 2013).

23. Mark Steele, and Ben Ward, *The crash of Bristol Beaufort AW288 at Roscroggan: In Memoriam*, http://213.228.233.205/aw288/, 2012 (accessed 6 January 2014).

24. The Association of Jewish Ex-Servicemen and Women, http://www.ajex.org.uk/, (accessed 13 December 2013)

25. Lesley Perry, Chesham researcher, unpublished work.

26. Z.T. Moreno, *To Dream Again: A Memoir*, New York, Mental Health Resources, 2012.

27. CWGC.

28. Princes Risborough Town Council, 'Memorials' http://www.princesrisborough.com/memorials.html (accessed 26 June 2014)

29. Dr D. Noy and J. Hunt, 'Winslow History', http://www.winslow-history.org.uk/twentiethc-aircrash.shtm, 2013, (accessed 25 November 2013).

30. G. Cannell and A Dishman, 'Roll of Honour' http://www.roll-of-honour.com/Buckinghamshire/WinslowBritishLegion.html, 2008, (accessed 25 November 2013).

31. *Buckingham Advertiser*, 1943.

32. H. Pollins, Jewish Civilian Deaths During World War II – JewishGen, http://www.jewishgen.org/jcr-uk/static/excludingthoselistedinstepneyregistry.pdf

33. Ibid.

34. The Marie-Louise von Motesiczky Charitable Trust, http://www.motesiczky.org/, J. Lloyd, *The Undiscovered Expressionist. A Life of Marie-Louise von Motesiczky*, Yale University Press, London and New Haven, 2007. The

catalogue raisonné is by Ines Schlenker: *Marie-Louise von Motesiczky 1906-1996. A Catalogue Raisonné of the Paintings*, Hudson Hills Press, Manchester and New York 2009, (accessed 23 June 2014). Special thanks to Frances Carey, (MLvM chairperson).

35. *Jewish Chronicle*, 27 October 1939.

36. ©David Jacobs/Jewish Museum London, Oral History Collection Transcript, interview with H Lipschitz

37. Elias Canetti, introduction, J. Adler, 'Party in the Blitz: The English Years', Random House, 2005, p.98.

38. Donna Krolick Hollenberg, 'A Poet's Revolution: The Life of Denise Levertov,' University of California Press, 2013.

39. Jill Lloyd, *The Undiscovered Expressionist: A Life of Marie-Louise von Motesiczky*, Haven, Yale University Press, 2007, p121.

40. N. Watkins, 'Harry Weinberger obituary: A trenchant defender of traditional painting with a melancholic and haunting style,' *The Guardian*, Friday 25 September 2009.

41. The Marie-Louise von Motesiczky Charitable Trust, Biography, http://www.motesiczky.org/biography/, (accessed 23 June 2014).

42. *Otto Loewi – Biographical*. Nobelprize.org. Nobel Media AB 2014. Web. (accessed 22 Nov 2014). http://www.nobelprize.org/nobel_prizes/medicine/laureates/1936/loewi-bio.html

43. Freud Museum London, The Sigmund Freud archive catalogues, http://www.freud.org.uk/archive/catalogue/letters/id/ASC/18/, (accessed 17 November 2013).

44. Josef Donnerer and Fred Lembeck (eds), *The Chemical Languages of the Nervous System: History of Scientists and Substances*, S. Karger AG, Publishers, Basel, Switzerland, Karger, 2006.

45. Ibid, p.25.

46. Recorded in *The Gazette* (*London Gazette*), issue 36145, 24 August 1943, https://www.thegazette.co.uk/London/issue/36145/page/3811/data.pdf, (accessed 23 December 2014).

47. Harvard Law School Library, Harvard University, Frankfurter, Felix. Letters to his sister Estelle, 1933-1964 http://oasis.lib.harvard.edu/oasis/deliver/~law00106, Call Number: HOLLIS 8149092 (accessed 23 December 2014).

48. Maurice Edelman, 'Small Town Theatre', Picture Post January 12, 1946, pp. 18-22. Ruth Abrams – permission.

49. Recorded in *The Gazette* (*London Gazette*), issue 1277, 18 March 1947, https://www.thegazette.co.uk/London/issue/37908/supplement/1277, (accessed 6 August 2013).

50. Charles Brasch, (1980), *Indirections: A Memoir 1909-1947*, Oxford University Press, Wellington. Chapter 14, The Abbey is also online, The New Zealand Electronic Text Collection, http://nzetc.victoria.ac.nz/tm/scholarly/tei-BraIndi-t1-body-d3-d2.html, (accessed 20 May 2015)

51. Dr Nathan Abrams, (2010), 'Hidden: Jewish Film in the United Kingdom, past and present', Journal of European Popular Culture 1: 1, pp. 53–68, doi: 10.1386/jepc.1.1.53_1)

52. Bernard Kops, *The World is a Wedding*, Five Leaves Publications, 2007.

53. Kendra Bean, 'Afternoon Tea with Renee Asherson', http://vivandlarry.com/general-discussion/afternoon-tea-with-renee-asherson/ (accessed 21 October 2013)

54. Dave Anderson, *Modern Houses In Buckinghamshire*, http://daveanderson.me.uk/houses/england/bucks.html, (accessed 26 August 2014)

55. Hughenden Manor, 2 July, 2014. Tour

56. Mark Lawley, 'Edmund Fredric Warburg (1908-1966)', http://rbg-web2.rbge.org.uk/bbs/Learning/Bryohistory/Bygone%20Bryologists/EDMUND%20FREDRIC%20WARBURG.pdf (accessed 27 August 2014)

57. *Bucks Examiner*, 13th January 1939.

58. Recorded in *The Gazette* (*London Gazette*), issue 2994, 5 May 1939, https://www.thegazette.co.uk/London/issue/34622/supplement/2994/data.pdf, (accessed 19 November 2014).

59. Hughenden Manor.

60. Hans Leeser, http://www.ratsgymnasium.de/ (accessed 26 November 2014).

61. Recorded in *The Gazette* (*London Gazette*), issue 38128, 21 November 1947, https://www.thegazette.co.uk/London/issue/38128/page/5513/data.pdf, (accessed 30 October 2014).

62. Dr Helen Fry, *Spymaster: The Secret Life of Kendrick*, Marranos Press, London, 2014, p265.

63. Elias Canetti, introduction, Jeremy Adler, 'Party in the Blitz: The English Years', Random House, 2005, p.70

64. Freedman Barnett, *A Dictionary of Modern and Contemporary Art* by Ian Chilvers and John Glaves-Smith. Oxford University Press Inc. Oxford Reference Online. Oxford University Press.

65. Slough History Online, 'Aspro History', www.sloughhistoryonline.org.uk/.../sl-sl-S000002706_aspros-d-00-000, (accessed 24August 2014).

66. Jewish Women's Archive, 'Rosalind Preston', http://jwa.org/encyclopedia/article/preston-rosalind, (accessed 14 August 2014).

67. Madeleine Albright, *Prague Winter: A Personal Story of Remembrance and War, 1937-1948*, Harper Collins Publishers 2012.

68. Czechs in Exile, http://www.czechsinexile.org/places/astonabbottsabbey-en. shtml, (accessed 25 June 2014).

69. Vernon Katz, *The Blue Salon and Other Follies: A Jewish Boyhood in 1930s' Rural Germany*, Xlibris Corporation, 2008).

70. T. Scarlett Epstein, 'Swimming Upstream: A Jewish Refugee from Vienna', Mitchell Vallentine & Company, 2005.

71. Buckinghamshire County Council, 'Allies and enemies', https://ubp.buckscc. gov.uk/SingleResult.aspx?uid=TBC554 (accessed 5 December 2013).

72. Walter Schellenberg and introduction by John Erickson, *Invasion, 1940: The Nazi Invasion Plan for Britain*, Little Brown Book Group and Imperial War Museum, 2001.

73. John Jagger, M.P., 'Obituary' The Times, London, 10 July 1942, p 7.

74. Oxford Dictionary of National Biography, David S. Katz, 'Margoliouth, Moses (1815–1881)', first published 2004; online, 2004, 1041 words, with portrait illustration, http://dx.doi.org/10.1093/ref:odnb/18055, (accessed 26 June 2014) and Haversham & Little Linford, http://www.havershamvillage. co.uk/stlenshisto.html, (accessed 26 June 2014).

75. Buckinghamshire County Council, 'Bombs over Bucks', http://www.buckscc. gov.uk/media/130641/WW2_bombs_over_bucks.pdf, (accessed 31 July 2013).

76. B'nai B'rith a humanitarian charity defending the vulnerable world-wide.

77. Extracts from *From There to Here: A Family's Journey*, Oxfordshire: Words by Design Ltd, 2013 (Author; Liz Ison, daughter of Clemens Nathan)

78. http://surveyresearch.weebly.com/mark-abrams.html

79. http://surveyresearch.weebly.com/an-interview-with-mark-abrams-transcripts.html

80. Principal Lecturer in Sociology and Unit Director, Survey Research Unit, Polytechnic of North London (1976-1992)

81. Professor Ruth Berman, *Dear Poppa: The World War II Berman Family Letters*, St. Paul: Minnesota Historical Society Press, 1997, pp127, 145, 152-153, 162, 198-200, 208-209, 212, 213, 218-219.

82. Nine chapters generously written for this book by Anne Zeto Kaye.

83. Socialist-Zionist youth movement

84. Bnei Akiva, Jewish youth movement

85. Denise Levertov, *Overland to the Islands: Illustrious Ancestors*, Jonathan Williams, Highlands, 1958.

86. Donna Krolik Hollenberg, *A Poet's Revolution: The Life of Denise Levertov*, Berkeley, University of California Press, 2013, p49.

87. Ibid, p52.

88. Ibid, p53.

89. D. Levertov, *Listening to Distant Guns*, Poetry Quarterly, 1940.

90. Dana Greene, *Denise Levertov: A Poet's Life*, Chicago, University of Illinois, 2012.

91. Greene, *Denise Levertov: A Poet's Life*, Information from her time at the ballet school is contained in letters from Denise Levertov to her parents. Denise Levertov to Paul and Beatrice Levertov, DLP, Series 1, Box 1, Folder 3, November – December 1939, Folder 5, July – December 1940, Folder.

92. Ibid, "My Prelude," LUTC, 244-53.

93. Ibid, "Hebert Reed Remembered", LUTC, 233 – 37.

94. Ibid. (Greene cited from Sutton, "A Conversation with Denise Levertov," and Packard, "Craft Interview with Denise Levertov").

95. Oscar Pressburger, The Wedding Ring, http://www.ajr.org.uk/journalpdf/1995_may.pdf, 1995, (accessed 10 July 2014). Note this was written by Oscar approximately ten years prior to his death.

96. Henry Werth, *Upstairs, Downstairs*, http://www.ajr.org.uk/index.cfm/section. journal/issue.Jun09/article=2833, (2009), (accessed on 21 October 2013).

97. Fritz Lustig, The Association of Jewish Refugees, 'Wilton Park: A very special PoW camp', http://www.ajr.org.uk/index.cfm/section.journal/issue. Aug09/article=3213, Aug 2009 Journal, (accessed 27 Feburary 2013).

98. Michael Zander, 'An Address by Michael Zander, Delivered at the Annual dinner of the Friends of the Hebrew University, Glasgow Branch, http://www.benjaminzander.com/walter/michael.php, 1994, (accessed 5 November 2013).

99. Walter Zander, Obituary, The Daily Telegraph 29 April 1993, (view at) http://www.walterzander.info/index.html, (accessed 5 November 2013).

100. Ibid, M. Zander, 'The Walter Zander Website'

101. *From Hitler's Hamburg to Hollywood: Growing Up in Germany* (2004) Editor, Lee Capristo, of *The Mulberry Tree*, and information from Steve's widow, Jill E. McGovern.

102. Rabbi Avrohom Katz, 'Gateshead Kolel History', http://www.gatesheadkolel. org/history.html, 2008, (accessed 25 August 2013).

103. *Dei'ah veDibur*, Mordecai Plaut, director and author Moshe Musman, (abridged from)'Torah For The Taking, Torah For The Giving: HaRav Zushe Waltner Zt'l', http://www.chareidi.org/archives5763/KRH63features2.htm, 25 Sivan 5763 – June 25, 2003 (accessed 2 October 2013).

104. Max Sulzbacher, Association of Jewish Refugees, Apr 2011 Journal, Letters to the Editor, 'No Nostalgia for the Blitz', http://www.ajr.org.uk/journal/ issue.Apr11/letters, (accessed 14 August 2013). Information kindly provided by AJR, The Association of Jewish Refuges.

105. Julie Summers, *When the Children Came Home: Stories of Wartime Evacuees*, Simon & Schuster UK Ltd, 2011.

106. Hilda Baxt, *The Listening Project: Brooklyn Practicing the Art of Listening one story at a time…* a project by Dempsey Rice, http://www.listeningprojectbrooklyn. com/participants/hilda-baxt/, (accessed 8 October 2013). Dempsey Rice's wonderful digital recordings of Hilda Baxt's memories, combined with our own interviews with Hilda.

107. Marina Calloni, "Body, Gender, Subjectivity" – Bologna, 28-9/ 1-10-2000 Section 8: "Refusing to forget" Politics, Moral Sentiments, Secular Judaism and Gender in an Autobiography by Amelia Rosselli Pincherle, http:// women.it/cyberarchive/files/calloni.htm, (accessed 11 June 2014).

108. Full account, edited by Jeremy Godden, can be viewed at: http://www.scribd. com/doc/24545683/The-Steinhardt-family-and-the-Cedar-Boys, (accessed 22 October 2013). Provided by editor with kind permission.

109. Professor Alice Shalvi, unpublished memoirs, (received 2014).

110. Brian Tesler adapted by the author from, *Before I Forget*, published by Mind Advertising Ltd, 2006.

111. S. Hatton, *A Wartime Hostel, Buckinghamshire Countryside*, May/June 2005 edition.

112. *Buckingham Advertiser*, 'Refugee's Fatal Ride to Work: Young Hostel Resident Dies from Injuries: Cycling to Chetwode Farm', 19 September 1942.

113. Ibid, "Jewish History: One of Persecution": 'Mr. A. Bryant and refugee's home: Husband Fighting for his Country: Strong Comments on Rural Housing Position', 22 February 1941.

114. *Buckingham Advertiser*, 'Alien's Change of Address: First Buckingham Summonses: German Jewess at Pabury': "Alien Fleeing from Nazi Oppression", 29 June 1940.

115. Yanky Fachler, *The Vow: Rebuilding the Fachler Tribe After the Holocaust: based on the journals of Eva and Eli Fachler*, Victoria, B.C. Trafford, 2003.

116. Dr Geoff Freed, 'Geoff Freed Online', http://www.geofffreed.com/2013/03/ post-11.html (accessed 15 January 2014).

117. Traute Morgenstern,Wycombe High School, Update From the Archive February 2013, 'A refugee from the Nazis at Wycombe High School 1941-1947', http://www. whs.bucks.sch.uk/explore/the-guild/archive', (accessed 21 November 2013).

118. Extract from Professor David Cesarani 'The London Jewish Chronicle and the Holocaust'. Robert Moses Shapiro (ed.), Why Didn't The Press Shout? American and International Journalism During the Holocaust. Yeshiva University Press/ Ktav, New York, 2003, pp. 175-195.